Nations, Nationalism and Patriotism in the European Past

Nations, Nationalism and Patriotism in the European Past

Edited by
Claus Bjørn, Alexander Grant and Keith J. Stringer

Academic Press-Copenhagen

Nations, Nationalism and Patriotism in the European Past
Edited by Claus Bjørn, Alexander Grant and Keith J. Stringer

© 1994, The Editors and Contributors severally, and Akademisk Forlag A/S
(Academic Press- Copenhagen)

Cover: "Danmark" ("Denmark") painted by Elizabeth Jerichau-Baumann (1851), Ny Carlsberg Glyptotek, Copenhagen. Design by Jens Lassen Landorph.

Printing: Reproset I/S, Copenhagen

ISBN 87-500-3196-1

Printed in Denmark 1994

This volume has its origin in two Colloquia held at the Universities of Lancaster (28 September – 1 October 1989) and Copenhagen (25 – 28 April 1990). Most of the speakers were drawn from Lancaster's Centres for Medieval Studies and for Social History and from Copenhagen's Center for Research in the Humanities, but the participants also included scholars from other universities in Britain, Denmark and Germany. The essays published here consist, in a revised form, of ten of the papers presented at Lancaster and Copenhagen, with the addition of two specially commissioned chapters. A second volume based on the Colloquia proceedings, *Social and Political Identities in Western History*, is also published by the Academic Press, Copenhagen.

The appearance of these two volumes marks an important stage in the joint Lancaster-Copenhagen research project, *Social and Political Identities in European Communities*, which continues to be pursued in both interdisciplinary and international contexts.

The editors and contributors gratefully acknowledge the generous financial support provided by the Danish Research Council for the Humanities for the publication of this volume and its companion, and towards the two Colloquia at Lancaster and Copenhagen which lie behind them.

Contents

Keith Stringer
Social and Political Communities in European History:
Some Reflections on Recent Studies...9

Dauvit Broun
The Origin of Scottish Identity..35

Troels Dahlerup
Danish National Identity, c.700–1700...56

Alexander Grant
Aspects of National Consciousness in Medieval Scotland......................68

Stanley Hussey
Nationalism and Language in England, c.1300–1500..........................96

Michael Lynch
National Identity in Ireland and Scotland, 1500–1640........................109

Ole Feldbæk
National Identity in Eighteenth-Century Denmark.............................137

Eric Evans
National Consciousness? The Ambivalence of
English Identity in the Eighteenth Century.....................................145

Jens Rahbek Rasmussen
Patriotic Perceptions: Denmark and Sweden, 1450–1850...................161

Ralph Gibson
The Intensification of National Consciousness in Modern Europe..........177

John Gooch
Nationalism and the Italian Army, 1850–1914................................198

Martin Blinkhorn
Euskadi: Basque Nationalism in the Twentieth Century.....................213

Contributors

Martin Blinkhorn is Professor of Modern European History at the University of Lancaster

Dauvit Broun is a Lecturer in Scottish History at the University of Glasgow

Troels Dahlerup is Emeritus Professor of History at the University of Aarhus

Eric Evans is Professor of Social History at the University of Lancaster

Ole Feldbæk is Professor of Social and Economic History at the University of Copenhagen

Ralph Gibson is a Senior Lecturer in French and History at the University of Lancaster

John Gooch is Professor of International History at the University of Leeds

Alexander Grant is a Senior Lecturer in History at the University of Lancaster

Stanley Hussey is Emeritus Professor of English Language and Medieval Literature at the University of Lancaster

Michael Lynch is Sir William Fraser Professor of Scottish History and Palaeography at the University of Edinburgh

Jens Rahbek Rasmussen is a Lecturer in English at the University of Copenhagen

Keith Stringer is a Senior Lecturer in History at the University of Lancaster

Social and Political Communities in European History: Some Reflections on Recent Studies

Keith Stringer

'Tis the social league, confederacy and mutual consent, founded in some common good or interest, which joins the members of a community and makes a people one.
                    Anthony Ashley Cooper, 3rd earl of Shaftesbury (1671 – 1713)[1]

They had nothing; not even their own bodies, which had become mere implements of warfare ... and yet they put their hands on each other's shoulders and said with a passionate conviction that it would be all right, though they had faith in nothing, but in themselves and each other.   Frederic Manning (1882 – 1935)[2]

Despite the current (or 1980s?) fashion for individualism, all individual lives are, and always have been, lived within layers of collective social groupings. In particular, five basic strata can readily be identified: the immediate (such as family, household, friends, comrades, neighbours, workmates); the local (such as village, parish, town, estate); the regional (such as lordship, diocese, county, province); the sovereign (such as principality, kingdom, state, nation); and the supra-national (such as Christendom, Empire, Commonwealth, European Community). The relationships and interactions among these various layerings have had the most profound influence on the history of Europe's past; they have largely determined the form of Europe's present, and it may confidently be assumed that they will continue to be of major significance in shaping Europe's future.

Both the present collection of essays and its companion volume, *Social and Political Identities in Western History*, are concerned with how solidarities based on community ties either developed or failed to develop. In consequence, they focus on the processes by which individuals were integrated into communities, on how identities were conceived, articulated

---

1 Quoted in J.H. Shennan, 'The Rise of Patriotism in 18th-century Europe', *History of European Ideas*, xiii (1991), p. 690.
2 Quoted by Sir Michael Howard in his Introduction to F. Manning, *The Middle Parts of Fortune: Somme & Ancre 1916* (London, 1986 edn), pp. v – vi.

and sustained, and on the contradictory pressures at work — some which enhanced community consciousness, others which militated against it. Social life is so multi-faceted, even chaotic, that the problems of definition and classification are manifold, and that point needs to be driven home at the outset. An individual will have plural attachments, loyalties and senses of identity; sometimes these will conflict with one another and sometimes not, 'so that', in Eric Hobsbawm's formulation, 'a man might have no problem about feeling himself to be the son of an Irishman, the husband of a German woman, a member of the mining community, a worker, a supporter of Barnsley Football Club, a Liberal, a Primitive Methodist, a patriotic Englishman, possibly a Republican, and a supporter of the British empire'.[1] Notoriously, 'patriotism' itself, the supposed embodiment of national identity, is a particularly nebulous and messy concept. It can be not only republican or royalist, but liberal or reactionary, bourgeois or aristocratic, Protestant or Catholic, state-led or subversive, revolutionary or counter-revolutionary. Moreover, to speak of 'love of country' automatically raises the question of which country. As Otto Dann has put it apropos of eighteenth-century Europe, 'was one's fatherland ... the territory of one's origin, the land of one's forefathers, or the country in which one felt most at home and with whose constitution one was most in sympathy?'[2] Again, to take the specific case of France, even the great Fernand Braudel found that the essence of French identity continually eluded him. In the event, he concluded that 'we are faced with a hundred, a thousand different Frances of long ago, yesterday or today'.[3] Similarly, writers on modern Italy have to cope with a powerful myth of national 'reunification' at one extreme, and continuing (and evidently increasing) political, social and regional divisions at the other.[4]

Nevertheless, these and other central problems have to be faced square on. What were the processes which made for effective state-formation? Was the development of nationalism a crucial element and, if so, is nationalism to be regarded as a purely modern phenomenon? Why were some countries better able than others to sustain genuine national movements? To what extent was a sense of national identity purely a state-orchestrated ideology?

1 E.J. Hobsbawm, *Nations and nationalism since 1780: Programme, myth, reality* (2nd edn, Cambridge, 1992), p. 123.
2 *Nationalism in the Age of the French Revolution*, ed. O. Dann and J. Dinwiddy (London, 1988), p. 3.
3 F. Braudel, *The Identity of France*, i: *History and Environment* (London, 1988), p. 5.
4 J.A. Davis, *Conflict and Control: Law and Order in Nineteenth-Century Italy* (London, 1988); D. Hine, *Governing Italy: The Politics of Bargained Pluralism* (Oxford, 1993); *Society and Politics in the Age of the Risorgimento: Essays in Honour of Denis Mack Smith*, ed. J.A. Davis and P. Ginsborg (Cambridge, 1991).

Social and Political Communities in European History

How were the symbols of nationalism created, propagated and manipulated? What interactions occurred between local communities and regions, and between regional society and the state? What roles were played by the law, education, religious practice and systems of military recruitment in shaping communal activity and communal spirit? How far was a sense of togetherness dependent on fear of dominant neighbours or internal political uncertainty? What interplay existed between language and identity? What were the economic and geographical stimuli or hindrances to the formation of collective groupings? How significant was ethnic self-awareness as a means of holding groups together? How successfully were problems of ethnic diversity overcome in plural societies? What relationship existed between material well-being, political contentment and senses of belonging?

During the past decade, such fundamental issues have been brought into much sharper focus thanks to the phenomenal upsurge of interest in human collectivities shown by historians, anthropologists, economists, historical geographers, philosophers, political scientists and sociologists alike. Since it is quite beyond the scope of a single essay to provide a comprehensive guide to the recent literature and the latest ideas, this chapter eschews *any* claims to thoroughness; it merely offers some sample thoughts, from a historian's point of view, based on a selection of English-language publications, most of which have appeared within the last five years. It should also be underlined that no attempt is made to take account of the ever-increasing volume of studies of group identities founded on class, gender, age or sexual orientation.

A medievalist might be permitted to mention first of all *Kingdoms and Communities*, the magisterial analysis by Susan Reynolds of community consciousness in the medieval kingdoms of England, France, Germany and Italy (Lombardy).[1] By highlighting the diversity and complexity of medieval collectivities, she has destroyed any notion that these early forms of collective association were any less significant and prevalent than those of modern times. Communities were here, there and everywhere, overlapping and intersecting within the framework of a wider and naturally independent entity, a *communitas regni* ('community of the realm'), that sophisticated concept of collective identity and interests which finally crystallised in the thirteenth century. Accordingly, nothing could be more misleading than the view of some modernists that medieval solidarities were essentially primitive, localised and fragmented, with only Christendom itself providing a wider sense of identity; on the contrary, they were 'much more like the different groups and networks to which modern people feel they belong than

---

1 S. Reynolds, *Kingdoms and Communities in Western Europe, 900–1300* (Oxford, 1984).

the sociological stereotypes admit'.[1] In sum, not only has *Kingdoms and Communities* helped to put group solidarities at the forefront of medieval research; but by demonstrating that medieval concepts of community were not so fundamentally different from modern ones, it encourages attempts, as in the present chapter, to range back and forth across the traditional medieval/modern divide.

In the medieval period, collective activity of all kinds was permeated by the ideas and values of family life, and the family, that central organ of social cohesion, for long remained at the core of community action and experience. Georges Duby and Lawrence Stone, among other intellectual heavyweights, continue to make outstanding contributions in their investigations of the relationship between wider social, legal, economic, political and cultural changes and the nature of family forms and strategies, kinship networks, the privileges and duties of family membership, and concepts of privacy and public manners.[2] Such studies have taken us afresh to the very heart of human relationships: 'private power', 'communal living', 'imagining the self', 'the use of private space', 'solitude', and so on.[3] This is far from saying that the history of the European family has ceased to be a source of lively contention, especially with regard to those old friends 'continuity' and 'change', the former much favoured by the 'Cambridge Group', to the consternation of its critics. Very recently, for example, a serious attack has been launched on the notion of nuclear family continuity in medieval English rural society.[4] Nevertheless, a 'younger generation' of scholars have risen to the challenge of synthesising the detailed case studies that have proliferated in recent years and, in doing so, have contributed in their turn to current debates by stimulating thought along new lines.[5]

As military historians have taught us, other 'families' include the regimental 'family'. National causes are now seen as nothing compared to

---

1   *Ibid.*, p. 335.
2   *A History of Private Life*, general editors P. Ariès and G. Duby (Cambridge, Mass., 1987–90). Lawrence Stone's recently completed trilogy on the history of marriage in England comprises: *Road to Divorce: England 1530–1987* (Oxford, 1990), *Uncertain Unions: Marriage in England 1660–1753* (Oxford, 1992), and *Broken Lives: Separation and Divorce in England 1660–1857* (Oxford, 1993).
3   These formulations are from *History of Private Life*, ii: *Revelations of the Medieval World*, ed. Duby.
4   Z. Razi, 'The Myth of the Immutable English Family', *Past and Present*, 140 (1993).
5   J. Casey, *The History of the Family* (Oxford, 1989), B. Gottlieb, *The Family in the Western World from the Black Death to the Industrial Age* (Oxford, 1993), and W. Seccombe, *A Millennium of Family Change: Feudalism to Capitalism in Northwestern Europe* (London, 1992), are major contributions.

the binding force of the regiment and its sub-units, and in particular the bonds forged by modern fighting soldiers with their immediate brothers-in-arms in the same rifle section or weapon group. On the one hand, this provides a classic illustration of the phenomenon of 'concentric loyalties', with allegiances to larger bodies tending to weaken in proportion to distance from the primary group; on the other, the sheer intensity of comradeship in war strikingly confirms the point that the more dangerous the perceived threat to individual well-being becomes, the more likely it is that men will act together with their fellows.[1] Military effectiveness, however, requires reinforcement by other conditions of the utmost relevance to the broader understanding of collective action: coercion, consent, convention, culture. The significance of this last aspect has been well brought out in a recent study of the remarkable fortitude of the British and Dominion troops in the First World War, who 'carried over from civilian life many institutions and attitudes which helped them to adjust to, and to humanize, the new world in which they found themselves'.[2] Most of these men came from towns, and in their rest areas they recreated the community spirit and cultural norms familiar to them from their shared urban experiences — which brings us at once to the issue of identity founded on localities.

Although over the past few years there have been some first-rate studies of individual manors, villages and rural parishes,[3] the European town, both medieval and modern, has arguably fared better at the hands of recent scholars. Thus, historians are exploring with renewed vigour the sources of fusion and fission within urban communities — notably the relationship between town and surrounding countryside, the development of neighbourhood solidarities, the cultural definition of civic identities as expressed in clubs, theatres, museums, statuary, street-names, and domestic and public architecture, processes of politicisation, and the interactions between

---

1 See especially R. Holmes, *Firing Line* (Harmondsworth, 1987). One of the most poignant and illuminating personal accounts of small group bonding in modern warfare is G.M. Fraser, *Quartered Safe Out Here: A Recollection of the War in Burma* (London, 1992). How such group solidarity might override even the most basic moral norms is frighteningly revealed in C.R. Browning, *Ordinary Men: Reserve Police Battalion 101 and the Final Solution in Poland* (New York, 1992).
2 J.G. Fuller, *Troop Morale and Popular Culture in the British and Dominion Armies 1914–1918* (Oxford, 1990), p. 175.
3 For example, Marjorie McIntosh's two-volume study of the changing pattern of community life in the Essex village of Havering: *Autonomy and Community: The Royal Manor of Havering, 1200–1500* (Cambridge, 1986); *A Community Transformed: The Manor and Liberty of Havering, 1500–1620* (Cambridge, 1991). On the English parish as a focus of both religious worship and communal belonging in the pre-industrial era, see more generally *Parish, Church and People: Local Studies in Lay Religion, 1350–1750*, ed. S.J. Wright (London, 1988).

the age-old underclass of 'outsiders' (petty thieves, beggars, prostitutes, unemployed workers, immigrants) and established residents or 'insiders'.[1] One significant merit of the latest urban 'biographies' is the importance they attach to 'history from below', focusing as they do on the values, beliefs, assumptions and prejudices that affected the everyday life of the not-so-anonymous humble folk as well as of urban elites; another is their elucidation of the complexity of social experience in urban communities, with their multiple sociabilities or 'worlds within worlds', to borrow Steve Rappaport's apt phrase,[2] provided by the home, neighbourhood, work, religion, education and recreation. At the same time, we are forcefully reminded of how degrees of social cohesion varied according to time and/or place. Often these variations are of great interest because of their unexpectedness, and offer much fresh food for thought about the problems of typicality and generalisation. To give one instructive example, a recent study has highlighted the strong communal identity of late medieval Westminster, despite a high level of social mobility and Westminster's place at the hub of English political life and government; very different were the results of an analysis of contemporary Durham, a small provincial capital well away from metropolitan influences, where that self-same quality was notable for its absence.[3]

Another pronounced feature of recent historiography concerns the continuing debate about what actually constituted a 'regional community', the evolution and inner workings of such collectivities, the degree of internal cohesion attainable, and the interconnections that existed between changing community perceptions, shifts in economic and institutional structures, and fluctuations in local balances of power. An ambitious undertaking is Longman's twenty-one-volume series, 'A Regional History of England', launched in 1986 under the general editorship of Barry Cunliffe and David Hey. Refreshingly, it recognises the impossibility of imposing clear-cut geographical patterns, stresses the extent to which the character of regional

---

1   To range no farther than France, see *Cities and Social Change in Early Modern France*, ed. P. Benedict (London, 1989); J. Dewald, *Pont-St-Pierre, 1398–1789: Lordship, Community and Capitalism in Early Modern France* (Berkeley, 1987); D. Garrioch, *Neighbourhood and Community in Paris, 1740–1790* (Cambridge, 1986); B. Geremek, *The Margins of Society in Late Medieval Paris* (Cambridge, 1987); T.W. Margadant, *Urban Rivalries in the French Revolution* (Princeton, 1992); J. M. Merriman, *The Margins of City Life: Explorations on the French Urban Frontier, 1815–1851* (Oxford, 1991).
2   S. Rappaport, *Worlds within Worlds: Structures of Life in Sixteenth-Century London* (Cambridge, 1989).
3   G. Rosser, *Medieval Westminster, 1200–1540* (Oxford, 1989); M. Bonney, *Lordship and the Urban Community: Durham and its Overlords, 1250–1540* (Cambridge, 1990).

Social and Political Communities in European History

identities altered over time, and endeavours not to overstate the importance of such identities at the expense of the common patterns of English provincial life. Still fashionable are studies of the seventeenth-century English 'county community' and regional studies of France during the Revolutionary period.[1] For medieval regions, Christine Carpenter, Tony Pollard and Nigel Saul for England, Benjamin Arnold for Germany, and Trevor Dean and Chris Wickham for Italy, to range no more widely, have opened up new lines of inquiry which are bound to influence future work in the field.[2] The special character and problems of socially undifferentiated or differentiated frontier societies (including colonial communities) continue to prove irresistible, especially perhaps to medievalists.[3] The Braudelian alliance between history and geography is reflected in significant studies reinforcing the importance of the natural environment, landscape and a 'sense of place' for the development and maintenance of communal structures, whether distinctively regional or sub-regional.[4] Equally, the relationship between community and social or political protest remains high on the agenda, as in discussions of the Maquis in southern France during the Second World War and strike action (or the lack of it) in the British coal

---

1   For important examples see, respectively, A.M. Coleby, *Central Government and the Localities: Hampshire, 1649–1689* (Cambridge, 1987), and A. Hughes, *Politics, Society and Civil War in Warwickshire, 1620–1660* (Cambridge, 1987); P.R. Hanson, *Provincial Politics in the French Revolution: Caen and Limoges* (Baton Rouge, 1990), and H.C. Johnson, *The Midi in Revolution: A Study of Regional Political Diversity, 1789–1793* (Princeton, 1986).
2   C. Carpenter, *Locality and Polity: A Study of Warwickshire Landed Society, 1401–1499* (Cambridge, 1992); A.J. Pollard, *North-Eastern England during the Wars of the Roses: Lay Society, War, and Politics 1450–1500* (Oxford, 1990); N. Saul, *Scenes from Provincial Life: Knightly Families in Sussex, 1280–1400* (Oxford, 1986); B. Arnold, *Count and Bishop in Medieval Germany: A Study of Regional Power, 1100–1350* (Philadelphia, 1991); T. Dean, *Land and Power in Late Medieval Ferrara: The Rule of the Este, 1340–1450* (Cambridge, 1988); C.J. Wickham, *The Mountains and the City: The Tuscan Appennines in the Early Middle Ages* (Oxford, 1988). L. Genicot, *Rural Communities in the Medieval West* (Baltimore, 1990), takes a broader look at the possibilities and problems of such approaches.
3   Two valuable contributions are *Medieval Frontier Societies*, ed. R. Bartlett and A. MacKay (Oxford, 1989), and *War and Border Societies in the Middle Ages*, ed. A. Goodman and A. Tuck (London, 1992). For the modern period, P. Sahlins, *Boundaries: The Making of France and Spain in the Pyrenees* (Berkeley, 1989), is a most stimulating study of the shifting meaning of state boundaries and their relationship to senses of identity.
4   See, among other studies, A. Everitt, *Landscape and Community in England* (London, 1985); P.P. Viazzo, *Upland Communities: Environment, population and social structure in the Alps since the sixteenth century* (Cambridge, 1989); A.J.L. Winchester, *Landscape and Society in Medieval Cumbria* (Edinburgh, 1987).

industry.[1]

In all these ways, and in numerous others besides, important fresh insights have been offered into the anatomies of 'grassroots' communities: how they differed one from another in their social make-up, peace-keeping mechanisms and other features, the importance of cultural traditions in shaping their self-image, and how concepts of unanimity, 'order' and corporate identity developed and were either advanced or endangered by the processes of political, religious and/or socio-economic change. One conclusion to be drawn about patterns of cooperation and conflict is that rural communities seem to have been rather less cosy and harmonious than was once thought, whereas pre-industrial urban communities were rather less polarised and tension-ridden than we have been led to suppose. Certainly, one is left with a much clearer awareness of the definitional problems associated with the term 'community', and of the key importance of local/regional studies for verifying generalisations about the development of social relationships as a whole.

Indeed, any commentary on the recent literature needs also to emphasise that underpinning or extending many of the works just mentioned are major comparative studies addressing in regional settings such central issues as the functions of landed power and the multiple ways in which landholding and lordship affected communal life during the feudal period and later on.[2] For its part, the ongoing discourse on modernity and late-modernity has resulted in a new crop of monographs from the social scientists on how far accelerated social change has 'de-centred' traditional forms of identity and encouraged the creation of more pluralistic and fragmented societies.[3] Furthermore, nowadays few 'localist' studies concentrate solely on their chosen communities, and most have the laudable aim of illuminating broader situations. Remarkable examples are Wendy Davies's and Guy Bois's microhistorical contributions to the general debate on the changing texture of

---

1 H.R. Kedward, *In Search of the Maquis: Rural Resistance in Southern France, 1942–1944* (Oxford, 1993); D. Gilbert, *Class, Community, and Collective Action: Social Change in Two British Coalfields, 1850–1926* (Oxford, 1992). For earlier periods see, for example, Y.-M. Bercé, *History of Peasant Revolts: The Social Origins of Rebellion in Early Modern France* (Cambridge, 1990); R.B. Manning, *Village Revolts: Social Protest and Popular Disturbances in England, 1509–1640* (Oxford, 1988).
2 J.-P. Poly and E. Bournazel, *The Feudal Transformation, 900–1200* (New York, 1991); *Landownership and Power in Modern Europe*, ed. R. Gibson and M. Blinkhorn (London, 1991).
3 For a selection of important recent work, see A. Giddens, *Modernity and Self-Identity: Self and Society in the Late Modern Age* (Cambridge, 1991); A. Giddens, *The Consequences of Modernity* (Cambridge, 1990); D. C. Thorns, *Fragmenting Societies? A Comparative Analysis of Regional and Urban Development* (London, 1992).

power relationships in early medieval society, offered from the perspectives of, respectively, village communities in ninth-century Brittany and a small village in the tenth-century Mâconnais.[1] Similarly, regional studies have enhanced our understanding of the ambiguities of communal life by giving due prominence to vertical as well as horizontal linkages, in other words, to the relationship at work and under strain between the 'local' and the 'central'. The notion of the English county community, for example, was important long before the seventeenth century; but the county itself was a royal creation at the service of central government as well as of county society, and a key point of contact between 'Court' and 'Country'. It is therefore appropriate to move on from 'small worlds' to the worlds of the nation and the state, whose relevance to what is meant by 'community' needs no underlining.

On states and 'super-states', nations and nationalism, the sheer bulk of recent research and publication is almost overwhelming. The European Science Foundation's mammoth project on 'The Origins of the Modern State in Europe, 13th−18th Centuries' is complemented by a plethora of independent studies, many of which break genuinely new ground in their discussions of the territorial, political, bureaucratic, economic, military and other aspects of state-formation, and of the varying degrees of success achieved in unifying lesser collectivities under the 'political roof' of the state. As a result, scholars have thrown into sharper relief the realities that lie behind theoretical formulations of the state: in particular, the actual nature of state power, and the intricacies of the two-way process whereby states affected society and society, in its turn, limited the freedom of action of the state itself.[2] Within these parameters, much attention has recently been paid to the problem of 'rise and decline', and to the factors that determined outcomes. An interesting slant is the stress placed on the importance of contingency, and some scholars have amused themselves by contemplating the different political patterns that might have emerged had circumstances been otherwise.[3] A good deal of research has also been devoted to 'centre-periphery' relations, with attention shifting back and forth between the heartland

---

1 W. Davies, *Small Worlds: The Village Community in Early Medieval Brittany* (London, 1988); G. Bois, *The transformation of the year one thousand: The village of Lournand from antiquity to feudalism* (Manchester, 1992).
2 *States in History*, ed. J.A. Hall (Oxford, 1986), strikes an especially productive balance between theoretical and historical approaches. See also C. Tilly, *Coercion, Capital, and European States, AD 990−1990* (Oxford, 1990), which includes an extensive guide to further reading.
3 For an example of this counter-factual genre, see M. Desai, 'Birth and Death of Nation States: Speculations about Germany and India', in *The Rise and Decline of the Nation State*, ed. M. Mann (Oxford, 1990).

and outlying, often autonomous regions, the better to understand the complexities of the interplay between them and the dynamics of expansion and incorporation.

Richard Kaeuper and John Brewer, for example, have fruitfully reexamined the pervasive significance of the demands of war in determining the growth of state power and the nature of its impact on local communities;[1] others have reassessed the role of military authority in subordinating territories, as well as the community responses military repression provoked.[2] At the same time, scholars have reconsidered the importance of the myriad non-violent forms of political dominance and control in penetrating and influencing society — forms ranging from royal pageantry and rituals[3] to what Anthony Giddens has termed 'the collection and storage of information' designed 'to co-ordinate subject populations'.[4] The admirable accounts by Rees Davies and Robin Frame of state-building in the medieval British Isles have the particular value not only of bringing England, Wales, Ireland and Scotland into a common comparative focus, but of giving due weight to the key roles played by interlocking factors such as colonisation and acculturation, language, ecclesiastical reform, economic dependence, and ties of patronage and clientage, all of which helped to secure dominion over local communities and, in some measure, to redefine their nature.[5] 'Conquest in the sense of a military act', Davies stresses, 'is only one of the routes to the domination of one society by another and not necessarily the most attractive, rewarding or important of such routes.'[6] A similar stress on the complex and varied processes by which medieval states could impose themselves on subject groups is developed in Robert Bartlett's panoramic study of European conquest and settlement between 950 and

---

1 R.W. Kaeuper, *War, Justice and Public Order: England and France in the Later Middle Ages* (Oxford, 1988); J. Brewer, *The Sinews of Power: War, money and the English state, 1688–1783* (London, 1989). See also, for instance, J.E. Cronin, *The Politics of State Expansion: War, State and Society in Twentieth-Century Britain* (London, 1991).
2 A recent comparative analysis is E. Carlton, *Occupation: The policies and practices of military conquerors* (London, 1992).
3 *Rituals of Royalty: Power and Ceremonial in Traditional Societies*, ed. D. Cannadine and S. Price (Cambridge, 1987), is concerned mainly (though by no means exclusively) with the extra-European world. See also *Rites of Power: Symbolism, Ritual, and Politics Since the Middle Ages*, ed. S. Wilentz (Philadelphia, 1985).
4 A Giddens, *The Nation-State and Violence* (Cambridge, 1985), p. 2. For the medieval period, see the second, substantially revised edition of Michael Clanchy's seminal work, *From Memory to Written Record: England 1066–1307* (Oxford, 1993).
5 R.R. Davies, *Domination and Conquest: The experience of Ireland, Scotland and Wales 1100–1300* (Cambridge, 1990); R. Frame, *The Political Development of the British Isles 1100–1400* (Oxford, 1990). See also *The British Isles 1100–1500: Comparisons, Contrasts and Connections*, ed. R.R. Davies (Edinburgh, 1988).
6 Davies, *Domination and Conquest*, p. 3.

1350, when the multi-state character of Europe was consolidated, albeit within a larger culture which was gradually transplanted to the outer fringes by the 'leading edge' of expansion. As Bartlett argues, 'Europe, [later] the initiator of one of the world's major processes of conquest, colonization and cultural transformation, was also the product of one'.[1] Again, conquest, integration and coalescence are the leading themes in a recent volume of essays on the states of early modern Europe, edited by Mark Greengrass.[2] A special strength of all these contributions is that they shift some of the emphasis away from 'winners' such as England, France, Russia and Spain to lesser studied 'losers' such as Béarn, Bohemia, Flanders, Ireland, Silesia and the Ukraine. But perhaps their greatest value lies in the new dimension they add to debates about the dynamics of state-formation by stressing the extent to which the modes and scale of domination, the centralising activities of the state, were dictated in practice by *local* situations.

The state, in brief, was but one force in society, and its influence was by no means all dominant when it came face to face with local communities and power structures. As Greengrass has put it in respect of early modern states:

> We discern how aware rulers were of the importance of sustaining local identities and accepting regional differences. We note how they ignored at their peril the will and determination of the local élites in the process of forging new loyalties ... So an important additional perspective is added with the hypothesis that local society could be a motive force in the formation and consolidation of the European state, that local notables were capable of both opposing and exploiting the state for their own ends, and that successful integration was not just the conquest and absorption of the small by the large but also the coalescence and continuity of local and wider interests within a larger political framework.[3]

These words could equally well have been written with regard to the nature of the medieval state, as the following summary by Gerald Harriss underscores:

> To attribute the development of late medieval government solely to royal policy, and to measure it by the growth of central institutions or the enlargement of royal power, is to mistake its nature and miss

---

1 R. Bartlett, *The Making of Europe: Conquest, Colonization and Cultural Change 950–1350* (London, 1993), p. 314.
2 *Conquest and Coalescence: The Shaping of the State in Early Modern Europe*, ed. M. Greengrass (London, 1991).
3 *Ibid.*, pp. 6–7.

its essential dynamic. This, I believe, is to be found in the development of the society which government had to serve. Government was moulded more by pressures from within political society than by the efforts of kings or officials to direct it from above. It was these pressures which shaped the institutions of government, the conventions of governing, and the capacity of kings to govern effectively.[1]

Last, but by no means least, we must mention Paul Kennedy's widely acclaimed blockbuster, *The Rise and Fall of the Great Powers*, which ranges from the sixteenth century to today and tomorrow, and far beyond the conventional political and diplomatic concerns.[2] His basic thesis is that expansionary cycles, often related to uneven patterns of economic growth, create hegemonic commitments that lead inevitably to exhaustion, and while the notion of unavoidable 'imperial overstretch' has its critics, Kennedy's systematic exposure of the limits to empire-building can be seen to fit well with the conclusions of Greengrass and others. Once again, the picture that emerges is less one of comprehensive control and direction from the centre than of how dominant powers were trapped by the internal constraints that confronted them on the ground. Taking a wider historical view, we are forcibly reminded that, for all their apparent might, imperial regimes have never managed to control the whole of Europe, or even to maintain a lasting pre-eminence *within* Europe. However compelling the unitary ideal has been in theory, in practice political plurality has prevailed. Indeed, the impressive staying-power of the European sovereign state after the collapse of Rome, compared to the fate of subsequent empires — the last of them, the Soviet empire, has disintegrated before our very eyes — is arguably the single most important aspect of our collective history.[3]

Now, while historians and political and social theorists fully recognise that no European state developed in exactly the same way as another, most accept as a commonplace that, by 1700 at the very latest, the concept of 'the state' had become firmly established. This is to say that already the state's

---

1   G. Harriss, 'Political Society and the Growth of Government in Late Medieval England', *Past and Present*, 138 (1993), p. 33.

2   P. Kennedy, *The Rise and Fall of the Great Powers: Economic Change and Military Conflict from 1500 to 2000* (London, 1988).

3   This generalisation is not intended to suggest that the historical significance of empires has necessarily been overrated, or that the rise of independent sovereign states was in any way predestined. But medievalists will not all be convinced by the imperialist arguments in D.J.A. Matthew, 'Reflections on the Medieval Roman Empire', *History*, lxxvii (1992). Cf., for example, Reynolds, *Kingdoms and Communities*, especially pp. 292ff.

basic legal, fiscal and administrative functions and agencies had attained their decisive form; the people, or rather the local elites, had achieved a high level of participation in the political process; and the state had gained the unquestioning loyalty of the majority of its subjects in return for the protection it afforded them. But to turn to what Gerald Aylmer has called 'the ethos of the state'[1] is to enter more difficult terrain, that of the nation, national identity and nationalism, and of how nation-building stood in relation to state-building. According to much conventional wisdom, the idea of the nation, insofar as it existed, was something that for long developed independently to the concept of the state, and not until after the French Revolution was it generally recognised that the one could not achieve its fullest expression without the support of the other. Thus, so it has seemed, only then was it perceived that the ideal political unit, the most perfect of all communities, was one based on a fusion of nation and state — the nation-state, reinforced or 'legitimised' by a single ideology, the phenomenon of nationalism.

There is, however, a growing awareness of the dangers of accepting at face value the orthodoxy that there are precise typological distinctions between the 'feudal' state, the pre-Revolutionary 'absolute' state, and the modern nation-state. Before we look again at nationalism, it is important to stress that, to some extent at least, the discernible variables over time are differences of degree rather than of kind; broadly speaking, the more 'modern' the state, the greater its administrative-bureaucratic reach and hence its ability to regulate social affairs. Even then, if we take our lead from recent work on the interaction between central and local power, there are serious problems about supposing that there was a neat-and-tidy progression from the 'primitive' to the 'advanced'. Increases in the *quantity* of government do not necessarily involve improvements in the *quality* of government, that is, in a state's capacity to accomplish those tasks it set itself. It cannot be assumed that modern authoritarian regimes were automatically 'strong', or that states lacking highly centralised institutions and complex bureaucracies were automatically 'weak'. The paradoxical blend of central control and local autonomy (or delegation), representative of what has been termed 'the inherent entropy of feudal arrangements',[2] could in fact work well, or at least better than many crown-centred interpretations have suggested.[3] And the fact that this characteristic duality was evidently more strongly reflected in early modern 'absolutist' states than has often

---

1 G.E. Aylmer, 'The Peculiarities of the English State', *Journal of Historical Sociology*, iii (1990), p. 104.
2 G. Poggi, *The State: Its Nature, Development and Prospects* (Cambridge, 1990), p. 38.
3 Harriss, 'Government in Late Medieval England', is particularly useful in this context.

been appreciated suggests in itself that the supposedly distinctive features of 'absolutism' have been overdrawn.[1] As in the feudal world, successful rule depended on acknowledging the limits to state power, on pragmatic compromise and adjustment between sovereign and community interests — not on breaking down local solidarities, but on flexible collective government which rested on consultation and consent, and which was, in short, based on the rules, conventions and assumptions working for community consensus at lower levels. Indeed, it was precisely when a ruler tried to act in a tyrannical manner and displayed contempt for local rights and traditions that central power was likely to reveal its weakness and inefficiency.

Within historical sociology, Michael Mann's attempts in his *Sources of Social Power* to develop a new twofold typology of states are most relevant to these considerations.[2] He distinguishes the relative degrees of 'despotic' and 'infrastructural' power; simply put, the extent to which there was organic coordination between the state and its 'civil society' or (in Gerald Harriss's terms) a 'close integration of monarchy and society'.[3] In pre-industrial Europe, Mann has argued, a *greater* concentration of power was created when central government cooperated with local power holders than when it attempted arbitrarily to impose itself on them, and in Western Europe it was 'the despotically weak state [that] proved the general model for the modern era'.[4] Thus, the distinction between these two faces of power continued to be crucial, and John Hall and John Ikenberry, pursuing the relevance of Mann's thesis for contemporary history, conclude that:

> The notion of state capacity is *not* straightforward: above all it is an error to equate the strength or autonomy of the state with the ability of state elites to ignore other social actors or to impose their will in any simple manner on society. If this were the case, totalitarian states, which seek to suppress the independence of other social actors, would be most capable of realizing state goals ... Such a conclusion is not justified: a deeper dimension of state power has more to do with the state's ability to work through and with other

---

1 Besides the essays collected by Greengrass, see N. Henshall, *The Myth of Absolutism: Change and Continuity in Early Modern European Monarchy* (London, 1992), whose main thesis is that 'absolutism' is a meaningless term, obscuring the traditional nature of state-society relations during the *Ancien Régime*.
2 M. Mann, *The Sources of Social Power*, i: *A History of Power from the Beginning to A.D. 1760* (Cambridge, 1986). See also M. Mann, *States, War and Capitalism: Studies in Political Sociology* (Oxford, 1988), chapter 1.
3 Harriss, 'Government in Late Medieval England', p. 56.
4 Mann, *States, War and Capitalism*, p. 27.

centres of power. The capacity of states to act rationally is furthered and not curtailed when the state co-ordinates other autonomous power sources.[1]

From these perspectives, it can be suggested that medievalists and modernists have more to learn from each other than has often been thought, and that point applies equally to the thorny problem of nationalism. While many commentators continue to regard nationalism as primarily an invention of nineteenth-century Europe, others have re-focused attention on earlier periods by firmly situating its origins in the emergence of the medieval state. One forthright champion of the longer historical perspective is Geoffrey Barrow, with the experience of the 'community of the realm of Scotland' particularly in mind. In a typically stimulating passage, Barrow remarks that

> the very idea of nationalism in the middle ages has become one of our most rigidly-observed taboos. But surely we must take things as we find them. No doubt personal and feudal loyalty counted for much, no doubt men responded more fervently to the call of religious faith or to the sanctions of some lawful institution (especially if it were ancient) than to their country as such. Nevertheless, country had begun to make its appearance, and whenever it coincided with an ancient institution and was reinforced by a common language and culture, the resulting mixture became practically irresistible.[2]

In a related context, Michael Clanchy has made a powerful case for the strength of national identity and awareness in thirteenth-century England, cemented by royal government (and misgovernment), the effects of war, xenophobic prejudices, hostility to papal imperialism, and reactions to stronger senses of 'Scottishness' and 'Welshness'.[3] Furthermore, Clanchy plays down the uniqueness of the English, or British, situation and concludes:

> Although medieval nations cannot be equated in terms of political power with the sovereign states of modern Europe, national identity was already in the thirteenth century an important element in a ruler's authority over his own subjects and in the assertion of power over his neighbours.[4]

---

1 J.A. Hall and G.J. Ikenberry, *The State* (Milton Keynes, 1989), p. 95.
2 G.W.S. Barrow, *The Anglo-Norman Era in Scottish History* (Oxford, 1980), p. 148.
3 M.T. Clanchy, *England and its Rulers 1066–1272: Foreign Lordship and National Identity* (London, 1983), especially chapter 10.
4 *Ibid.*, p. 257.

It is also helpful to summarise the central features of the positions adopted by two other distinguished medievalists. Bernard Guenée has stressed that in the West by c.1300 there was a general correspondence between people, nation and state, so that 'with more or less success the later medieval States ... were concerned ... to rely on one language and the conviction of their inhabitants that they constituted a "nation". These States were undoubtedly "nation" States.'[1] For his part, Karl Ferdinand Werner, in one of his most recent contributions, argues that even in the early Middle Ages ideas about peoples and states were not unlike modern ideas about nation-states.

> 'Nations' ... have existed in both 'ancient' and 'medieval' times ... They are not our present-day nations — and this is why modern nations have had difficulties in recognizing them as true nations — and they are not yet aware of the self-determination (real or pretended) of contemporary nations ... This said, from the sixth century onwards one knew, and it was said, that a people that is not politically, or as a state, embodied in a *regnum* is condemned to disappear. Today we know that even the period of the migrations was followed immediately by an act of 'territorialization' that gave to the mixed populations resulting from these large-scale movements a political identity in a precise territory, namely the ability to be a *gens* in a *patria*.[2]

One basic way of illuminating concepts of nationhood in medieval and post-medieval Europe has been to locate individual 'nations' in their relevant historical and ethnic-cultural contexts. Notable here is the Blackwell's 'Peoples of Europe' series, edited by James Campbell and Barry Cunliffe, which aims at demonstrating the most significant and tenacious aspects of their corporate identities, the relationships they developed with states, and how their political independence was thereby sustained or ended. Volumes have already been published on the Basques, Bretons, English, Franks, Germans and Mongols, and others are promised on, for example, the Celts, Normans, Sicilians and Spanish. As for recent country-by-country studies, modern Europe has been particularly well served. The debate about the origins and development of the Irish nationalist movement continues to

---

1 B. Guenée, *States and Rulers in Later Medieval Europe* (Oxford, 1985), especially chapter 3; quotation at p. 54.
2 K.F. Werner, 'Political and Social Structures of the West, 300–1300', in *Europe and the Rise of Capitalism*, ed. J. Baechler, J.A. Hall and M. Mann (Oxford, 1988), p. 180.

reverberate.[1] The nature of 'British' identity has become a major preoccupation.[2] Nationalism in France remains a no less topical subject.[3] The same can be said of nation-building in Germany;[4] and, predictably, the climactic events of 1989–91 have kindled general interest in nationalities within the former Soviet empire.[5]

Viewed in comparative perspective, much of this recent work underlines the *diversity* of patterns of nationalism in the European nation-states, and how various the paths to 'national unity' actually were. In modern (and in medieval) states, policy makers and shapers were confronted with a variety of alternatives, some of which were less exclusive than others. At the liberal end of the spectrum lay non-doctrinaire regimes which specifically allowed for, and safeguarded, plural traditions and customs. 'Nationality', as Wolfgang Mommsen has written, 'was defined here in terms of the subjective political option by the individuals concerned rather than by "objective" factors like language, ethnicity and/or religion.'[6] To anyone familiar with the unitary and pluralistic features of medieval Britain, it will come as no surprise that this 'subjective' aspect of national unity was the hallmark of the composite British state (England, Scotland, Wales) created by the Treaty of Union in 1707. The net result, as Keith Robbins in particular has shown, was that a stronger sense of collective 'British' loyalty

1 For example, T. Bartlett, *The Fall and Rise of the Irish Nation: The Catholic Question 1690–1830* (Dublin, 1992); J. Fulton, *The Tragedy of Belief: Division, Politics, and Religion in Ireland* (Oxford, 1991); *The Revolution in Ireland, 1879–1923*, ed. D.G. Boyce (Basingstoke, 1988).
2 See most recently L. Colley, *Britons: Forging the Nation, 1707–1837* (New Haven, 1992); *Patriotism: The Making and Unmaking of British National Identity*, ed. R. Samuel (London, 1989).
3 See above all B. Jenkins, *Nationalism in France: Class and Nation since 1789* (London, 1990); *Nationhood and Nationalism in France: From Boulangism to the Great War 1889–1918*, ed. R. Tombs (London, 1991); *Searching for the New France*, ed. J.F. Hollifield and G. Ross (London, 1991).
4 The most important recent contributions include M. Hughes, *Nationalism and Society: Germany, 1800–1945* (London, 1988); H. James, *A German Identity, 1770–1990* (revised edn, London, 1990); *Nation-Building in Central Europe*, ed. H. Schulze (Leamington Spa, 1987); H. Schulze, *The Course of German Nationalism: From Frederick the Great to Bismark, 1763-1867* (Cambridge, 1991); *The State of Germany: The National Idea in the Making, Unmaking and Remaking of a Modern Nation-State*, ed. J. Breuilly (London, 1992).
5 For example, N. Diuk and A. Karatnycky, *New Nations Rising: The Fall of the Soviets and the Challenge of Independence* (New York, 1993); *The Nationalities Question in the Soviet Union*, ed. G. Smith (London, 1990); P.S. Wandycz, *The Price of Freedom: A history of East Central Europe from the Middle Ages to the present* (London, 1992).
6 W.J. Mommsen, 'The Varieties of the Nation State in Modern History: Liberal, Imperialist, Fascist and Contemporary Notions of Nation and Nationality', in *Rise and Decline of the Nation State*, ed. Mann, p. 213.

emerged in the nineteenth century not so much despite, but because of, the willingness to recognise older allegiances and sentiments, at least to a significant degree — and it went on to withstand the ordeal of the First World War under the leadership of a Prime Minister (David Lloyd George) whose first language was not English, but Welsh.[1] The success of this strategy (however flawed it seems with hindsight) serves only to reinforce arguments that a state can often achieve a greater measure of stability and strength when it recognises its limitations, is sensitive to local interests, and refrains from imposing inflexible demands from the centre. Yet the British path of development was scarcely the most typical one, and that brings us back to nationalism's Janus-like character, whether liberal-unificatory, repressive-exclusive, radical-democratic, or otherwise. How far particular kinds of nationalism were encouraged by certain political features such as strong citizenship rights and parliamentary traditions, or the lack of them, may be an issue worth exploring further. The same applies to the significance of geopolitical power politics, the importance of other factors that served to intensify feelings of 'us' and 'them', and the possibility that despotic forms should be understood (to extend Michael Mann's proposition) as an indication of the relative weakness of a state rather than of its strength.[2] Certainly, while a good deal has already been learned, plenty of challenges remain to be taken up if we are fully to account for the various nationalisms that emerged at different times and in different contexts.

Another striking feature of recent studies is how firmly political approaches are married to explorations of modern varieties of cultural nationalism as sources of solidarity and community: for example, the cultural values that shaped and reflected identity and nationhood in the seventeenth-century Dutch Republic;[3] or what, in a British context, has been called 'the splendid public spectacles of monarchy, the Royal Tournament, the Henry Wood Promenade Concerts, the old school tie, the Wimbledon tennis championships, Test Match cricket and Sherlock Holmes'.[4] Accordingly, much new light has been shed on the central issues of how distinctive

---

1 K. Robbins, *Nineteenth-Century Britain: Integration and Diversity* (Oxford, 1988); reissued as *Nineteenth-Century Britain. England, Scotland and Wales: The Making of a Nation* (Oxford, 1989).
2 The role of 'geopolitical rivalry, and [how] this impacted on every stage of the development of nationalism', have recently been discussed by M. Mann, 'The emergence of modern European nationalism', in *Transition to Modernity: Essays on power, wealth and belief*, ed. J.A. Hall and I.C. Jarvie (Cambridge, 1992).
3 S. Schama, *The Embarrassment of Riches: An Interpretation of Dutch Culture in the Golden Age* (London, 1987).
4 D. Cannadine, 'Gilbert and Sullivan: The Making and Unmaking of a British Tradition', in *Myths of the English*, ed. R. Porter (Cambridge, 1992), p. 25.

cultural traditions reinforced national identification; the ways in which they were articulated, transmitted and changed; the connections that have existed between cultural developments and fluctuations in the all-important socio-economic and political contexts, including oscillations in national power, prestige and alignments; and the extent to which national cultures were in fact formed by, as Ernest Gellner has argued, 'the general imposition of a high culture on society, where previously low cultures had taken up the lives of the majority, and in some cases of the totality, of the population'.[1]

The formation of a modern national culture through uniform administrative and educational systems, communications networks and technologies, linguistic standardisation, and other cultural agencies was, of course, also a matter of collective identities being influenced and fashioned by symbols, memories, images and vocabulary with the ability to conjure up the idea of a nation in the mind's eye: in Benedict Anderson's famous phrase, the nation is an 'imagined community'.[2] But we can no longer have any illusions that the discourse of national culture necessarily played the same role in the mentality of certain groups or classes as it did for others.[3] Put another way, every nation needs to manufacture a national history, blotting out painful episodes and glorifying past triumphs; but a nation's history can be variously understood and exploited in the 'national interest', depending on one's social, intellectual and/or political agenda — as graphically demonstrated by the recent (and very heated) German *Historikerstreit* about national credentials.[4] Likewise, we now need little reminding that the myths, rituals, slogans and other cultural representations that today underpin senses of nationhood are often relatively recent creations.[5] But earlier equivalents have been detected, for instance, in Shakespeare's plays,[6] in the national cults of

---

1 E. Gellner, *Nations and Nationalism* (Oxford, 1983), p. 57.
2 B. Anderson, *Imagined Communities: Reflections on the Origin and Spread of Nationalism* (revised edn, London, 1991). See also *Nation and Narration*, ed. H.K. Bhabha (London, 1990), one of several recent studies stimulated by Anderson's work.
3 M. Hroch, *Social Preconditions of National Revival in Europe: A Comparative Analysis of the Social Composition of Patriotic Groups among the Smaller European Nations* (Cambridge, 1985), is a seminal study of the social structure of modern 'patriotic communities'.
4 C.S. Maier, *The Unmasterable Past: History, Holocaust, and German National Identity* (Cambridge, Mass., 1988).
5 The classic discussion is still *The Invention of Tradition*, ed. E. Hobsbawm and T. Ranger (Cambridge, 1983).
6 A.J. Hoenselaars, *Images of Englishmen and Foreigners in the Drama of Shakespeare and His Contemporaries: A Study of Stage Characters and National Identity in English Renaissance Drama, 1558−1642* (London, 1992).

late medieval and Renaissance France,[1] in the cultivation of 'Englishness' by King Alfred the Great,[2] and in the earliest *origines gentium* (origin and descent myths) produced by the European peoples, which 'are not essentially different' from the 'legends that modern nations have created for themselves in their respective historiographies'.[3]

The fact remains, however, that any attempt to characterise the dynamics of a national culture is highly problematic. Major questions have been raised about the state and the emphasis often placed on the importance of its role as an 'inventor' of nations, as if the forging of national individuality was due exclusively to the activity and power of elites. Although some nations were much more obviously constructed from above than others, that emphasis sometimes seems to stem from the fallacy that national loyalties and cultures, being distinctly 'modern' curiosities, had necessarily to be superimposed. In any case, a statist view threatens to underestimate the extent to which the 'national community' was present at its own making as an active participant, rather than as some kind of dehumanised mass moulded by the state or (as in some functionalist arguments) by the engines of modernisation and industrialisation.[4] It is, indeed, important to remember the crucial reservation about the influential notion of 'invented traditions' — that they were most successful when they built on sentiments that were already present. Elite ideas may thus have evolved partly in response to messages from below.[5] And this corresponds well with Anthony Smith's significant qualifications of the 'states-make-nations' approach when he stresses the indispensability of a previously well-defined historic culture or ethnic core for the emergence of a strong national political culture and

---

1 C. Beaune, *The Birth of An Ideology: Myths and Symbols of Nation in Late Medieval France* (Berkeley, 1991); R.E. Asher, *National Myths in Renaissance France* (Edinburgh, 1993).

2 *Alfred the Great: Asser's Life of King Alfred and other contemporary sources*, ed. S. Keynes and M. Lapidge (Harmondsworth, 1983).

3 Werner, 'Political and Social Structures', pp. 180–1. For modern parallels, see most notably *Historians as Nation-Builders: Central and South-East Europe*, ed. D. Deletant and H. Hanak (Basingstoke, 1988).

4 For a recent critique of Gellner's stress on the cardinal significance of industrialisation, see P. Anderson, 'Science, politics, enchantment', in *Transition to Modernity*, ed. Hall and Jarvie, especially p. 208: 'there is a sense in which Gellner's theory of nationalism might be described as immoderately materialist. For what it plainly neglects is the overpowering dimension of collective *meaning* that modern nationalism has always involved: that is, not its functionality for industry, but its fulfilment of identity.'

5 *Invention of Tradition*, ed. Hobsbawm and Ranger, *passim*. Also useful to this argument is the emphasis on the mutual interaction between high and low culture in A. Gurevich, *Medieval Popular Culture: Problems of Belief and Perception* (Cambridge, 1988).

community.[1] Although Smith regards nationalism as a modern phenomenon, he nevertheless argues that:

> The 'nation' is not, as we see, built up only through the provision of 'infrastructures' and 'institutions', as 'nation-building' theories assumed; but from the central fund of culture and symbolism and mythology provided by shared historical experiences.[2]

Taking a broad historical view, Smith also writes:

> There were wide differences in ethnic cultures, despite the unifying bond of Catholicism, throughout the medieval era, and this 'ethnic mosaic' provided an important base for the subsequent [sic] consolidation of national states, first in western Europe, and later in central and eastern Europe.[3]

From a rather different standpoint, it is also useful to be reminded that state-sponsored compulsory education, as an instrument of nation-building, was a double-edged weapon and did not always achieve the desired results.[4] In this context, the point to be emphasised is the dangers, once again, of being mesmerised by the formal powers of centralist bureaucracies, and, still more, of assuming that the most effective state policy was a rigorous, doctrinaire insistence on a mono-cultural conception of the nation. Such a programme was beyond the coercive might of even the most authoritarian regimes, was likely to be at odds with 'popular' needs, and could fall far short of its objectives. As Mary Fulbrook has underlined in her recent discussion of twentieth-century German political culture,

> the interventionist nature of the Nazi state, in which 'total' claims were made on the lives of citizens, tended to produce a widespread 'inner emigration', as people learned to lead a double life, conforming in public and reserving their authentic feelings for private spaces and private lives. This phenomenon, frequently termed a *Nischengesellschaft* (niche society), has been widely observed in a number of East European societies which — in different ways — also tended to make total claims on their citizens.[5]

---

1   A.D. Smith, *The Ethnic Origins of Nations* (Oxford, 1986); A.D. Smith, 'State-Making and Nation-Building', in *States in History*, ed. Hall.
2   *Ibid.*, p. 258.
3   *Ibid.*, p. 245.
4   See especially J. Van Horn Melton, *Absolutism and the Eighteenth-Century Origins of Compulsory Schooling in Prussia and Austria* (Cambridge, 1988).
5   M. Fulbrook, *The Divided Nation: A History of Germany, 1918–1990* (Oxford, 1992), pp. 308–9.

Continuing in this vein, Fulbrook goes on to argue that

> structural conditioning does not mean that actual political cultures are necessarily those desired by political elites: modes of adaptation may be quite subversive, and, despite certain elite theories of history, elites have by and large proved to be notoriously bad at social engineering.[1]

In sum, we badly need to know more about what impact 'official' doctrine had on popular mentalities and, indeed, how far the latter left their imprint on the former. In this field, regional research has a basic importance for testing generalisations, and for the modern period two recent contributions, by Celia Applegate and Vicki Caron, deserve special mentions.[2]

Another issue strongly reflected in the recent literature is nationalism's built-in limitations as the basis of a group identity capable of transcending alternative sources of solidarity. As the British case shows, localism, regionalism, and other particularist attachments were not always incompatible with national loyalties. Nevertheless, some national identities were (and are) notably less unified and more rudimentary than others. At one extreme, 'a common symbolic universe was interpreted in divisive and conflict-laden ways by different social, regional and confessional groups, turning the representation of national unity into a vehicle for the expression of social, confessional and political antagonisms'.[3] Furthermore, a national culture inevitably involves exclusion from the 'family of the nation' as well as inclusion within it. Thus, just as scholars are re-examining the ethnic-cultural factors that helped to mould national communities, so they are re-evaluating the extent to which those self-same factors worked *against* national unity and cohesion within the state. After all, very few states, even European ones, have fitted the nation-state model exactly. As manifest cultural hybrids, many have contained within their boundaries large minority communities whose presence has often been a source of deep divisions. Much depended, of course, on the tone of the dominant nationalist ideology — on whether or not it was impatient of linguistic, religious and other differences, and sought to obliterate rather than subsume them. But some states, like Czechoslovakia or Yugoslavia, founded as a collection of minorities in 1918, were ethnic mixes leaving a country with little sense of common nationhood at all, and a precarious multi-national structure

1 *Ibid.*, p. 316.
2 C. Applegate, *A Nation of Provincials: The German Idea of Heimat* (Berkeley, 1990); V. Caron, *Between France and Germany: The Jews of Alsace-Lorraine, 1871–1918* (Stanford, 1988).
3 J. Sperber, 'Festivals of National Unity in the German Revolution of 1848–1849', *Past and Present*, 136 (1992), p. 137.

vulnerable to disintegration on today's pattern of seemingly endless ethnic-nationalist fission in Eastern Europe. Particularly timely, therefore, is another major interdisciplinary project sponsored by the European Science Foundation, 'Comparative Studies on Governments and Non-dominant Ethnic Groups in Europe, 1850-1940', which has helped to clarify, in Michael Thompson's words, 'the problem created by imposing the concept of the nation-state on a mosaic of frequently intermingled peoples of differing religion, language, and culture, whose geographical distribution and pattern of settlement simply did not conform to the abstract specifications assumed by the concept'.[1]

Few scholars, however, have been as bold as Eric Hobsbawm, who in his *Nations and nationalism since 1780*, first published by Cambridge University Press in 1990 and reissued in a second edition in 1992, has provided a succinct dissection of the phases of modern nationalism and a controversial assessment of its relevance in today's world. After the Age of Revolution (1780−1830) and the Age of Liberalism (1830−1870) came, in Hobsbawm's periodisation, the Age of Transformation (1870−1918), when two interconnected movements accelerated and ultimately propelled Europe into the mass slaughter of the First World War. One the one hand, rapidly expanding state bureaucracies engaged in 'ideological engineering' to encourage stronger senses of nationhood. On the other, the capitalist dynamic and democratisation generated major social tensions, especially among the petite bourgeoisie, who abandoned liberal ideas and espoused a militant form of nationalism characterised by anti-semitism, chauvinism and xenophobia. The next phase, the Apogee of Nationalism (1918−1950), was inaugurated by President Wilson's flawed attempt to revive liberal principles and solve the problems of Eastern Europe on the basis of national self-determination, which had two unintended but far-reaching results. First, it led with barbaric logic to the deportation and mass murder of minorities — Hitler, in Hobsbawm's view, was a Wilsonian nationalist *par excellence*. Second, after 1945 Wilsonian ideology helped to stimulate anti-imperial liberation movements in the Third World — though the pluri-ethnic entities emerging from decolonisation were structurally different from the 'standard' Western pattern of the nation-state.

Hobsbawm's final phase, the Decline of Nationalism, saw, in his view, a decisive marginalisation of the nation due to the bipolarisation of the world during the Cold War and the progressive undermining of the autonomy and

---

1 This project's findings have been reported in a series of eight volumes, the last published being *Governments, Ethnic Groups and Political Representation*, ed. G. Alderman in collaboration with J. Leslie and K.E. Pollmann (Aldershot, 1993); quotation from Thompson at p. xv.

competence of nation-states by international capitalism and the other forces of globalisation. According to this analysis, originally developed in the 1980s and still staunchly defended in 1992, nation-states and nationalism can be seen to have lost their former dominance, and the old nationalist yearnings must be written off as irrational and unrealistic programmes, irrelevant to the big issues of the day, and 'no longer a major vector of historical development'.[1]

To Hobsbawm's critics, even from the standpoint of 1990, these were provocative and questionable conclusions. Now, after the final death-throes of the Soviet Union, with the racism that has erupted in the newly reunited Germany, and with the intense reassertion of national identities in the Baltic states, the Ukraine, Georgia, Azerbaijan, Armenia, Hungary, Bulgaria, and the former Czechoslovakia and Yugoslavia — not to mention renewed nationalist enthusiasm among the Scots, Corsicans, Basques, Catalans, and seemingly countless others — the demise of nationalism seems to be as far away as ever. As we approach the second millennium, commentators can differ over their explanations of this 'rebirth of history'[2] — whether, for example, the resurgence of East European nationalism was a cause or (in Hobsbawm's view) a mere consequence of the collapse of Soviet power. They can disagree over whether the new movements owe most to the 'emancipatory' ideology of liberal nationalism or to the repressive features of exclusive national ideals. They can also dispute whether the newly independent nation-states are viable self-supporting entities or mere 'balalaika republics' likely to fall apart as rapidly as they have appeared.[3] But what *is* incontestable is that nationalist fervour is transforming the political map of Europe in the most profound and startling ways.

And, finally, while state frontiers multiply in Eastern Europe, today's political debate in Western Europe is dominated by the so-called 'fast tracking' of the processes of European integration. Self-evidently, one major problem for the European Community's grand vision of itself as a powerful super-state is which post-communist democracies to exclude and how to keep them excluded; another is the acute difficulty of reconciling the conflicting demands of federalism and national sovereignty. The rejection of

---

1 Hobsbawm, *Nations and nationalism* (1990 edn), p. 163. For the 1992 edition, Hobsbawm's last chapter, 'Nationalism in the late twentieth century', was rewritten in the light of events since 1989, but with renewed stress on 'the *decline* [Hobsbawm's emphasis] of nationalism as a vector of historical change' (p. 163).
2 M. Glenny, *The Rebirth of History: Eastern Europe in the Age of Democracy* (2nd edn, Harmondsworth, 1993).
3 For a measured (and optimistic) assessment of the future prospects of the Baltic states, see J. Hiden and P. Salmon, *The Baltic Nations and Europe: Estonia, Latvia and Lithuania in the Twentieth Century* (London, 1991).

the Treaty of Maastricht in the first Danish referendum (2 June 1992) and the deep ambivalence of British attitudes towards the rest of Europe — quite apart from the present Community-wide inability to agree common economic, social, foreign and security policies — are proof enough that centrifugal forces are no less strong than centripetal ones. Indeed, it is perhaps the supreme irony that in Belgium itself, the supposed epicentre of the new Europe, nationalist feelings are gaining ground in both the Dutch-speaking Flemish and the French-speaking Walloon communities, marginalising the traditional unifying role of the monarchy and threatening political chaos. At the risk of oversimplifying, it is as if the prospect of closer European union has served only to reactivate historic antagonisms and reinforce national loyalties

For all these reasons, the problem of 'identity' in Western and Eastern Europe has never had greater relevance, and the contradictory processes at work in the present inevitably compel us to review the balance and direction of our approaches to the past. Why is the notion of European integration strongly contested in the West and why did the party-state system fail in the East? Have national sovereignties and identities embarked on a losing battle against 'progressive' forces? How should 'Europe' be defined? What is meant by a 'European' identity, and can it ever resolve conflicting concepts of community? For the historian, the main implications of these questions seem to be twofold. First, it is not enough to try to find some kind of answer to today's problems in the history of medieval empires or of the composite states of early modern Europe, stimulating though such approaches have been.[1] What is needed is a more concerted dialogue between medievalists and modernists concerning the historical development and character of political communities — in particular, the factors that made some European states, however constituted, more (or less) stable, durable and successful than others, and the extent to which central power could afford to cut across forces emanating from within society itself. Second, the movement for greater European unity, however problematic it remains, seems bound to refuel efforts to debate issues from a more pronounced pan-European perspective; not (it is to be hoped) by developing some spurious all-European model that ignores the historical cleavages, diversities and contrasts, but by giving proper weight both to the distinctive qualities of national histories and to those transnational economic, political and cultural interrelationships that have shaped people's lives in Europe as a whole. For the present, however, there is still some way to go before we come fully to grips with the challenges of this current 'crisis of historiography', not

---

1 Matthew, 'Medieval Roman Empire'; J.H. Elliott, 'A Europe of Composite Monarchies', *Past and Present*, 137 (1992).

only in our own researches but in the curricula devised for schools and universities.[1]

1 This concluding paragraph owes much to Keith Robbins's thought-provoking article, 'National Identity and History: Past, Present and Future', *History*, lxxv (1990), reprinted in K. Robbins, *History, Religion and Identity in Modern Britain* (London, 1993). For contributions which respond expressly to the challenge of contemporary events, see most recently *National histories and European history*, ed. M. Fulbrook (London, 1993), and *The National Question in Europe in Historical Context*, ed. M. Teich and R. Porter (Cambridge, 1993).

The Origin of Scottish Identity

Dauvit Broun

It is often said that Scotland is in origin a 'hybrid' kingdom, consisting of an amalgam of four peoples — the Scots, the Picts, the Britons of Strathclyde and the Angles of northern Bernicia — who were gradually 'united' over two centuries in a process which began in about 843 when the king of the Scots, Cináed mac Ailpín (Kenneth mac Alpin), also became king of the Picts.[1] Cináed is usually reckoned to have been the first of a line of kings reigning over what had been the territories of the Picts and Scots, defined generally as the land-mass north of the Firths of Forth and Clyde. This 'Scoto-Pictish' kingdom is generally referred to as *Scotia* or *Alba* — as it was, indeed, by contemporaries. *Scotia* and *Alba*, of course, now mean 'Scotland' in Latin and Gaelic respectively. It is no surprise, therefore, that Cináed mac Ailpín is sometimes represented as the first king of Scotland.[2] In the view of Archibald Duncan, however, it is anachronistic to regard

---

1 See, for instance, W.C. Dickinson, *Scotland from the Earliest Times to 1603*, revised by A.A.M. Duncan (Oxford, 1977), pp. 23, 26; J.D. Mackie, *A History of Scotland* (revised edn, Harmondsworth, 1969), pp. 33, 38; also A.P. Smyth, *Warlords and Holy Men: Scotland 80–1000* (London, 1984), p. 210, and E.J. Cowan, 'Myth and Identity in Early Medieval Scotland', *Scottish Historical Review*, lxiii (1984). The phrase 'hybrid kingdom' is used by A.A.M. Duncan, 'The Kingdom of the Scots', in *The Making of Britain: The Dark Ages*, ed. L.M. Smith (London, 1984), p. 136.
2 Scottish kings are traditionally numbered from Cináed mac Ailpín ('Kenneth I'), so that 'Constantine I' is Constantín mac Cináeda (862–77), not Constantín mac Fergusa (king of *Fortriu*, 789–820); 'Donald I' is Domnall mac Ailpín (858–62), not Domnall Brecc mac Echdach (king of *Dál Riata*, 629–42); and 'Malcolm IV' (1153–65) is the fourth King Máelcoluim to succeed Cináed mac Ailpín: also see, e.g., Mackie, *Scotland*, p. 38; F.J. Byrne, *Irish Kings and High-Kings* (London, 1973), p. 260; G. Donaldson and R. Morpeth, *A Dictionary of Scottish History* (Edinburgh, 1977), p. 233. In this essay, where I refer to pre-12th-century Scottish kings, I have preferred to use their Middle Gaelic names and patronymics rather than the traditional English forms (where those exist), namely:

Cináed mac Ailpín	= Kenneth mac Alpin / Kenneth I (843–58)
Domnall mac Ailpín	= Donald I (858–62)
Constantín mac Cináeda	= Constantine I (862–77)
Áed mac Cináeda	= Aed (877–8)
Domnall mac Constantín	= Donald II (889–900)
Constantín mac Áeda	= Constantine II (900–43)
Cináed mac Máelcoluim	= Kenneth II (971–95)

[continued overleaf]

Cináed as 'king of Scotland', because his rule did not include the area within present-day Scotland south of the Forth.[1] As far as Duncan (and others) are concerned it is axiomatic that 'Scotland', whatever the period, is more than just the original *Scotia* or *Alba*. For him, therefore, when Cináed mac Ailpín's successors succeeded in extending their kingdom south of the Forth in the mid-tenth century, 'Alba had become Scotland'.[2] Even so, when the 'hybrid' Scottish kingdom, which included both Strathclyde Britons and Angles south of the Forth, took shape in the eleventh century, Duncan argues that the 'unity of Scotland', 'the sense of being one people', was still another two centuries in the future, during which time the ethnic mix had become further complicated by the immigration of French, English and Flemings in the twelfth century and by the annexation of the Gaelic-Scandinavian Western Isles in 1266.[3] According to this widely accepted view, it was as subjects of an increasingly effective kingship in the twelfth and thirteenth centuries that these different peoples were welded together to form 'one kingdom and one people': in Duncan's words, 'it was as kingdom

Máelcoluim mac Cináeda = Malcolm II (1005–34)
Macbethad mac Findlaích = Macbeth (1040–57)
Máelcoluim mac Donnchada = Malcolm III (1058–93)

The genealogical descent to Constantín mac Áeda is as follows:

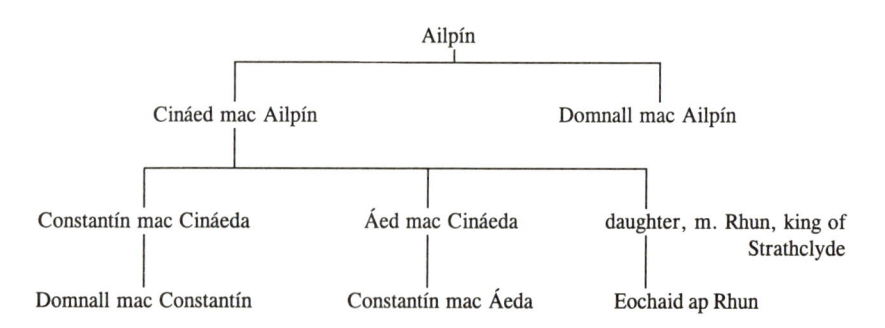

```
                        Ailpín
            ┌──────────────┴──────────────┐
      Cináed mac Ailpín              Domnall mac Ailpín
            │
   ┌────────┼────────────────┐
Constantín mac Cináeda   Áed mac Cináeda    daughter, m. Rhun, king of
                                                    Strathclyde
       │                        │                    │
Domnall mac Constantín   Constantín mac Áeda    Eochaid ap Rhun
```

---

1 Duncan, 'Kingdom of the Scots', p. 135. For his other work on the subject, see the following two notes, and also A.A.M. Duncan, *Scotland: The Making of the Kingdom* (Edinburgh, 1975).
2 A.A.M. Duncan, 'The making of the kingdom', in *Why Scottish History Matters*, ed. R. Mitchison (Edinburgh, 1991), p. 7.
3 Duncan, 'Kingdom of the Scots', p. 144; A.A.M. Duncan, 'The Making of Scotland', in *Who Are the Scots?*, ed. G. Menzies (London, 1971), p. 138; Duncan and Dickinson, *Scotland from the Earliest Times*, p. 33.

The Origin of Scottish Identity

and then as community, that Scotland was put together'.[1]

In the light of these comments it might be expected that a discussion of the origins of Scottish identity should focus on the thirteenth century. After all, according to the current view, it is only in the second half of that century, when contemporary Scots began to refer to the area south of the 'Forth-Clyde line' as part of *Scotia*,[2] that we see 'the first emergence of "Scotland" in a modern sense'.[3] A chronicler at Melrose, recording events which occurred in 1216, applied the term 'Scot' particularly to the inhabitants of the original 'Scoto-Pictish' *Scotia*, north of the Forth, and regarded them as sacrilegious hooligans, much as was the wont of English commentators.[4] By the second half of the century, however, all subjects of the king of Scots were 'Scots', regardless of their antecedents or location within his realm.[5] While this process certainly involved a change of identity for those living south of the Forth, it cannot, however, be said to represent the coining of a new identity as such; rather, it is better understood as an extension of the existing identifiers *Scotia* and *Scoti* ('Scotland' and 'Scots') to apply to those beyond the original *Scotia* who had been ruled without interruption since 1124 by a succession of kings who described themselves as 'kings of Scots'.[6] As far as contemporary Scots were concerned, the existence of 'Scotland' and its people the 'Scots', corresponding with the 'kingdom of the Scots', were not invented in the thirteenth century. All these terms related to the original *Scotia*, 'Scotland' north of the Forth; the description of the kingdom of the Scots in *De Situ Albanie* (1165×1184)

---

1   Duncan, 'The making of the kingdom', p. 13; see also G.W.S. Barrow, *Kingship and Unity: Scotland 1000–1306* (London, 1981), p. 153; R. Mitchison, *A History of Scotland* (2nd edn, London, 1982), p. 14. For a different view, see M. Lynch, *Scotland: A New History* (London, 1991), p. 49, who talks of the Scottish *regnum* and *gens* coming together by 1034, when Máelcoluim mac Cináeda (Malcolm II) at his death is referred to by one contemporary as 'king of *Scotia*'.

2   Barrow, *Kingship and Unity*, p. 153; Duncan, 'Making of Scotland', p. 129.

3   G.W.S. Barrow, *Robert Bruce and the Community of the Realm of Scotland* (3rd edn, Edinburgh, 1988), p. 6.

4   In A.O. Anderson, *Early Sources of Scottish History A.D.500–1286*, i (Edinburgh, 1922), pp. 407–9.

5   Barrow, *Kingship and Unity*, p. 153; Duncan, 'Making of Scotland', p. 138; Duncan, 'The making of the kingdom', p. 13. William I's chapel was the first to address the king's subjects indiscriminately as 'Scots' (rather than as 'French, English and Scots' or suchlike); this became established practice from as early as 1179: *Regesta Regum Scottorum*, ii: *The Acts of William I, 1165–1214*, ed. G.W.S. Barrow (Edinburgh, 1971), p. 77.

6   Duncan, 'Making of Scotland', pp. 129–30; *Regesta Regum Scottorum*, i: *The Acts of Malcolm IV, 1153–65*, ed. G.W.S. Barrow (Edinburgh, 1960), p. 69, where it is noted that the style 'king of Scotland' was also used, but only very occasionally; *Regesta Regum Scottorum*, ii, p. 75.

as north of the Forth would have raised few eyebrows.[1] It would not be surprising, though, if in time this original sense of the Scottish kingdom was no longer felt to be appropriate for a kingship which had established its rule as far as the Tweed and Solway. Geoffrey Barrow has drawn attention to how areas beyond the original *Scotia* were first referred to as being in the 'kingdom of the king of Scots' or simply the 'kingdom of Scotland' as early as 1161/2, and how this usage became common from the 1190s.[2] There was, therefore, an intermediate stage of more than half a century in which contemporaries commonly regarded the Scottish kingdom as consisting of more than just 'Scotland' (*Scotia*) and the 'Scots', before the meaning of 'Scotland' automatically corresponded once again with the kingdom and the entire people of the kingdom were identified again as 'Scots'.

If contemporary Scots were familiar with 'Scotland', the 'Scots', and a corresponding kingdom of the Scots before the thirteenth century, then I would argue that we should not be squeamish about talking of Scotland or Scottish identity before the terms 'Scotland' and 'Scots' came to be applied to what we can recognise (roughly speaking) as 'modern Scotland'. To insist that Scotland was not a meaningful concept, or that Scottish identity did not exist before the end of the thirteenth century, would surely be to allow our modern idea of Scotland to take precedence over the view of contemporaries. Indeed, strictly speaking, 'Scotland' cannot be said to have emerged in a modern sense until the Northern Isles became part of Scotland in the aftermath of their cession by the king of Denmark in 1468−9. The argument that Scotland only came into being once Scottish identity was adopted by the inhabitants of the lands between the Forth-Clyde line and the Tweed and Solway, or when the rule of the kings of *Scotia* or *Alba* was first extended beyond *Scotia* in the tenth century, therefore simply reflects the view of modern historians about what they regard as crucial ingredients of modern Scotland (in this case Lothian and the south-west, but not the Northern Isles). It hardly needs to be said, however, that the territories of kingdoms and states are flexible and that identities change and develop. If we eschew any tendency towards taking a determinist view, we should recognise that, while Scotland and Scottish identity developed significantly in the thirteenth century, both were by then already well established in the minds of contemporaries. In this essay, I shall discuss when this Scottish identity first appeared and what it then signified, and offer some suggestions

---

1 Edited in M.O. Anderson, *Kings and Kingship in Early Scotland* (2nd edn, Edinburgh, 1980), pp. 240−3; translated in Anderson, *Early Sources*, i, pp. cxv−cxix.
2 G.W.S. Barrow, *The Anglo-Norman Era in Scottish History* (Oxford, 1980), pp. 153−4.

about how it can be understood.

*

When the 'Scots' are mentioned as part of the 'ethnic mix' which, according to the usual account, came together to form 'modern Scotland', the people who are thereby referred to are the kin-based group who called themselves the *Dál Riata* and who identified themselves, along with the inhabitants of Ireland, as *Gáedil* ('Gaels'). The *Gáedil* were called *Scoti* in Latin, hence the learned origin-legend which described how they were descended from *Gáedel Glas* ('Mr. Gael', as it were) and his wife (or mother) *Scota* ('Ms. Gael').[1] It is well known, however, that by the eleventh century *Scoti* could be used to refer specifically to the inhabitants of Scotland, the kingdom of *Scotia* north of the Forth.[2] The term *Scotia* itself had undergone a similarly radical change, having once been a common term for Ireland (or, more correctly, 'Gaeldom').[3] Clearly, such a change represents more than just a development of an existing identity. Although the *literati* (at least) of eleventh-century Scotland still identified themselves as Gaels, *Scoti* and *Scotia* now signified something markedly different; a new identity had appeared — the identity of the Scots and Scotland which subsequently extended south of the Forth-Clyde line in the thirteenth century.

This change of identity is seen most clearly in the change in what the learned Latin term *Scoti* denoted in Middle Gaelic, the Scots' own language: *Scoti* no longer meant simply *Gáedil*, but could now be translated as *fir Alban* or *Albanaig*, the 'men of Scotland'.[4] The key word is *Alba*, which has remained the Gaelic term for 'Scotland' ever since. It was not always translated as *Scotia* in Latin, but was sometimes Latinised simply as *Albania*, especially in the oldest extant Scottish Latin works relating to the Scottish kingdom and its history.[5] Like *Scotia*, however, *Alba* had not always meant 'Scotland'; it was originally the Gaelic for the island of Britain. Again, therefore, an existing term — this time in the Scots' own language — under-

---

1 D. Brown, 'The Scottish Origin-Legend before Fordun' (Edinburgh University Ph.D. thesis, 1989), pp. 378 ff.
2 W.F. Skene, *Celtic Scotland: A History of Ancient Alban*, i (Edinburgh, 1876), p. 2, and p. 3 n. 4.
3 *Ibid*. *Scotia* was, indeed, used to refer to Ireland. Its literal meaning is, however, 'Gaeldom'; hence, as T.F. O'Rahilly (*Early Irish History and Mythology* [Dublin, 1946], p. 86 n.2) pointed out, Bede was able to refer to Iona as part of *Scotia*. It would appear that Dicuil (writing in the first half of the 9th century) used *Scotia* in this sense in his *De Mensura Orbis Terrae* when he talked of hermits travelling from Ireland as leaving *nostra Scotia*.
4 O'Rahilly, *Irish History and Mythology*, p. 386 and n. 2.
5 Skene, *Celtic Scotland*, i, p. 3 and n. 4, referring in particular to the *Old Scottish Chronicle* (which he calls the 'Pictish Chronicle') and to *De Situ Albanie*.

went a dramatic transformation in order to denote 'Scotland'. Such a radical change again surely signifies an attempt to articulate a new identity.

The initial articulation of this new identity (among the learned orders, at any rate) is best appreciated with reference to the term *Alba*. Not only is it found unambiguously denoting 'Scotland', either as *Alba* or Latinised as *Albania*, earlier than the term *Scotia*, but it is (unlike *Scoti* or 'Scots') the keyword of this new identity in the native language of the people concerned. It is more accurate, therefore, to say that 'Scotland' or *Scotia* denotes *Alba*, rather than the other way round.

It has long been noted how, in Irish annals, the first contemporaneous reference to *Alba* meaning Scotland is in the notice of the death in 900 of Domnall mac Constantín (Donald II, 889–900), who is described as *rí Alban*, 'king of Scotland'. This title was thereafter used regularly to describe Domnall's successors. In contrast, Domnall's predecessors, from his grandfather Cináed mac Ailpín (d. 858) to his uncle Áed mac Cináeda (d. 878), are each referred to as *rex Pictorum*, 'king of the Picts'. (The Irish annals give no notice of the death or deposition of Domnall's immediate predecessor, who was either his cousin Eochaid ap Rhun or a certain Giric.)[1] Both the *Annals of Ulster* and the *Chronicon Scotorum*, the chief witnesses in this period of the lost 'Chronicle of Ireland' (from which all the Irish annal-collections are ultimately derived), switch from the terminology 'king of the Picts' to 'king of Scotland' in 900.[2] It is likely, therefore, that this change appeared in the 'Chronicle of Ireland' itself. Moreover, since it has been shown that the 'Chronicle of Ireland' continued only as far as 911,[3] it may be suggested that it was a contemporary annalist who in 900 for the first time wrote 'king of Scotland' rather than 'king of the Picts'.

This new terminology for the kingdom of Cináed mac Ailpín's successors was not, however, simply dreamt up by an Irish annalist. A strikingly similar change in terminology can also be seen in the so-called *Old Scottish Chronicle*, which covers the second half of the ninth century and the first three-quarters of the tenth century and is the chief Scottish source

---

1 See Anderson, *Early Sources*, i, pp. 287 and n. 3, 290 and n. 6, 277 and n. 2, 356, 395 and n. 2, 451 and n. 3, and the following pages thereafter.
2 *The Annals of Ulster (to A.D. 1131)*, ed. S. Mac Airt and G. Mac Niocaill (Dublin, 1983); *Chronicon Scotorum: a chronicle of Irish affairs from the earliest times to A.D.1135, with a supplement, 1141–50* (London, 1866), ed. W.M. Hennesy. See K. Hughes, *Early Christian Ireland: an introduction to the sources* (London, 1972), pp. 97–115. For convenience, I shall use Anderson, *Early Sources*, to give references to the Irish annals.
3 K. Grabowski, 'The Annals of Innisfallen, A.D.431–1092: sources, structure and history', in K. Grabowski and D. Dumville, *Chronicles and Annals of Mediaeval Ireland and Wales: The Clonmacnoise-group Texts* (Woodbridge, 1984), pp. 53–6.

for this period.[1] Up to the reign of Domnall mac Constantín, the *Chronicle* (written almost entirely in Latin) regularly describes the region ruled by Cináed mac Ailpín and his successors as *Pictavia*, 'Pictland'; but thereafter it calls it exclusively *Albania*, using this term for the first time in its account of the Danish devastation caused by the grandsons of Ivar in 903.[2] It is very likely that this change in terminology is attributable to a contemporary Scottish witness. The *Chronicle* survives only as part of a fourteenth-century English collection of Scottish historical pieces which, Marjorie Anderson has argued, were originally compiled between 1165 and 1184.[3] But since it represents chiefly a history of the Scottish kingdom from Cináed mac Ailpín to Cináed mac Máelcoluim (Kenneth II, 971–95), whose reign-length is left blank, it would seem that the *Chronicle* more or less assumed its present proportions some time during the reign of Cináed mac Máelcoluim. The basic pattern of the *Chronicle* consists, furthermore, of naming each king with his reign-length and noticing some events which occurred during his reign, usually relating to the kingship and mainly in the east of Scotland from modern Clackmannanshire to Atholl and Angus. From 849 to 952 these events are commonly noted according to the year of the king's reign;[4] it would appear, therefore, either that the *Chronicle* is itself a more-or-less contemporary source for this period,[5] or (which is more likely) that it represents what is probably a selection from a set of Scottish annals,

---

1 Edited in Anderson, *Kings and Kingship*, pp. 249–53; edited and translated in B.T. Hudson, 'The *Old Scottish Chronicle*' (forthcoming). See also E.J. Cowan, 'The Scottish Chronicle in the Poppleton Manuscript', *Innes Review*, xxxii (1981).
2 Anderson, *Early Sources*, i, pp. 444 and 399.
3 Anderson, *Kings and Kingship*, p. 236; M.O. Anderson, 'The Scottish Materials in a Paris Manuscript, Bib. Nat. Latin 4126', *Scot. Hist. Rev.*, xxviii (1949), p. 34. M. Miller, 'Matriliny by treaty: the Pictish foundation-legend', in *Ireland in Early Mediaeval Europe: Studies in memory of Kathleen Hughes*, ed. D. Whitelock *et al.* (Cambridge, 1982), pp. 139–42, suggests a dating 1202×14 (but see Brown, 'Scottish Origin-Legend', pp. 13–17), and argues persuasively that the compilation was put together at Scone.
4 The deaths of Cináed mac Ailpín and his brother Domnall are dated precisely to the day, suggesting a contemporary record; see, however, Anderson, *Early Sources*, i, p. 288 n. 7. Precise datings are also given for Olaf's arrival and departure in 866, and for an eclipse in 885 (see *ibid.*, p. 364 n. 3).
5 As B.T. Hudson suggests, '*Old Scottish Chronicle*' (forthcoming). Given the evidence for the continuing use of Pictish terminology to describe the kingdom, and for a Pictish king-list written in Scotland which terminated with Constantín mac Cináeda (see Anderson, *Kings and Kingship*, pp. 78–9, 83), I find it difficult to believe that a 9th-century chronicler, never mind a contemporary of Cináed mac Ailpín's, would have regarded Cináed as the first king of a new kingship. The fact that the contemporary record, as it appears in the *Chronicle*, has variations in spelling and gaps in its dating is not inconsistent with its being derived from a set of annals.

now lost, which was kept from approximately the mid-ninth to the mid-tenth centuries in the heartland of the kingdom of Cináed mac Ailpín and his successors.[1] Accordingly, the change from *Pictavia* to *Albania* in the *Old Scottish Chronicle* can be explained with some confidence as the work of a Scottish annalist working in *c.*900.

Our evidence for contemporary Scottish terminology in this period is, however, probably greater than simply the annalistic element in the *Old Scottish Chronicle*. The coincidence that the changeovers from *rex Pictorum* to *rí Alban* in what was the 'Chronicle of Ireland', and from 'Pictland' to *Alba* by an annalist in the heart of the Scottish kingdom, both occur in *c.*900 is particularly striking. The most attractive explanation is that annalists working on the 'Chronicle of Ireland' and the Scottish annals were in close contact with each other. Indeed, among the selection from the Scottish annals which survive in the *Old Scottish Chronicle* there is a series of entries concerning the Uí Néill 'kings of Tara' from the death of Máel Sechnaill mac Máel Ruanaid in 862 to the death of Niall Glúndub mac Áeda in 919, and also entries noting the deaths of Domnall mac Áeda, king of Ailech, in 915[2] and Cormac mac Cuilennáin, king of Munster, in 908. This suggests that contact between Scottish and Irish annalists could have been active (though not necessarily continuous) throughout most of the second half of the ninth century and well into the first quarter of the tenth. (Although the 'Chronicle of Ireland' is no longer a common source for all Irish annal-collections after 911 this, of course, does not mean that its text ceased to be updated and developed, only that the work of updating and developing survives independently from more than one *scriptorium*.[3]) On the other hand, there is a formal possibility that this contact between Scottish and Irish annalists was not contemporaneous. There is nothing to suggest that the *Old Scottish Chronicle* has derived its annalistic material from a set of Irish

---

1 That the *Chronicle* is a selection from a contemporary record, rather than the original contemporary record itself, could explain how an event in Constantín mac Cináeda's fourteenth year (875) is described in the *Chronicle* as occurring 'shortly after' (*paulo post*) an event in his third year. Cowan, 'Scottish Chronicle', p. 18, describes the *Chronicle* as the conflation of a king-list with a set of annals. As Professor Duncan has pointed out to me, however, it is more likely that the king-list element was also derived from the same set of annals; for, in any event, the most obvious way in which a king-list would have been constructed was from an annalistic source. Professor Cowan suggests that the *Chronicle* was composed at Brechin and edited at Loch Leven.

2 B.T. Hudson, '*Elech* and the Scots in Strathclyde', *Scottish Gaelic Studies*, xv (1988), pp. 145–9.

3 For the most detailed discussion of when it can be said that the ancestor of the Clonmacnoise group of annals began to be written independently of the source it shares ultimately with the *Annals of Ulster*, see D. Dumville, 'When was the "Clonmacnoise Chronicle" created? The evidence of the Welsh annals', in Grabowski and Dumville, *Chronicles and Annals*; he dates it 911×54.

annals cognate with the *Annals of Ireland* or the *Chronicon Scotorum*, but it is not inconceivable that Scottish entries in these and related Irish annal-collections were ultimately derived at a later date from the same set of Scottish annals as the *Old Scottish Chronicle*. Whether or not, however, the evident contact between Scottish and Irish annalists occurred in the second half of the ninth and first half of the tenth centuries, we can (either way) be confident that the change in c.900 from *rex Pictorum* to *rí Alban* in the *Annals of Ulster* and the *Chronicon Scotorum* reflects the terminology of a contemporary Scottish source. It is probable, therefore, that these Irish annal-collections record contemporary Scottish terminology in their Scottish entries relating to this period, probably from at least their notice of the death of Cináed mac Ailpín, *rex Pictorum*, in 858.[1]

This is important if we wish to argue that a new terminology was adopted in Scotland to denote not only the kingship of Cináed mac Ailpín's successors and their kingdom, but also the people they ruled. The problem is that the *Old Scottish Chronicle* refers to them (with one exception)[2] as *Scoti*; the first instance is in its notice of the defeat of Constantín mac Cináeda (Constantine I, 862–77) by the Danes at Dollar in 875. It may not be too significant that *Albani* (or suchlike) does not appear, but there is certainly a need to explain why the Picts are mentioned only in the second sentence of the *Chronicle*. Here we are told that *Pictavia* is called after the Picts whom Cináed mac Ailpín destroyed, and explains that God deigned to deprive them of their heritage 'because they not only spurned the Lord's mass and precept, but also refused to be held equal to others in the law of justice'. That reads more like a stock piece of moralising than a contemporary statement;[3] it is an elaborate gloss on *Pictavia*, possibly by the person who, in the last third of the tenth century (as was suggested above), drew on material from a set of Scottish annals to create the *Old Scottish Chronicle*. If this is the case, a purpose would not be difficult to suggest. By his time the kingship would have been securely monopolised by Cináed mac Ailpín's dynasty. In its format, the *Old Scottish Chronicle* is self-consciously a

---

1 In the first half of the 9th century the *Annals of Ulster* consistently refer to kings who appear in the Pictish king-list as 'kings of *Fortriu*', or to their people as 'men of *Fortriu*' (see also Anderson, *Early Sources*, i, pp. 262 n. 2, 266, 268); such a specific title would appear to reflect contemporary Scottish terminology. The Scottish material in the Irish annals, and its relationship to the *Old Scottish Chronicle*, will be the subject of an important study in J. Bannerman, *Studies in the History of Scotia* (forthcoming).
2 In Domnall mac Ailpín's reign it says that the *Goedeli* (Gaels) made *iura et legis regni*: Anderson, *Kings and Kingship*, p. 250.
3 M. Miller, 'The Last Century of Pictish Succession', *Scottish Studies*, xxiii (1979), p. 59; for a different view, see Anderson, 'Scottish Materials in a Paris Manuscript', p. 38.

history of their kingdom; and it is, furthermore, the first surviving text which portrays Cináed mac Ailpín as the founding-figure of the Scottish kingship. The statement about Pictish destruction and deprivation could thus be an attempt to project Cináed mac Ailpín, the apical ancestor of the royal dynasty, as the founder of the political order of his own day. And the notion that Cináed destroyed the Picts could have suggested itself as a credible device to represent the creation of the political order of the late tenth century because, by then, there was no-one called a Pict; there were only *Scoti*. His desire to represent Cináed mac Ailpín as the destroyer of the Picts, however, would obviously have made him unwilling to refer to the people of the kingdom thereafter as Picts. It is not difficult to suppose, therefore, that the preponderance of the term *Scoti* in the *Old Scottish Chronicle* reflects its author's view of the identity of the kingdom's people since its 'foundation' by Cináed mac Ailpín, rather than the terminology of its Scottish annalistic source. Thus, if any knowledge is to be gained of the terminology used for the people of the kingdom by the set of Scottish annals which lies behind the *Old Scottish Chronicle*, and of how this might have changed in *c.*900, recourse must be made to Irish annal-collections.

Unfortunately, the *Chronicon Scotorum* as it stands does not show much interest in Scottish events, which makes it difficult to reconstruct with confidence the original readings of the 'Chronicle of Ireland' for this period. The *Annals of Ulster*, however, are not so disappointing. In line with the terminology used to describe the kingship of Cináed mac Ailpín and his successors, the people they ruled are described as *Picti*, 'Picts', until the tenth century; they are then referred to as *fir Alban* or *Albanaig*, the 'men of Scotland', and the term 'Pict' is abandoned for ever. Thus the *Annals of Ulster*'s description of a Pictish slaughter at the hands of the Danes in 875 surely refers to the defeat of Constantín mac Cináeda at Dollar noted in the *Old Scottish Chronicle*. Earlier, both the *Annals of Ulster* and the *Chronicon Scotorum* tell how the Danes had brought Angles and Britons as captives to Ireland in 871; but the *Annals of Ulster* add that Picts were also among the captives, as probably did the original 'Chronicle of Ireland', judging from the fact that the *Annals of Clonmacnoise* (related to the *Chronicon Scotorum*) describe the Danes as bringing captives back from 'Pictland'.[1] In 918,

---

1 *The Annals of Clonmacnoise, being annals of Ireland from the earliest period to A.D.1408, translated into English, A.D.1627 by Conell Mageoghagan*, ed. D. Murphy (Dublin, 1896), p. 141; also Anderson, *Early Sources*, i, p. 303 n. 1. In view of the fact that the Annals do not know of *fir Alban* until the 10th century, Alfred Smyth is surely mistaken to argue (*Warlords and Holy Men*, pp. 191–2) that the Picts were singled out for attack by Olaf of Dublin from 866–71 while the *fir Alban* were spared; see also A.A.M. Duncan's review of A.P. Smyth, *Scandinavian Kings in the British Isles 850–880* (Oxford, 1977), in *Scot. Hist. Rev.*, lviii (1979), p. 96.

The Origin of Scottish Identity

however, the *Annals of Ulster* describe in some detail how Constantín mac Cináeda's cousin, Constantín mac Áeda (Constantine II, 900−43), led the *fir Alban* into battle against the Danes on the banks of a River Tyne.[1] The Picts are never mentioned in the tenth century or thereafter. The change in terminology from 'Picts' to 'men of Scotland' in the *Annals of Ulster* is not entirely clean, however, for they use another phrase — *fir Fortrenn*, the 'men of *Fortriu*' — to describe Constantín mac Áeda's army in its defeat of the Danes in 904. This battle is located in Strathearn in the *Old Scottish Chronicle*, which, if Strathearn was indeed in *Fortriu*, might explain the use of the phrase 'men of *Fortriu*' on this occasion.[2]

*

It appears, therefore, that in c.900 some lost Scottish annals dropped the Pictish terminology relating to the kingdom of Cináed mac Ailpín's successors and its people, and in its place adopted a new vocabulary based on the word *Alba*. What does this change signify, and how can it best be understood? In many accounts, the 'kingdom of Alba' is seen simply as the result of a 'Scoto-Pictish union' achieved by Cináed mac Ailpín, king of *Dál Riata*, when he established himself as *rex Pictorum* in the 840s.[3] The earliest witness of this event, however, is the *Old Scottish Chronicle* composed four generations later, whose account of such a sensitive subject as the origin of the kingship of *Alba* (I have suggested) is likely to owe rather more to the political realities of the late tenth century than to those of the mid-ninth. Nevertheless, there is no mention anywhere of a king of *Dál Riata* later than Cináed; that could be because of Cináed's 'union' with the Picts.[4] The

---

1 See Anderson, *Early Sources*, i, pp. 406−7. There are River Tynes in Lothian and Northumberland; Smyth, *Warlords and Holy Men*, p. 197, locates the battle on the Northumbrian Tyne at Corbridge, while B.T. Hudson, '*Old Scottish Chronicle*', sites it on the Lothian Tyne in the Lammermuirs.
2 See Anderson, *Early Sources*, i, pp. 399, 444. There is no need to believe that *Fortriu* consisted only of Strathearn and Menteith, one of the seven divisions of Scotland described in *De Situ Albanie*. A new discussion of what was meant by *Fortriu* will appear in Bannerman, *History of Scotia* (forthcoming).
3 Such a 'union' (whether violent or otherwise) is envisaged, for instance, by W.F.H. Nicolaisen, *Scottish Place-names: their study and significance* (London, 1976), p. 156; D.P. Kirby, 'The Problem of the Picts', in *Who are the Scots?*, ed. Menzies, pp. 59−60; J. Bannerman, 'The Scots of Dalriada', in *ibid.*, p. 76; Anderson, *Kings and Kingship*, p. 204; Byrne, *Kings and High-Kings*, p. 260; O'Rahilly, *Irish History and Mythology*, p. 386. See also Duncan, *Making of the Kingdom*, pp. 56−9; I. Henderson, *The Picts* (London, 1967), pp. 96−103; and above, p. 35 n. 1. For the most recent detailed discussion see M.O. Anderson, 'Dalriada and the creation of the Kingdom of the Scots', in *Ireland in Early Mediaeval Europe*, ed. Whitelock *et al.*
4 In the *Old Scottish Chronicle*, Cináed is said to have 'received the kingship of *Dál Riata* two years before he came to Pictland'. The *Dál Riata* themselves do not disappear, but

45

contemporary annalistic evidence discussed above, however, suggests that the 'kingship of the Picts' did not become the 'kingship of *Alba*' until two generations after Cináed mac Ailpín. Admittedly it is often maintained that Cináed's 'union' of the two kingships was accompanied by a Gaelic take-over of (at least) the upper echelons of Pictish society which, once it became established, might have led to the abandoning of Pictish terminology and the coining of *Alba* as a term for 'Gaelic Britain'.[1] It does not necessarily follow, however, that even a complete take-over of the top level of society would cause a change of name for the kingship and its people, far less the coining of a new identity. A spectacular example of such continuity, of course, is the preservation of the title 'king of the English' after the conquest of England by the duke of Normandy, and the gradual adoption of English identity by the incoming French, who almost entirely displaced the English from the upper echelons of society.

The most serious problem, however, with any attempt to explain the new terminology focused on *Alba* in terms of Cináed mac Ailpín's alleged *Dál Riata*-Pictish 'union' or the Gaelicisation of the Picts is that the minimum definition of *Alba*, up to the twelfth century, does not seem to have denoted a kingdom of Gaels in Britain incorporating 'Pictland' plus *Dál Riata* (or, at least, mainland Argyll); in its narrowest sense *Alba* evidently meant the territory between the River Spey in the north, the River Forth in the south and the range of mountains known as *Druim Alban* (the 'Ridge of Britain')[2] in the west dividing Perthshire and Argyll. W. J. Watson drew attention to place-name evidence for this minimum definition of *Alba*.[3] In particular, he noted place-names referring to an *Albanach* or Scot in Sutherland, Easter Ross and Moray in the north, and in Lanarkshire in the south, which were presumably named by people who regarded themselves as different from the *Albanaig*, the 'inhabitants of *Alba*'; another example of such an *Albanach* name is *Coire an Albanaich*, 'Corrie of the Scotsman', preserved in the mountain-name 'Stob Coir' an Albanaich', an impressive peak overlooking Glen Etive in Argyll. We can note also that in one version of the twelfth-century Irish text *Cogad Gáedel re Gallaib* Brian Bóruma is described (with

---

it is not always easy to tell whether the *Dál Riata* in Scotland or Ireland are intended: see Anderson, *Kings and Kingship*, pp. 199–201, and Anderson, *Early Sources*, i, pp. 489, 494.

1 It has been suggested that the Picts could already have been Gaelicised by the mid-9th century: W.J. Watson, *History of the Celtic Place-Names of Scotland* (Edinburgh, 1926), p. x; see also Bannerman, 'The Scots of Dalriada', p. 76.
2 *Dorsum Britannie* in *Adomnán's Life of Columba*, ed. A.O. and M.O. Anderson (Edinburgh, 1961), book i, chapter 34; ii, 31, 42, 46; iii, 14.
3 Watson, *Celtic Place-Names*, pp. 12–13.

The Origin of Scottish Identity

typical exaggeration) as taking tribute 'from Saxons and Britons, and from the Lennox, and *Alba*, and all Argyll', implying that neither Argyll nor the Lennox was part of *Alba*.[1] This restricted sense of *Alba* is also found to apply to *Scotia* (which, as we have seen, was one of the two Latin terms denoting *Alba*). That was observed by W. F. Skene, who noted that the author of *De Situ Albanie* (writing in 1165×1184) refers to what must be *Druim Alban* as 'the mountains which divide *Scotia* from Argyll', while a law called *Claremathan*, attributed to William I (1165 – 1214), delineated the central core of the kingdom as between the Spey and the Forth and between *Druim Alban* and the Forth.[2] Skene also pointed out that both Orderic Vitalis and Ailred of Rievaulx made a distinction between *Scotia* and Moray, while we can also note that the Lennox (in the west) is the only earldom north of the Forth-Clyde line absent from *De Situ Albanie*'s breakdown of *Scotia* into fourteen constituent parts.[3] It appears that this minimum definition of *Alba* must have been fairly well entrenched for it to be visible in place-names and to have survived into the late twelfth century, by which time it bore little relationship to any political or ethnic reality. It is probably most easily explained as referring to the original kingdom of *Alba*, before it expanded south to include Edinburgh in the mid-tenth century or in the north encompassed Moray, whose ruling family put in a strong claim to the kingship of *Alba* itself in the eleventh century, most successfully in the person of Macbethad mac Findlaích (famous as King Macbeth, 1040 – 57). Be that as it may, the fact that (for instance) Argyll and Moray could, within a couple of centuries, be regarded as separate from *Alba* militates strongly against the possibility that *Alba* was coined as a term signifying 'Gaelic Britain'; and, equally, the fact that *Alba* could exclude the territory of *Dál Riata* runs counter to the argument that *Alba* was originally meant to denote a new united 'Scoto-Pictish' kingdom.

The adoption of *Alba* to replace the kingdom's Pictish terminology can, however, be explained in terms of political change of another kind — the articulation of a new type of kingship. John Bannerman points out that the use of a territorial term, *Alba*, to identify a kingdom and its people is different from the usual kin-based or people-oriented terms such as *Ulaid*, *Dál Riata* or *Cenél Loairn*; *rex Pictorum* and *Pictavia*, ('king of the Picts', 'Pictland') thus contrast with the territorially focused terms *rí Alban* and *fir Alban/Albanaig* ('king of *Alba*', 'men/inhabitants of *Alba*').[4] This is a key observation, for it will be argued below that the adoption of a terminology

---

1 *Cogadh Gáedhel re Gallaibh*, ed. J.H. Todd (Rolls Series, 1867), p. 136.
2 Skene, *Celtic Scotland*, i, p. 3 and n. 4.
3 Anderson, *Kings and Kingship*, p. 242; Anderson, *Early Sources*, i, p. cxvi.
4 Bannerman, *History of Scotia* (forthcoming).

47

focused on *Alba* for the kingship and its people represents the development of a new, primarily territorial, idea of kingship.

*

In order to have any more certainty about what this new *Alba* terminology signified it would, of course, be of enormous value if a contemporary Scottish statement defining *Alba* could be identified. Although no Scottish manuscript survives from this period, there is a legend of Scottish provenance, found in late-medieval Irish and English manuscripts, which defines *Alba* in exclusively Pictish terms. This contrasts with the *Old Scottish Chronicle*, which (as we have seen) saw the kingdom of *Alba* as originating with the destruction of the Picts by Cináed mac Ailpín; and it also contrasts with the tenth-century edition of the *Senchus Fer nAlban*, which sought to provide the *fir Alban* with a *Dál Riata* genealogical definition consistent with its statement that Fergus Mór, Loarn Mór and Óengus Mór (and their doublets) 'took *Alba*'.[1] Furthermore, the legend employs area-names that were becoming obsolete in the tenth century, such as *Fortriu* and *Círcenn*, neither of which, it seems, is found in contemporary sources after the beginning of the tenth century (*Fortriu* is used for the last time in the *Annals of Ulster* in its notice of Constantín mac Áeda's victory over the Danes in 904).[2] It would appear, therefore, that this legend bears the hallmarks of being one of the first statements defining *Alba* in its new sense.

The legend survives in two forms.[3] The longer is found at the beginning of Pictish king-lists derived from a late ninth-century archetype. It reads:

> Cruithne son of Cinge, father of the Picts living in this island, reigned 100 years. He had seven sons. These are their names: Fíb, Fidach, Foltlaid, Fortrenn, Caitt, Cé, Círcinn. Círcinn reigned 60 years; Fidach 40; Fortrenn 70; Foltlaid 30; Gatt 12; Cé 15; Fíbaid 24.[4]

---

1 J. Bannerman, *Studies in the History of Dalriada* (Edinburgh, 1974), pp. 41, 47, 118–19.
2 *Fir Alban* and *fir Fortrenn* are occasionally used interchangeably in a passage describing the battles against the Danes in 904 and (possibly) 918 in Dubhaltach Mac Firbisigh's annalistic fragments: 'Annals of Ireland: three fragments copied from ancient sources by Dubhaltach Mac Firbisigh', ed. J. O'Donovan, in *Miscellany of the Irish Archaeological Society* (Dublin, 1860), pp. 228–30; see Anderson, *Early Sources*, i, pp. 407–8. *Fortriu* appears in the late-11th-century *Prophecy of St Berchán*, but this is a deliberately obscure work which is likely to have used terminology that would not have been readily understandable at that time.
3 The legend's text-history is discussed in detail in my 'The Seven Pictish Provinces and the Origins of *Alba*' (forthcoming).
4 Note that list 'A' reads 'Floclaid' rather than 'Foltlaid', and 'Got' rather than 'Caitt'/

The list continues with six more kings and their reign-lengths before reaching 'Brude Bont, from whom thirty *Brude* ruled Ireland and *Albania* for the space of 150 years'; it then lists the 'Brudes' in pairs (in the fashion 'Brude X, Brude Ur-X'), but without reign-lengths.

The key section in this pseudo-history is the opening passage concerning Cruithne and his seven sons. *Cruithne* is simply the Gaelic for 'Pict', and is clearly meant to be the Picts' eponymous ancestor.[1] It has long been recognised, furthermore, that at least some of the names of Cruithne's seven sons correspond to Pictish districts: 'Fíb' is Fife in medieval Gaelic; 'Fortrenn' is the genitive form of *Fortriu* (as in *fir Fortrenn*, 'the men of Fortriu', and *rí Fortrenn*, 'king of *Fortriu*', in the Irish annals);[2] 'Caitt' survives in Caithness ('Cat-ness'), and in the modern Gaelic for Sutherland, *Cataibh* (from *i Cataib*, 'among the "Cats"'); 'Círcinn' appears twice (as *Círcenn*) in the *Annals of Tigernach*, as the site of a battle and as the land in which another battle was fought 'between Picts on both sides'; and 'Foltlaid' can be construed as a misreading of *Fótla* ('Ireland'), and could refer to Atholl, which is *Athfotla* ('New Ireland') in medieval Gaelic.[3] The remaining two, 'Fidach' and 'Cé', were no doubt also names of Pictish districts, though they are not named in any record contemporary with the Picts.[4] The seven sons of Cruithne thus appear to be intended as eponyms of

---

'Gatt'; I have preferred list 'C''s readings in these instances because there are examples elsewhere in the Poppleton manuscript's collection of Scottish pieces of 't' being misread as 'c', of metathesis, and of 'c' being misread as 'g' (e.g. 'Fergar' for 'Fercar', i.e. *Ferchar*: Anderson, *Kings and Kingship*, p. 253, comparing line 17 with line 15). There is no critical edition of king-list 'P'.

1 There were also *Cruithni* in Ireland (the *Dál nAraide*), but the statement that Cruithne was *pater Pictorum habitantium in hac insula* clearly excludes them. Marjorie Anderson notes that it would be unnecessary to qualify *Picti* as 'those living in this island', for the term *Picti* was only used to denote the *Cruithni* in Britain, and surmises that the whole passage may originally have been in Gaelic: Anderson, *Kings and Kingship*, p. 80.
2 A. Macquarrie, 'Early Christian religious houses in Scotland: foundation and function', in *Pastoral Care before the Parish*, ed. J. Blair and R. Sharpe (Leicester, 1992), p. 121 n. 58, argues that it is unnecessary to interpret *Fortrenn* as the genitive of an unattested feminine *n*-stem noun **Fortriu*; however, as O'Rahilly, *Irish History and Mythology*, pp. 463–64, points out, **Fortriu* can be deduced with confidence because not only its genitive form *Fortrenn*, but also its accusative and dative singular form *Fortrinn*, are attested in the *Annals of Ulster* in the 7th and 8th centuries.
3 Watson, *Celtic Place-Names*, pp. 100, 108, 113–14, 228–9.
4 See *ibid.*, pp. 114–15, for a discussion of these names. M. Dobbs, 'Cé: the Pictish Name of a District in Eastern Scotland', *Scottish Gaelic Studies*, vi (1949), pp. 137–8, identifies *Benn Cé* and *Magh Cé* in the title of a lost Irish tale with, respectively, Bennachie, a hill overlooking the strath of the River Urie, and the strath of the River Urie itself. Perhaps *Cé* was an earlier name for the Garioch.

Pictish areas; and the purpose of this legend seems to have been to portray these different Pictish regions, from Caithness to the Firth of Forth, as belonging to a single Pictish kingdom from the beginning of Pictish history. The legend is notably different, however, from other eponymous tales in which regions take their names from sons of a common father (such as that of the sons of Cunedda relating to north-west Wales); instead of the sons' names being *bona fide* personal names applied to a region (such as Ceredig, eponym of Ceredigion), it is evidently the other way round, with actual area-names being applied, however incongruously, as personal names. The legend, therefore, seeks to define the kingdom explicitly in territorial terms. What is more, when a term is required to denote this kingdom, as in its statement that the thirty 'Brudes' ruled it and Ireland, the word it employs is not *Pictavia* (as one might expect) but *Albania*, the original Latin for *Alba* when it came to mean 'Scotland'.

This image of a single territorial entity, termed *Alba*, which unites all Picts, is even clearer in the shorter version of the legend. This consists of a single stanza of Gaelic poetry which deals only with Cruithne and his seven sons:

> Seven children of Cruithne
> Divided *Alba* into seven shares;
> [Those of] Cat, Cé, Círech, children with hundreds [of possessions],
> Fíb, Fidaid[?], Fótla, Fortriu;
> And the name of each one of them is borne by his land.[1]

It is striking how the names of the seven Pictish regions in the legend of Cruithne's sons are remarkably alliterative; four begin with 'F', and the other three with 'C'. It would be remarkable if the Picts, in reality, were divided up at any time into provinces whose names began only with the letters 'F' and 'C'. Such alliteration, however, would be perfectly natural in Gaelic poetry, where it is a stylistic requirement. It is even more remarkable that these seven names should form two alliterative groups of four and three, which fit so comfortably into a poem, given that it would take two lines in most metres to name all seven; the number seven itself could quite readily have been selected to symbolise a unity (like the seven orders of churchmen).[2] When the seven names are first given in the king-list, they

---

1 The translation is adapted from Watson, *Celtic Place-Names*, p. 107. The names appear to be genitive in the stanza; they are given in nominative forms in the translation; 'Fidaid' is Watson's conjectured nominative form of 'Fidach'.
2 See *Uraicecht na Ríar*, ed. L. Breatnach (Dublin, 1987), pp. 84–7. Duncan, *Making of the Kingdom*, p. 48, notes how the alliterative nature of the names, and the number seven, arouse suspicion.

The Origin of Scottish Identity

appear in these two alliterative groups, and, furthermore, they appear within each alliterative group in the same order as in the stanza; this is more significant than the fact that the 'C' group precedes the 'F' group in the stanza, while the 'F' group precedes the 'C' group in the king-list. It is difficult not to believe that Cruithne's seven sons were designed originally to fit into a Gaelic poem, and that the king-list used this poem as its source. We need not look further than the stanza for such a poem.

*

If the stanza is the ultimate source for the division of the Picts into seven coterminous provinces, then this, it would seem, should best be regarded not as a record of Pictish political geography, but as a literary device designed, through the medium of alliterative verse, to express the new concept of *Alba*, 'Scotland'. Those historical maps which, for instance, make 'Fidach' the name of a region stretching from the Spey to the Oykell, or 'Cé' the name of a region stretching from the Mounth to the Spey are, more likely than not, misguided. These names in the stanza (and, for all we know, others) could well represent in reality much smaller districts chosen by the poet for their initial consonant as much as anything else. On the other hand, *Fortriu*, which is the name given in the Irish annals to the kingdom ruled by Bridei son of Bile, victor at Dunnichen (685), and by Constantín mac Fergusa and his family from 789 to 839, may never have been merely Strathearn and Menteith, as is often supposed.[1] Nor do all these area-names necessarily refer to political units; some could be purely geographical. The sevenfold division of the Picts by the sons of Cruithne should be recognised, therefore, as a political fiction projecting the image of a single territorial entity which bound together all the Picts from Caithness to Fife. And the novelty of this political fiction is suggested by the use of what must have been a new term to denote this territorial unit: *Alba*.

The evidence thus suggests that the legend of Cruithne's seven sons in the stanza and king-list should be regarded as the earliest surviving statements which define *Alba* in its new sense of 'Scotland' in any detail. They show that *Alba*, 'Scotland', was not conceived as a term for Gaelic Britain, nor for a 'united kingdom' of *Dál Riata* and 'Pictland', but was conceived with reference to the Picts alone. The legend of Cruithne's sons, therefore, amplifies what is implied by the change of terminology of a Scottish chronicler in *c.*900: that the new identity focused on *Alba*

---

[1] On the basis of the description of this sevenfold division in *De Situ Albanniae* (1165×84), according to the political geography of its own time. This text inspires no confidence as a source for Pictish political geography: see further my 'Seven Pictish Provinces and the Origins of *Alba*' (forthcoming).

represented a redefinition of Pictish identity into one that was, to a new degree, territorial and unifying. The contemporary annalistic evidence suggests that this new identity was essentially political, relating to the kingdom of Domnall mac Constantin's successors in the tenth century; and, indeed, *Alba* — as defined in the legend of Cruithne's sons — can readily be understood as the focus for a centralising political identity, but does not seem appropriate for a primarily ethnic identity. The fact, therefore, that the Picts 'disappeared' after they became *fir Alban*, 'men of Scotland', would seem to indicate that the Pictish identity which developed into this new, 'Scottish', identity had been essentially political as well; no doubt there had been a Pictish cultural identity (focused on their language if nothing else) which, by the end of the ninth century, could already have given way to the cultural identity of Gaelic-speakers.[1] The final disappearance of the Picts and the origins of Scottish identity can, therefore, be seen as first and foremost a political phenomenon which should be explained in relation to Pictish politics.

*

One of the most striking features of Pictish politics in the ninth century is the appearance of dynastic kingship. The first certain instance of the son of a Pictish king succeeding to the kingship is Drest, son of Constantín mac Fergusa (789–820), who was joint king from 832/4 to 836. Furthermore Drest, who had succeeded his uncle, Óengus mac Fergusa (reigned 820–832/4), was in turn succeeded by his cousin, Eóganán mac Óengusa. For the first time the Pictish kingship (or kingship of *Fortriu*, as the *Annals of Ulster* more precisely refer to it in this period) was retained by successive kings of the same agnatic kindred over more than one generation.[2] The success of the descendants of Fergus mac Echdach (himself a king of *Dál Riata* in 778–81) was, however, short lived: the *Annals of Ulster* record that in 839 the Scandinavians defeated the 'men of *Fortriu*' in battle, killing Eóganán mac Óengusa and his brother Bran. The resulting power vacuum

---

1   Some indication of how long Pictish may have survived might be suggested by the fact that the Pictish king-list which rendered kings' names according to Pictish orthography, and forms the basis of much of king-list 'P', terminated with Bridei son of Uurad who was king in 842/3. The learned Cormac mac Cuilennáin (king of Munster, 902–8) referred to *bérla Cruithnech*, 'the language of the Picts' (O'Rahilly, *Irish History and Mythology*, p. 355 n. 3).
2   There is no evidence that Pictish society in general was matrilineal. Indeed, the designation of Pictish kings in the regnal lists as sons of their fathers (rather than of their mothers) suggests that, if royal succession was matrilineal, it operated between patrilineages. See especially W.D.H. Sellar, 'Warlords, Holy Men and Matrilineal Succession', *Innes Review*, xxxvi (1985), p. 41.

The Origin of Scottish Identity

seems to have led to conflict and instability, judging from the fact that each of the two groups of extant Pictish king-lists offers different accounts of the succession. Whichever account is read, however, dynastic kingship seems to have been established on the Pictish political agenda. According to the 'Q' group of Pictish king-lists, Eóganán was succeeded by Uurad son of Bargoit (a Pict), who, after a three-year reign, was succeeded by his sons Bridei (for a month) and Ciniod (for a year). This family's hold on the kingship was briefly interrupted by another Bridei for two years, before Drest, another son of Uurad, reigned for three years (?845−8).[1] The 'P' group of lists record the reigns of Uurad and his son Bridei (whom it reckons to have reigned for a year), but then makes Cináed mac Ailpín king for sixteen years.[2] Cináed appears eventually to have asserted his control over the kingship, which all the sources confirm was retained by his family into the next generation; he was succeeded by his brother Domnall mac Ailpín (Donald I, 858−62), who was followed in turn by Cináed's sons Constantín (862−77) and Áed (877−8). The hold of Cináed's dynasty on the kingship was interrupted by his daughter's son Eochaid ap Rhun and/or a king called Giric for eleven years before the succession of his grandson, Domnall mac Constantín in 889; and in 900 the kingship passed to Domnall's cousin Constantín mac Áeda, and remained with the male descendants of Cináed mac Ailpín throughout the tenth century (and beyond).

The nature of Pictish kingship has been the subject of much controversy;[3] but, whatever it may have been before the ninth century, it is clear that during that century it came to be dominated as never before by individual families — if at first only for a spell of a couple of generations — until, by the tenth century, it was monopolised by the descendants of Cináed mac Ailpín. This suggests an increasing concentration of political power in which the kingship would have been able to develop a more effective, rigid and onerous structure of subordination.[4] In short, the new pattern of dynastic kingship allows for a new type of kingship characterised by the exercise of territorial lordship to a greater extent than before. The legend of Cruithne's seven sons, with its emphasis on how the Picts belonged to a single territorial entity, can, therefore, be seen as an attempt to articulate

1 Anderson, *Kings and Kingship*, pp. 266, 273, 281, 287, 292.
2 *Ibid.*, pp. 249, 263; Skene, *Chronicles*, p. 400.
3 Sellar, 'Warlords, Holy Men and Matrilineal Succession', pp. 35−41, is an excellent discussion.
4 A study of the distribution of Class II and Class III symbol-stones in Strathmore, Strathearn and areas adjacent to the Firth of Tay suggests an increasing concentration of patronage and power, in this area at least, from the 8th century: M. Cottam and A. Small, 'The Distribution of Settlement in Southern Pictland', *Medieval Archaeology*, xviii (1974).

this new political order; while the adaptation and extension of this legend into a single line of succession in the king-list's version may be seen as relating this idea more explicitly to a dynastic kingship of *Alba*. At the same time, the coining of a new territorial term for the kingship suggests that it was seen not only as more intense, but also as more extensive than before; it is notable in the legend of Cruithne's sons that the term *Fortriu*, which had been applied to the kingship of Constantín mac Fergusa and his dynasty in the early ninth century, became only one of seven parts of the kingdom of *Alba*. The kingdom of *Alba*, of course, could in *c*.900 have extended from the Pentland Firth to the Firth of Forth only in the minds of the first Scottish historians (and, no doubt, the self-conceit of their royal patrons). The apparent fact, however, that the area between the Spey, the Forth and *Druim Alban* became known as *Alba* suggests not only that this represented the original bounds of the 'new' kingdom, but that the territory controlled by this kingdom was more extensive than could be denoted by any existing geographical or political term.

The coining of the new political identity focused on *Alba* can, therefore, be readily understood in terms of an increasing concentration of political power and the rise of a more extensive territorial kingship. Not only churchmen who wrote history, however, seem to have assumed this new identity, but also the people who experienced this new political order — the men who left their mark as *Albanaig* on the consciousness of those they met beyond its bounds in Moray, Ross and Argyll. The footsoldiers of this kingdom's 'common army' would, no doubt, have shouted '*Albanaig, Albanaig!*' just as their successors did at the battle of the Standard in 1138. It is impossible to say, however, which came first; whether the *literati* moulded a new political identity for their patrons which people came to adopt, or whether the new vocabulary had *already* been coined in the language of people all too aware of a new kind of kingship.

*

Yet to claim that Scottish identity emerged as an expression of a new political order is perhaps only to view the surface-stirrings of deeper social and economic developments. Scottish identity was born at a time of not merely political change: the death of the Pictish language, the appearance of new place-names with the element *pett*, 'piece [of land]', and the repeated Scandinavian incursions from 839 to 904, all point to this period as a time of social and economic upheaval which cannot as yet be gauged or properly understood.[1] Moreover, the Pictish kingdom was not alone in developing a more territorial or centralised political identity; for instance, the 'men of

---

1 *Ibid.*, and Duncan, 'Kingdom of the Scots', pp. 136, 141.

Ireland' first appear in contemporary annals in 858,[1] while the notion that people from Gwynedd, Powys, or Dyfed were foreigners beyond their region was finally replaced in the ninth and tenth centuries by an increasing recognition of everyone Welsh as *Cymro*, a 'fellow citizen'.[2] This raises the question of whether the emergence of Scottish identity was part of a general process. Such a process need not relate simply to the appearance in this period of identities which developed into the nations of today, of course. Taking Gaeldom — Scotland and Ireland — as a whole, the development of the dynastic, territorial kingship which produced 'Scotland' should probably be compared with the rise of a dynastic polity and territorial lordship from the eighth century in provinces such as Connacht and Leinster, and among the Northern and Southern Uí Néill, rather than with the emerging kingship of Ireland itself. Might we ask, for instance, if there are any grounds for comparing the emergence of 'Scotland' with the rise of 'territorial principalities' in West Francia during the same period?[3]

1 *Fir Érenn*, as well as the phrase *rí Érenn*, 'king of Ireland': see F.J. Byrne, *The Rise of the Uí Néill and the High-Kingship of Ireland* (Dublin, 1970), p. 13; D. Ó Corráin, 'Nationality and Kingship in pre-Norman Ireland', in *Nationality and the Pursuit of National Independence*, ed. T.W. Moody (Belfast, 1978), p. 8. The phrase *rex Hibernie* appears a couple of times in the 7th-century annals, but this seems to reflect Adomnán's precocious political ideas: see Byrne, *Kings and High-Kings*, pp. 257, 259.
2 T. Charles-Edwards, 'Some Celtic Kinship Terms', *Bulletin of the Board of Celtic Studies*, xxiv (1970−2), pp. 117, 122.
3 I should like to thank Dr John Bannerman and Professor Archie Duncan for their helpful comments on an earlier draft of this essay, and Dr Nerys Ann Jones for her kind advice and support; also the British Academy for the post-doctoral Research Fellowship which enabled me to research the subject.

Danish National Identity, c.700−1700

Troels Dahlerup

Generally speaking, we Danes do not consider ourselves to be at all nationalistic, even if in our aloof contempt for the rather ostentatious expressions of other national cultures we may find our very special feeling of superiority, that is to say our traditional self-sufficiency, mistaken by foreigners for politeness. As aliens will not and cannot be Danes, it is not their fault, and they cannot help it!

Possibly this sense of self-sufficiency is connected to an inherent feeling of continuity in Danish history. We do not know when Danes first came to Denmark, because we all feel that we, through our ancestors, have *always* been here. When we do have evidence of the earliest inhabitants of Denmark, there are no biological reasons to suppose that their skeletal remains are foreign,[1] and that trend of continuity runs right through our history. For instance, the first evidence of the language is from the runic inscriptions on the 'Golden Horn' (c.400−450): this language is 'old' Danish, and decidedly unlike its Teutonic Saxon or Gothic cousins.[2] In 811, when Charlemagne's army was halted at the Danish border, he made a treaty with the then king of Denmark; but, thanks to recent archaeological excavations, we now know that the border fortifications, the famous *Danevirke*, had already been in existence for about eighty years, as they have been dated by dendrochronology to 737. At about that time a Frankish missionary visited a king of Denmark, whose ability to build this enormous earthwork shows that he must have been in a much stronger position than that of a mere tribal chief.[3]

Thus, even if 'Danepride' may have got its present expression through nineteenth-century, German-influenced nationalism, it goes together with the inbred sense of continuity. Common culture, language and law in one indivisible state give in themselves a certain identity, but often in such a matter-of-fact way that it can be difficult to find expression of it in the sources. When our eighteenth-century writer Ludvig Holberg, in his picaresque *Peder Paars*, made the inhabitants of a small and remote island

---
1 T. Dahlerup, *11 Kapitler af Danmarks Historie* (Rirge, 1987), p. 8; cf. S. Müller, *Vor Oldtid* (Copenhagen, 1897), p. 188.
2 P. Skautrup, *Det Danske Sprogs Historie* (Copenhagen, 1944−53), i, p. 23.
3 H.H. Andersen, H.J. Madsen and O. Voss, *Danevirke I−II* (Copenhagen, 1978).

Danish National Identity, c.700-1700

profess their religious views, they declared that 'their faith is as pure as when King Dan was reigning' — Dan being an epynonymous Hengist-like hero king from c.500 BC![1] This joke would have been meaningless if most of Holberg's audience, like present-day Danes, had not possessed a strong sense of continuity with the far-distant Danish past.

It is obvious that the Vikings were full of pride, and with good reason. Thanks to the spread of Christianity, the Viking age ended in the eleventh century, and then began the period of the German threat. Nothing gives such a sense of national feeling as hostilities with neighbours (witness modern football matches). Accordingly, our great historian Saxo in his *Gesta Danorum* (c.1210)[2] constantly found it necessary to remind the endangered nation about its glorious past, a theme which recurs for the next hundred years. A typical example comes from the border monastery of Ryd, in an annal for 1288: 'observe that Germans have never got the upper hand without treason or falsehood'.[3] In 1329, during German occupation, one clerk wrote his famous lament, *Geme, plange, moesto more, dolorosa Dacia* ('Sigh and weep as by a graveside, sorrowful Denmark'), and exhortations such as 'once you conquered Saxony, Lombardy and England'[4] are disturbingly like the jingoistic poetry of the nineteenth century. During the unique interregnum of 1332–40, in which this period of Danish-German tension culminated, there is a reference in an episcopal appropriation to the necessity for its royal confirmation by 'the king of Denmark, who by the grace of God will always be among us'.[5]

Suddenly international conditions changed, and Danish border problems became more dynastic when, by means of marriages and wars, the German counts of Holstein took possession of the duchy of Schleswig. But the numerous dukes and counts of northern Germany could never become a general political threat to Denmark, since for the next five hundred years Germany was more a geographical than a political term. When the great Queen Margaret established the Scandinavian Union (1397), she simply replaced a Mecklenburg pretender with her great-nephew from Pomerania, whose international standing deserves to be stressed, as he was to marry an English princess.[6]

---

1 Ludvig Holberg, *Peder Paars* (Copenhagen, 1719).
2 *Gesta Danorum*, ed. J. Olrik and H. Ræder (Copenhagen, 1931–57).
3 *Annales Danici Medii Ævi*, ed. E. Jørgensen (Copenhagen, 1920–1), p. 107.
4 *Scriptores Minores Historiæ Danicæ Medii Ævi*, ed. M. Gertz (Copenhagen, 1917–22), i, p. 480.
5 Dated 1336: *Diplomatarium Danicum*, 2nd series, xi (1950), no. 335.
6 T. Dahlerup, *De fire Stænder, 1400–1500* (Gyldendals og Politikens Danmarkshistorie, vi, 1989), pp. 41 ff.

In the fifteenth century, on the other hand, Denmark experienced an enormous influx of German culture, and the language adopted more low German words than present-day Danish has mid-Atlantic ones.[1] Art, dynasties and especially queens generally came from the north of Germany, together with numerous settlers (though beside Hanseatic merchants we also find an important group of Scottish immigrants in the towns around the Sound[2]). In particular, Hanseatic commerce and capital was of fundamental importance, but represented no political threat. Legislation in the fifteenth century required foreign merchants to choose between being 'guests' who could do only wholesale business, or settling as ordinary citizens in the towns; the result was that the the settlers soon became totally 'Danised'. Also, practically no foreigners were accepted among the dominant landowning aristocracy in the period from c.1410 to 1520.[3] Among the few exceptions were some Swedish refugees and the Pomeranian vassals of the see of Roskilde.

During this period, when the external political threat had relaxed, only a few instances of historical interests are to be found, and these are generally of a poetic or general sort. This, at first sight, is rather surprising, because in fifteenth-century Sweden a very important tradition of historical writing developed.[4] At the Council of Basle during the 1440s, the Swedish representatives protested about their being seated behind the Spanish delegation: in a magnificent speech the Swedish bishop claimed that his people were descendants of the Gothic tribes who had destroyed the Roman Empire — to which the Spaniards caustically answered that the Spanish aristocracy considered themselves the descendants of those Goths, whereas the Swedes could be only descendants of their lazy and cowardly cousins who had stayed at home![5] The growing wealth of Swedish, and strange lack of Danish, historical writings may, however, have a very simple explanation. As the impossibilities of the Danish-dominated Scandinavian Union became evident in the latter half of the fifteenth century, when the constitutional struggle between the royalist and constitutionalist aristocracies gradually changed for Sweden into a nationalistic propaganda war, the Swedes had an urgent need for a history of their own, and accordingly they had to construct one.

Such a thing is of course totally un-Danish, as there is no need to

1   Skautrup, *Det Danske Sprogs Historie*, ii, pp. 31 ff.
2   See T. Riis, *Should Auld Acquaintance be Forgot ... Scottish-Danish Relations c.1450–1707* (Odense, 1988).
3   T. Dahlerup, 'Danmark', in *Den nordiske Adel i Senmiddelalderen* (Raporter til det nordiske historikermøde, 1971), p. 55.
4   *Kulturhistorisk Leksikon for Nordisk Middelalder*, vi (1961), cols. 587–591.
5   B. Losman, *Norden och reformkonsilierne 1408–1449* (Gothenburg, 1970), p. 209.

convince Danes of their Danishness. In 1502 a low German edition of the abridged *Gesta Danorum* was printed, and it was claimed that in this book one could learn that, since the days of Abraham, Denmark had always been a sovereign state under its own independent kings, and could read about all the wonderful deeds of the Danes.[1] Earlier, before the middle of the fifteenth century, a Danish bishop had translated the Jutland Law of 1241 into Latin, with learned annotations, and claimed that this might help other nations — probably because more and more Roman Law had to be insinuated into the German courts to make them function. In some instances he even claimed that Danish law was much better than both Roman and Canon Law.[2]

Legal aspects may in fact have been of great importance to national identity. For example, a 'townlaw' (*stadsret*) was both a local law and, at the same time, a royal privilege for the town's inhabitants, which would have given them a greater feeling of belonging to the national community ruled over by the king. And, although the exclusiveness of the secular aristocracy may have had its origin simply in the common feeling of hating to share privileges with royal (and foreign) favourites, a sense of common law as a feature of identity can certainly be found when in 1421 King Erik the Pomeranian wanted to prove that Sønderjylland (Schleswig) was purely Danish, and not a fief in possession of the Holstein counts. He based his argument partly on the fact that Danish was spoken there, but even more emphasis was placed on the fact that Danish law was in use throughout the whole territory.[3] Furthermore, however unjust the propaganda against the deposed King Christian II may have been (after 1523), his enemies lost no opportunity to stress that by his legal reforms he had allowed Danish law and custom to be superseded by foreign laws.[4] That is a rare instance of Danish xenophobia in the sixteenth century — to which there is an interesting Swedish parallel, when in c.1550 a Finnish peasant lost his case in a Swedish court; angered, he declared this to be an example of 'Jute Law', and for this 'high treason' (in other words for describing Swedish common law as 'Danish') he was fined forty marks, the traditional fine in capital cases.[5]

1 Dahlerup, *De fire Stænder*, p. 330.
2 S. Iuul, 'Jyske Lov i Retslitteraturen før 1683', in *Med lov skal man Land bygge*, ed. E. Reitzel-Nielsen (Copenhagen, 1941), pp. 139 ff.
3 Arild Huitfeld, *Chronologia*, iii (Copenhagen, 1603, reprinted 1977), pp. 302 ff.
4 T. Dahlerup, 'Ukritiske bemærkninger over Christiern IIs rigslovgivning', in *Middelalder, Metode og Medier: Festskrift til Niels Skyum-Nielsen* (Copenhagen, 1981), pp. 271 ff.
5 *Dombock för Nedre Satakunta 1550–1552*, ed. J. Roos (Finlands äldsta Domböcker, 1964), p. 197.

Following the Reformation, the Danish-Norwegian state felt reasonably secure, and through the development of printing the national language acquired a fixed standard. As educated Norwegians understood Danish, the old Norwegian language or languages became just local *patois*, but that should not be taken to imply the operation of some greater 'Danish nationalism'; after all, Iceland during the Reformation gained its own typefaces for its old and difficult language. And although the northern half of Sønderjylland (Schleswig) spoke Danish, for administrative reasons German became important as the language of the Church. Thus the Oldenburg monarchy ruled a multi-national, multi-lingual state; but Denmark was its central part, the home of the king, the court and an ever-growing bureaucracy. That meant that German officers of state were forced to have some knowledge of Danish.[1]

During the Renaissance, a certain national pride flourished, especially among the aristocracy, whose ladies collected ballads or folk songs. Local traditions, monuments and the like were collected or recorded in a Camden-like antiquarian fashion, as, for example, when the king in 1624 ordered a questionnaire from the learned professor Ole Worm to be sent to all parsons in order to obtain information about rune stones and other historically important remains.[2]

When in 1617 a young Danish nobleman on his grand tour from one European university to another visited Normandy, his reason for doing so was to study the common law of Normandy. There he was happy to read those normally unintelligible glosses of *vrag* and *ran* ('wreck' and 'unlawful seizure'), which for a Dane were easy and self-explanatory.[3] At the same time Danish science flourished. King Christian IV built the *Rundetårn* as an observatory for the astronomer Longomontanus, a pupil of Tycho Brahe, and Longomontanus's works were even translated into Chinese during his own lifetime.[4] Danish medicine in particular experienced a golden age, and when Samuel Pepys heard that his nephew intended to study medicine, the kind uncle sent him a *Bartholin* for, as everyone knew, this was the *Gray's Anatomy* or *Spalteholz* of those days.[5] Music flourished at the court of

---

1   V. Winge, *Geschichte der deutschen Sprache in Dänemark* (Heidelberg, 1992), chapter 4, gives an instructive instance of council business in 1663 recorded in both languages.
2   *Præsteindberetninger til Ole Worm*, ed. F. Jørgensen, i–ii (Copenhagen, 1970–4), especially i, introduction, pp. ix ff.
3   'Extracts from the diary of Jørgen Seefeldt', *Personalhistorisk Tidsskrift*, 6th series, iv (1913), p. 238.
4   K. Hashimoto, 'Longomontanus' astronomia Danica in China', *Journal for the History of Astronomy*, xviii (1987) (I am most grateful to Lecturer K.P. Moesgaard for this reference).
5   *Diary of Samuel Pepys* (various editions), entry for 12 September 1660.

Danish National Identity, c.700-1700

Christian IV to such an extent that if the musicians of northern Europe wanted to succeed, they had to go to Copenhagen, as did John Dowland and Heinrich Schütz.[1] A composer of international fame was *Der gewaldige Däne* Didrik Buxtehude, whose name indicates that his family was of Holstein origin. When he died in 1707, after a long and famous career spent in the German *Reichstadt* of Lübeck, a local newspaper stated that he had always claimed Denmark as his fatherland (*Patriam agnoscit Daniam*), a statement which would have been meaningless if he had not settled in a free imperial city *outside* the extended borders of the king's domains.[2] As for Danish literature — little known outside Denmark proper — the court poet Lyskander and especially the Baroque poet Thomas Kingo (son of a Scottish immigrant) constantly stressed a national pride of 'old virtue and Danish simplicity', as opposed to alien duplicity and so on.[3]

But it is only from the middle of the seventeenth century that we begin to have sources that provide some information about the 'common man'. We have, for example, several impressions from observant foreigners, especially the much-quoted Viscount Molesworth, whose *An Account of Denmark as it was in the Year 1692* gives a most depressing picture of Danish society, even though he did at least admire Danish law (the modern *Danske Lov* was promulgated in 1683). Molesworth found all Danes to be virtually alike, with no significant differences between noble counts and common peasants — he considered them all of rather low intellect and extremely boring. But he did admit, albeit grudgingly, that 'the common people do generally read and write'.[4] (I am not quite sure if he did not mistakenly equate a general ability to read with an ability to write.)

Of course the correct definition of nationalism is a question in itself — perhaps 'royalism' is better, or simply 'a sense of solidarity with the existing political order'. In Molesworth's time, the traditional enemy was the rising Sweden, and an enemy is always useful to give a sense of national identity. After it was ceded to Sweden by the Peace of Roskilde in 1658, the inhabitants of the island of Bornholm continued their own national resistance to the Swedish occupation, and carried out a successful rebellion in order to go on being Danes.[5] Similarly, their less fortunate neighbours in Swedish-

---

1 See, e.g., the useful entries for Dowland and Schütz in the *Encyclopedia Britannica*.
2 *Dansk Biografisk Leksikon* (3rd edn, Copenhagen, 1979-84), iii, p. 94.
3 For further information on the literary renaissance of the 17th century, see H. Ilsøe, 'Danskerne og deres fædreland: Holdninger og opfattelser *c*.1550−1700', in *Dansk Identitetshistorie*, ed. O. Feldbæk (Copenhagen, 1991-2), i, pp. 27ff.
4 Robert Molesworth, *An Account of Denmark as it was in the Year 1692* (London, 1694, reprinted 1976), p. 257.
5 K.V. Jespersen, *Danmarks Historie*, iii (Gyldendal, 1979), pp. 137 ff.

occupied Scania waged a somewhat Basque-like resistance for about two generations.[1] As for the rest of Denmark, although ironically the Danes' allies in the later seventeenth-century wars, the Poles and Brandenburgers, also caused disasters for the ordinary people — the Poles brought the devastating plague of 1658−9, while 'Brandenburger' is still remembered in local dialects as a name for pests who eat up the harvest[2] — nevertheless it was always the Swedes who were the enemy. Every Danish child knows of the famous *Gøngehøvding* (nowadays a television programme based on a popular novel from the middle of the last century), who led a gang of *snaphaunces* in a successful guerila fight in 1658−60.[3] And scholars, at least, have heard of Jacob Daneferd, who single-handedly captured a Swedish vessel and took it safely to beleaguered Copenhagen, thereby strengthening the city's morale in the dangerous winter of 1659−60.[4]

Nor were these isolated acts of heroism. Thanks to a seventeenth-century church register from an ordinary Zealand parish, where the parsons for once gave not only dates of births, marriages and deaths, but also short obituaries of all the deceased, we are able to observe how the 'common people' reacted to the wars with Sweden.[5] When war broke out in 1658, a distant relation of the vicar who had some military experience went as a substitute for his nephew to the army. Soon he was taken prisoner by the victorious Swedes, but thanks to his rank (probably corporal) he ingratiated himself with the Swedes and was placed in command of 400 prisoners, who were to be shipped to Riga as reinforcements for the far-off Swedish front in Russia. Exploiting his position of trust he overwhelmed the guard, armed the other prisoners and, like the famous Jacob Daneferd, took his ship to Copenhagen too. This man was no doubt one of many forgotten war heroes — even if locally it seems to have been remembered that he had not paid his war taxes in full! In 1661 peace arrived, and now we hear about the local *snaphaunce*[6] of the village. He had joined a group which operated from the woods in central Zealand, but was killed in an unsuccessful ambush. In order not to reveal the bases of this resistance movement to the Swedes, his comrades

---

1 *Ibid.*, pp. 156, 260 ff., and references given there.
2 *Ordbog over det Danske Sprog*, ii (1920), col. 1099. Cf. a contemporary complaint from 1660, where the Brandenburger and Polish allies were considered to be doing greater harm than the Swedes: *Levnedsløb i Sørbymagle og Kirkerup 1646−1731*, ed. O. Højrup (Copenhagen, 1963−8), no. 246.
3 *Dansk Biografisk Leksikon*, ix, pp. 494 ff.
4 *Ibid.*, iii, pp. 569 ff.
5 *Levnedsløb i Sørbymagle og Kirkerup*, nos. 250, 414.
6 It is not without interest that, whereas the term *snaphaunce* in Danish simply means *a freedom fighter*, much of the Swedish literature uses the term as *terrorist* (see the material cited in Jespersen, *Danmarks Historie*, iii, pp. 156, 260 ff.).

Danish National Identity, c.700-1700

buried him in haste and great secrecy. But they remembered where, so that later his body was retrieved and transferred to his own cemetery.

In another slightly later parish register, from the border area between northern and southern Jutland (Vonsild parish), we find additional entertaining stories of many local heroes who were present at, for example, the battles of the Boyne, Blenheim, Oudenarde and especially Ramillies, where Danish farm boys rode down the *Maison du Roi* (the musketeers and gendarmes of the French court who fought as a cavalry division).[1] Through these parish registers we realise that — at least in the traditions written down by the vicars — the common people did have a sense of the past, which was close to being a sense of history. When one farmer died in c.1670 the vicar noted that the new copyholder was not related to the deceased, even though this farm was said to have been in possession of the same family for more than 300 years.[2] That would give us a perspective back to the fifteenth century, and although I have some reservations about this story, it is not its accuracy but the feeling of tradition and continuity that is of importance here. Another obituary tells us about a man whose long-deceased father had witnessed a battle in the neighbouring parish which happened during the civil war of 1534–6, that is, about 150 years earlier.[3] The Jutland vicar tells us about a farmer from a very good family whose ancestors should have been buried, in Cistercian habits, in the distant but famous monastery of Lögum (*Locum Dei*), which gives us another instance of a family memory of about 200 years. Strangely enough, a relative of this man was illiterate, and that had to be explained: he must have been born in c.1615, 'and in those days learning was not taken as seriously as in our times', the vicar tells us.[4]

In my view, from the middle of the seventeenth century the majority of the common people were able to read (if not to write, notwithstanding Viscount Molesworth's opinion). One of the earliest pieces of evidence of this is found in an outlying district of Scania (north Halland), where a Lutheran bishop made his visitation in 1624. Instead of returning a report on the instruction of the local youths, he simply recorded (in Latin), 'Not a few could read in books!'[5] To him this was a remarkable and singularly

---

1 *Vonsild kirkebog 1659–1708*, ed. H.H. Worsøe (Copenhagen, 1982), e.g., pp. 332 (Flanders), 425 (Hochstadt). Cf. W.L.S. Churchill, *Marlborough, his Life and Times* (London, 1933–8), where the presence of Danish auxiliaries is repeatedly mentioned.
2 *Levnedsløb i Sørbymagle og Kirkerup*, no. 845 (1724).
3 *Ibid.*, no. 182.
4 *Vonsild kirkebog*, pp. 240, 160.
5 *Visitatsbog for Lunde Stift, 1611–1637*, ed. B. Kornerup, in *Lunds stifts Herdaminne*, i (1), ed. G. Carlquist (Lund, 1942), p. 151.

happy finding, even if a few years later the unfortunate clergyman of the place complained to his bishop that as an unexpected result of his efforts, his parishioners did not study the ever-growing number of printed religious tracts, but went through the law book, starting proceedings not only among themselves but against the parson, too![1]

The supporters of the traditional belief in illiteracy at that time very often draw attention to the absence of any mention of books in the settlements of deceased farmers' estates. Yet books are rarely found in present-day settlements, except those of book collectors and learned professors. In any case, in making such settlements the courts of the seventeenth century did not think in terms of providing wonderful sources for modern ethnologists. Their main concern was to settle the debts of deceased farmers, and to collect outstanding rents and especially the fees due to the officers of the court. The published court books of the most westerly hundred of Jutland (near modern Esbjerg) mention books on only three occasions in the period 1636–40, but each time in a significant way. One very wealthy local yeoman had a son, who was intended to have an expensive education which would enable him to administer a noble estate (in similar cases this study, of accounting, took place at Hamburg). That yeoman is recorded as possessing the law book, and with it (but probably only because the law book was considered worth noting) some religious books and tracts.[2] The second case lists no books, but a written pledge for ten *rixdollar* has a note that the debt was augmented by another half dollar, as the debtor wanted to be able to buy the new hymn book.[3] Such a thing is normally never mentioned, for the very simple reason that used and second-hand books are of little commercial value. Most important for the modern scholar, however, is the third instance, where an extremely pedantic clerk writes: 'any books found should be divided among the children', exactly the way in which we proceed today in Denmark.[4]

What did the common people actually read? The valuable almanacs and calendars of the beginning of the seventeenth century not only listed market days and similar mundane matters, but could contain other interesting material such as agricultural advice of an almost 'medieval' character. But as most of the early popular literature is a kind of 'soft porn', very little is preserved. In 1638, 'having learned that even in our churches are sold ballads, love songs, *Eulenspiegel* and several other awful and immoral

1   *Ibid.*
2   *Skast Herreds Tingbøger, 1636–40*, ed. P. Rasmussen (Copenhagen, 1955–66), 1639: 447; cf. 1640: 143.
3   *Ibid.*, 1638: 449.
4   *Ibid.*, 1639: 122.

Danish National Identity, c. 700-1700

books', the king placed a total ban on the sale of such things *in churches*, though they could still be bought from market stalls. Brief religious tracts, however, are preserved in such quantities that they must have been common, together with a growing number of works of 'popular science' — tracts on folk medicine and herbs, not to mention the best-selling cookery books.[1]

By accident I rediscovered an old publisher, the failed scholar Jens Sørensen Nørnissum, who not only sold but edited books. If he wanted a type of book which did not exist, he commissioned it to be written, or else wrote it himself.[2] To give just one instance of the deficiencies of our sources, I found in a stocklist from the greatest Copenhagen dealer in 1666 seven titles (all brief religious tracts) by this Nørnissum, of which only one, very miserable, copy still exists. The rest are known only from the stocklist.[3] Now this dealer had a special love of history, being a member of the circle of the astronomer Longomontanus, who as a master of chronology was surrounded by others with historical interests.[4] In 1635 Nørnissum published a popular edition of the so-called *Prison Chronicle* (concerning the Investiture Contest in thirteenth-century Denmark), which was easily done because the great amateur historian and statesman Arild Huitfeld (royal justiciar, able counsellor, and administrator of the noble school of Herlufsholm) had produced an edition at the end of the sixteenth century.[5] At the same time this distinguished nobleman finished his publication of a ninevolume *History of Denmark*; and not being a scholar but only a nobleman, he wrote his work in Danish (but based it on a wealth of documents, which gives it an immortal importance).[6] In *c.*1600 this great work could expect a reading public only among the better classes, but Huitfeld's commonsense political interpretations, found mostly in his preambles to individual volumes, are of great interest: for example, 'as we are one people with a common language, one king and one faith, why should we not have just one law?' But even if literacy was growing, this nine-volume work was heavy reading. Accordingly, in 1645 Nørnissum produced his own *Short History of Denmark from King Dan to the Present Times for the Use of the Common Reader*, in 138 pages. This must have been an extraordinary success, for a

---

1 *Bibliotheca Danica* (Copenhagen, 1877–1902): a complete inventory of all books in *Det Kongelige Bibliotek*, The Royal Library, Copenhagen.
2 H. Ehrencron-Müller, *Forfatterleksikon*, vi (Copenhagen, 1929), pp. 132 ff.; cf. *Dansk Biografisk Leksikon*, x, p. 624.
3 I. Ilsøe, 'Boghandleren Joachim Moltke og hans virksomhed, 1626–64', *Fund og Forskning*, xxiv (1979–80), pp. 86 ff.
4 T. Dahlerup, 'Den folkelige historieskrivings fødsel', *Skalk*, vi (1986), pp. 24 ff.
5 *Bibliotheca Danica*, iii, col. 1126.
6 *Dansk Biografisk Leksikon*, vi, pp. 598 ff.

second, corrected edition came out in 1645, and a reprint in 1649.[1] There was clearly, therefore, something of a market for Danish history among the common people of seventeenth-century Denmark.

In the same period, townsfolk adopted the modern European custom of having pictures hung on their walls. Religious motifs seem to have been extremely popular, but in Denmark pictures of members of the royal family came a close second.[2] The dean of Zealand (another member of Longomantanus's circle) produced a very popular series of royal portraits, and this idea was borrowed by the bookseller-publisher Jens Lauridsen Wolf, who furnished these cartoons with a text giving a cannibalised version of Nørnissum's *History*. But Nørnissum had his revenge when in 1655 he produced another, still extant, edition of his *History*, updated to include the new king, Frederick III (acceded 1648).[3] This, of course, used Wolf's 'borrowed' pictures; but that perhaps made the book too expensive, for subsequent editions (which were produced into the following century) are without pictures. It should be remembered, however, that existing editions are only the tip of the iceberg. I was happy to be able to prove that point when a scholar with an interest in the history of mentalities challenged me. The University Library at Aarhus was founded at the turn of this century by buying up some of the greatest private collections, especially that of *Geheimearchivar* Wegener, and in the Wegener collection we found an edition of Nørnissum's book which until then had been overlooked.[4]

As Danish authors in those days had to rely on sponsors' support or royal grants, they constantly complained about not being able to get into print without promising the publishers substantial security. So it is of interest that the university printer Joachim Moltke dared in 1650−2 to re-edit the important work of Huitfeld in a two-volume folio edition, carried out, as he proudly stressed, at his own expense.[5] Might it not have been the success of Nørnissum's humble book that inspired him and made him realise that there really was a demand for popular history, as long as it was the history of Denmark? The last known edition of Nørnissum's book appeared as late as 1750,[6] notwithstanding the recent work of Professor Ludvig Holberg, who had tried to replace Huitfeld's study with his own three-

---

1   *Ibid.*, x, p. 624; Ehrencron-Müller, *Forfatterleksikon*, vi, pp. 132 ff.
2   P. Eller, *Bogerne og billedkunsten på Christian IVs tid* (Hillerød, 1975), pp. 116 ff.
3   Dahlerup, 'Den folkelige historieskrivings fødsel', p. 25.
4   *Ibid.*
5   His pride is underlined in the preamble to the 1650−2 edition; cf. Ilsøe, 'Boghandleren Joachim Moltke og hans virksomhed', p. 71.
6   Ehrencron-Müller, *Forfatterleksikon*, vi, pp. 132 ff.

volume history (published 1732−5). Holberg does not seem to have been very happy about all this popular reading, and in one of his much-admired comedies he complains about a lazy peasant who did not try to improve his holding but sat instead all day with pipe in mouth reading the good book of 'Doctor Huitfeld'.[1]

*

In recent years the 'struggle between classes' has more or less been superseded by a growing interest in the history of mentalities, a very difficult theme. I claim no deep knowledge of the thoughts of seventeenth-century Danes, and have tried only to explore some issues as evidence of their sense of national identity, even if 'loyalism' or 'patriotism' might be better terms. At the end of his reign, King Christian IV ran short of money to hire mercenaries, and was forced on the advice of his noble council to form a peasant militia. In the court books concerning the estates of deceased farmers in Zealand in the 1640s we thus find rifles with live ammunition on one farm after another.[2] But neither the king nor his noble council, nor the Danish peasants, were able to imagine that such rifles might be used for anything other than shooting Swedes — always a nice and completely legal pastime of the Danes![3]

1 Ludvig Holberg, *Erasmus Montanus* (Copenhagen, 1731).
2 *Bondeskifter fra Smørum og Lille herred, 1644−48* (Copenhagen, 1984), pp. 33, 74, 95, 119, 136.
3 I wish to acknowledge my gratitude to the editors, Sandy Grant and Keith Stringer, for their kindly corrections of my faulty English prose.

Aspects of National Consciousness in Medieval Scotland

Alexander Grant

We may begin conventionally, with contemporary political theory. The most striking theoretical expression of national consciousness in medieval Scotland is in that remarkable letter of 1320 to Pope John XXII, commonly known as the Declaration of Arbroath, which stated the case for Scottish independence in the names of the earls, the barons and the rest of the Scottish community.[1] Its fundamental point emerges from its description of the pope as 'the earthly representative of God — He who makes no distinction between Jew and Greek [i.e. Gentile], between Scotsman and Englishman'. Here, God is seen as giving divine sanction to national diversities: in His eyes the Scots were no better than the English, and *vice versa* — and so there was no justification for one to conquer the other. Therefore, the Declaration sought papal support for the Scots against the king of England, who, it stated, should be satisfied with what belonged to him (it used to satisfy seven kings!), and should leave Scotland to the Scots. The case was substantiated by an appeal to the history of the Scottish nation, which was said to have originated in Scythia; to have been converted and taken into his protection by St Andrew (brother of the first pope); and subsequently to have travelled to Scotland, where it enjoyed a long history of unconquered freedom in a kingdom ruled by 113 kings of its own royal stock, uninterrupted by any alien king.

---

1 *The Acts of the Parliaments of Scotland* (Edinburgh, 1814–75), i, pp. 474–5. There are various translations; I generally, though not exclusively, follow that of A.A.M. Duncan, in his *The Nation of Scots and the Declaration of Arbroath* (Historical Association Pamphlet, 1970), pp. 34–7. For discussions, see *ibid.*; A.A.M. Duncan, 'The Making of the Declaration of Arbroath', in *The Study of Medieval Records*, ed. D.A. Bullough and R.L. Storey (Oxford, 1971); G.W.S. Barrow, *Robert Bruce and the Community of the Realm of Scotland* (3rd edn, Edinburgh, 1988), pp. 302–11; G.W.S. Barrow, 'The Idea of Freedom in Late Medieval Scotland', *Innes Review*, xxx (1979); G.G. Simpson, 'The Declaration of Arbroath revitalised', *Scottish Historical Review*, lvi (1977); S. Reynolds, *Kingdoms and Communities in Western Europe, 900–1300* (Oxford, 1984), pp. 273–6; and, most recently, A.A.M. Duncan, 'The War of the Scots', *Transactions of the Royal Historical Society*, 6th series, ii (1992), and N.H. Reid, 'Crown and Community under Robert I', in *Medieval Scotland: Crown, Lordship and Community*, ed. A. Grant and K.J. Stringer (Edinburgh, 1993).

The Declaration drew on long-established notions of Scottish history. In Scotland as elsewhere the development of origin myths, and hence of the consciousness of a country's own history, is a significant feature of the twelfth and thirteenth centuries;[1] and, as Dauvit Broun shows (see above), they go back much earlier. The authors of the Declaration thus had a straightforward argument: the legitimation of the existence of separate kingdoms on the grounds that they had *always* existed independently. From this, they continued that although the Scots had been attacked wrongfully by the kings of England, their liberty had been restored by Robert I (Robert Bruce), whom all Scots now acknowledged and accepted as their king.

> Yet if he should give up what he has begun, seeking to make us or our kingdom subject to the king of England or to the English, we would strive at once to drive him out as an enemy and a subverter of his own right and ours and we would make some other man who was able to defend us our king; for, as long as a hundred of us remain alive, we will never on any conditions be subjected to the lordship of the English. For we fight not for glory, nor riches, nor honours, but for freedom alone, which no good man gives up except with his life.

The argument was not simply that of one king against another; it was clearly expressed in terms of the Scottish people against the English.

The Declaration was, of course, a piece of government propaganda, and hence is easily dismissed. Nevertheless, its ideas are worth taking seriously, particularly in the context of a volume of essays such as this. After all, the Declaration has the existence of separate national identities as its basic premise. Then there are the appeals to history, to the facts and fictions about origins which were and are essential for any viable nation. Again, although it was addressed to the papacy, its message was also aimed at domestic consumption. As Susan Reynolds has pointed out, presumably the men who allowed their seals to be attached to the letter

> knew what it said, at least in outline, so that its contents were intended to appeal to them, as much as to the pope. This suggests that, for all its flourishes, it is likely to have been based on ideas which were widely shared, at least among the Scots, if not, as it turned out, at the papal curia.[2]

---

1 See E.J. Cowan, 'Myth and Identity in Early Medieval Scotland', *Scot. Hist. Rev.*, lxiii (1984); and, more generally, S. Reynolds, 'Medieval *Origines Gentium* and the Community of the Realm', *History*, lxviii (1983).
2 Reynolds, *Kingdoms and Communities*, p. 275. Cf. also her comment: 'Arguments [against taking the Declaration seriously] ... spring from that curious historical cynicism — almost a sort of inverted naïvety — which is determined not to take any

Admittedly, not all the signatories were convinced; within a few months, four were found guilty of involvement in a conspiracy against Robert I. Yet that probably strengthens Reynolds's suggestion: if, as has been suggested, the Declaration was partly intended as a test of Scottish nobles' loyalty to the Bruce regime,[1] that would hardly have been done by presenting completely novel ideas.

This may be taken further. Despite its impressive argument, the Declaration of Arbroath achieved relatively little at the papal curia, because the pope was under heavy English political pressure.[2] The point is that no matter how eloquent a theory may be, to be effective it has to be in tune with political realities — and the political realities of the papal curia in the 1320s told against the Scots. But that point must apply to Scotland as well. In the context of Scottish political realities, the Declaration was an attempt to articulate a theory in order to account for and justify events which had already taken place during the past thirty years.

Between 1284 and 1290 a tragic sequence of deaths in the royal family had brought Scotland to the brink of civil war between rival claimants to the throne. To avert that calamity, the Scottish political community asked Edward I of England to adjudicate. Edward did so, on condition that he was accepted as feudal overlord of Scotland; when that was eventually conceded, his court found in favour of John Balliol of Galloway, who was the nearest heir by strict primogeniture. But after King John was crowned in 1292, Edward's active exercise of the principles of feudal superiority proved unacceptable. In 1295 Scottish political leaders imposed an executive council on King John, renounced English overlordship, and entered into an alliance with France. War with England followed: Edward I defeated the Scots in 1296 and made King John abdicate. But the following year Scottish rebellion broke out, led initially by Andrew Murray and William Wallace; this lasted, in King John's name, more or less successfully until 1303-4, when a massive campaign by Edward I forced Scottish submission. Then, in 1306, there was a fresh revolt, this time headed by Robert Bruce, earl of Carrick (grandson

---

statement of feeling or principle at face value.' Both a formal, sealed, top copy and a preliminary draft of the Declaration were kept in Scotland: Duncan, 'Making of Declaration of Arbroath', pp. 180−2.

1 Barrow, *Robert Bruce*, pp. 309−10; but cf. Duncan, *Nation of Scots*, p. 28, and also his 'War of the Scots', pp. 127−31, where he suggests that the 1320 conspiracy was provoked by the collection of seals for attachment to the Declaration. We must remember, however, that only a few Scottish nobles were involved in the conspiracy. See also Reid, 'Crown and Community under Robert I', pp. 204−9, 215−18.
2 G. Donaldson, 'The Pope's Reply to the Scottish Barons in 1320', *Scot. Hist. Rev.*, xxix (1950).

of Balliol's main rival in 1290-2), who had himself crowned king. After initial setbacks, Robert I proved victorious, both against John Balliol's supporters and against the English (with whom the Balliol faction joined). By the end of 1314, when Robert defeated Edward II of England at the battle of Bannockburn, English occupying forces had been almost completely expelled. But Edward II would not recognise Scottish independence, and, among other things, manipulated the pope into both imposing the ecclesiastical sanction of an interdict — prohibiting religious activity — on Scotland, and declaring that Scottish oaths of allegiance to King Robert were invalid. The Declaration of Arbroath was written to persuade the pope to lift the interdict, and also probably to counter any weakening of loyalties to Robert I among the Scottish nobles.[1]

Now, although John Balliol had ceased to be *de facto* king of Scots in 1296, there had been no formal Scottish renunciation of allegiance to him until Robert Bruce took over the crown ten years later. Strictly speaking, therefore, Bruce was a usurper, who in 1306 had deposed King John.[2] That was certainly how the Balliol faction viewed what had happened: hence the Bruce-Balliol civil war. In such circumstances it was imperative to produce a theoretical legitimisation of Bruce kingship. This was done, initially, at Robert I's first parliament in 1309.[3] The argument was, basically, that the Scottish political community followed the king's lead: John Balliol had been made king by Edward I and recognised him as his superior; the community had therefore accepted Balliol and the ensuing English overlordship; but once Edward had removed Balliol in 1296 the community was able to turn to the rightful heir, Robert Bruce, who should have been king all along. This was in line with traditional medieval political theory, according to which political authority descended from God to popes and kings and thence downwards to the various peoples. But it had two flaws: John Balliol's hereditary right to the throne was actually better than Robert Bruce's, which must have been widely known; while the idea that Balliol had been king only because, and so long as, Edward I had wanted him virtually recognised Edward's claims to superiority over the Scottish crown. Therefore, when the need to justify Bruce kingship arose again in 1320, a very different argument was put forward, which used newer theories of political authority coming

---

1 Barrow, *Robert Bruce*; or, more briefly, R. Nicholson, *Scotland: The Later Middle Ages* (Edinburgh, 1974), chapters 2−5.
2 A point made most cogently by E.J. Cowan in a paper delivered to the Conference of Scottish Medieval Historical Research in January 1975.
3 *Acts of the Parliaments of Scotland*, i, pp. 460−1; Barrow, *Robert Bruce*, pp. 184−5, 363; Duncan, 'War of the Scots', pp. 131−5; see Duncan, 'War of the Scots', 125−35, for the impossibly difficult choices faced after 1306 by those who supported both Balliol kingship and the cause of Scottish independence.

from God to the various peoples and then *ascending* to their kings.[1] According to the Declaration of Arbroath, Scotland's independence had been restored, after Edward I's attacks, by Robert I, king through 'divine providence, the succession to his right according to our laws and customs ..., and the due consent and assent of us all'; but Robert was accepted as king by the Scottish community only because he was carrying out his duty of maintaining Scottish independence, and were he to fail in that he would not remain king. The problem of John Balliol's right to the throne was solved by ignoring him;[2] implicitly, Balliol was not a proper king of Scots, because he agreed to English overlordship. It is, of course, Bruce propaganda; but it also seems to have been much closer to the political realities of the Scottish resistance to English conquest.

That applies not only to events after 1306, but also to the 1290s, at the start of the crisis of Scottish kingship. When, in 1291, Edward I stated that he would adjudicate only if he were accepted as Scotland's overlord, the Scottish negotiators answered that Edward's demands were a matter for their king, and in his absence they could give no response; that followed the orthodox political theory of the community's taking the king's lead. But Edward produced what might nowadays be called a 'Catch 22': he demanded that each of the 'Competitors' to the throne should recognise him as overlord. Naturally they did so; each knew that otherwise he would have no chance of being chosen as king. Therefore Edward could return to the leaders of the Scottish community and point out that all the Competitors, including whoever was rightfully king, had recognised him as overlord; therefore the king of Scots had done so; and therefore, by their own argument, the leaders of the Scottish community had to do so, too. That was reluctantly accepted by the Scots; they were no doubt swayed by the fact that an English army was nearby, but at the time they probably also regarded English overlordship as a lesser evil to that of possible civil war.[3] As has been said, however, within three years the exercise of Edward's overlordship provoked an upheaval in Scotland: power was seized from King John, and Edward I was defied. No political theory was specifically invoked in 1295, simply the realities of the political situation.[4] It was not, in fact,

---

1 For descending and ascending theories of kingship see, e.g., W. Ullmann, *Principles of Government and Politics in the Middle Ages* (4th edn, London, 1978), especially pp. 19–26.
2 John Balliol was not mentioned in the Declaration of Arbroath.
3 Barrow, *Robert Bruce*, pp. 30–6; A.A.M. Duncan, 'The community of the Realm of Scotland and Robert Bruce', *Scot. Hist. Rev.*, xlv (1966), pp. 190–2.
4 Or, at least, no theoretical justification survives, apart from the later chronicle comment that 'guardians' were appointed to defend the freedom of the kingdom: John Fordun, *Chronica Gentis Scotorum*, ed. W.F. Skene (Historians of Scotland, 1871–2)

until twenty-five years later that a theory was produced to justify this overturning of the crown-community relationship, by which it was up to the political community, not the king, to determine Scottish independence or subjection. But eventually, in 1320, that is what was stated in the Declaration of Arbroath.

The point is, therefore, that while the ideas or theories of politics are easily accessible, very interesting, and obviously highly important to historians, they would only have much contemporary force if they were in tune with what was actually happening. If, in the late thirteenth and early fourteenth centuries, no Scots had been prepared to fight against the English and risk death in battle; or if, having been defeated once, they had submitted to alien rule — as in effect happened with the Norman Conquest of England after the battle of Hastings in 1066 — then there would have been no meaning to the rhetoric of the Declaration of Arbroath, and indeed no occasion for it. The fight for independence came first, before its theoretical justification of it. As this shows, political theories do not initiate political action; at best they help to consolidate and legitimise what is happening.

*

The argument relates not just to the Declaration of Arbroath, but to all the rest of the intellectual apparatus associated with the growth of national consciousness during the Middle Ages[1] — in Scotland as elsewhere. Consider, for example, medieval historical writing, through which the origin myths and narratives of significant events were established and formalised in the various west European nations, thereby defining the separate histories of each of the countries and their peoples. That helped to shape perceptions of the past and mould common identities, but it could not have been done in a vacuum. It is impossible to write the national history of a non-existent nation — or even to invent one, because that could be done only for an audience consisting of people who believed or were prepared to believe that the nation actually existed. And although such histories are obviously propaganda, if the audience were indifferent or uninterested their effect may be doubted.

[hereafter *Chron. Fordun*], i, p. 327. But there was more to it than that; as Barrow has commented, 'Now there were to be Guardians during the "incapacity" or "incompetence" of the sovereign' (*Robert Bruce*, p. 64), which was a revolutionary step for the Scottish political community, as revolutionary as the imposition of a baronial council on Henry III of England in 1258, with which there are obvious parallels.

1 Usefully sketched in chapter 3 of B. Guenée, *L'Occident aux xive et xve siècles* (2nd edn, Paris, 1981): translated as *States and Rulers in Later Medieval Europe* (Oxford, 1985); see especially *ibid.*, pp. 58–62, 'Nation and history'.

Propaganda of that sort works best, surely, when it defines and articulates beliefs and theories which are already there, albeit in a half-baked form — in other words when it is a matter of preaching to the converted, or at least the semi-converted.

That is certainly the case in Scotland. It may be seen most clearly in the major works of Scottish history produced from the late fourteenth to the mid-fifteenth centuries: John Fordun's *Chronica Gentis Scotorum* (Chronicle of the Scottish Race, *c*.1365–85); Andrew Wyntoun's *Orygynale Cronykil of Scotland* (*c*.1410–20);[1] and Walter Bower's *Scotichronicon* (Scots' Chronicle, *c*.1440).[2] Together, these produced the standard history of medieval Scotland, which has held sway until the middle of the present century. But, to the frustration of current historians, much of their work dealt with the far distant, mythological past — because Fordun, Wyntoun and Bower saw themselves as historians, not contemporary annalists. Wyntoun's title, for instance, denoted that he was putting Scotland into the context of world history by going back to the 'Origins', that is, to the Creation. And none of them invented the concept of Scotland; instead, they were justifying the country's right to exist by producing a definitive history for the people of Scotland. The last words of Bower's *Scotichronicon* make the point: 'Christ! He is not a Scot who is not pleased with this book.'[3] That could have been said of all three works; Fordun, Wyntoun and Bower were all strongly, and in Bower's case virulently, nationalist. What they were writing was a consolidation of Scottish beliefs about the past. They were trying to give the Scots their history; but they were not setting out to produce a Scottish national consciousness. That had already been displayed in the Wars of Independence; had it not been in existence then there would have been no Scots for Fordun, Wyntoun and Bower to write for. Thus, certainly in Scotland's case, the production of national histories was a reflection of the current state of affairs. Fordun, Wyntoun and Bower were indeed preaching to the converted.

The actual significance of theories of nationhood, origins, history and so on is also illuminated by comparing medieval Scotland with medieval Wales and Ireland. Well-articulated origin myths, firm beliefs in racial solidarity, and an eloquently expressed hatred of foreigners are as evident in Wales and Gaelic Ireland as in Scotland, and from an earlier period. In Ireland, for instance, the Gaelic term for the native Irish was *Gaedhil*, while all who

---

1 Ed. D. Laing (Historians of Scotland, 1872–9); ed. F.J. Amours (Scottish Text Society, 1903–14) [hereafter *Chron. Wyntoun*].
2 Ed. W. Goodall (Edinburgh, 1759); ed. D.E.R. Watt (Aberdeen, 1987– , in progress) [hereafter *Chron. Bower*].
3 'Non Scotus est Christe cui liber non placit iste.' *Chron. Bower* (Watt), viii, pp. 340–1.

National Consciousness in Medieval Scotland

were not of native stock were called *Gall* — foreigners or incomers — no matter whether they were Danish, Norwegian, English or Norman; it was a distinction between the natives and the rest, irrespective of the latter's race. Native Irish hatred of foreigners was expressed at its most virulent in the twelfth-century Irish Gaelic text *Cogadh Gaedhel re Gallaibh*, a history of 'The War of the Gael with the Gall' (in that case, the Norse).[1] As for Wales, between the seventh and the tenth centuries the standard Welsh term for the native Welsh changed from *Brytaniaid*, or Briton, to a term with a much greater sense of racial solidarity: *Cymry*, meaning people of the same region, or 'compatriots'.[2] Since the early Middle Ages, the Welsh have described themselves to themselves literally as *the people*.[3] Furthermore, the peoples of medieval Wales and Ireland also had their own native systems of law,[4] and their Welsh and Gaelic languages, both of which accentuated their sense of racial togetherness in the face of English, Scandinavian or French-speaking outsiders; with respect to language, they were much better off than the inhabitants of medieval Scotland, where, as we shall see, there was great linguistic diversity. Thus during the Middle Ages the Welsh and the Irish surely had at least as strong a concept of racial or national solidarity as the Scots, and much more linguistic solidarity. Yet, between the eleventh and the thirteenth centuries, the whole of Wales and very substantial parts of Ireland were conquered by the English; subsequently, both countries experienced many anti-English rebellions, but neither was ever liberated from foreign rule. The contrast with what happened to Scotland is obvious — and demonstrates that success or failure in maintaining independence cannot simply be explained in terms of racial consciousness, nationalist myths, common language and the like.

The maintenance of medieval Scotland's independence is particularly interesting, since in terms of the medieval and some of the modern ideas about nationhood, Scotland was a mess, having no racial or linguistic unity

---

1   Ed. J.H. Todd (Rolls Series, 1867); the Scandinavians are described as 'a furious, ferocious, pagan, ruthless, wrathful people. In short, until the sand of the sea, or the grass of the field, or the stars of heaven are counted, it will not be easy to recount ... what the Gaedhill all, without distinction, suffered from them' (p. 43, quoted in Cowan, 'Myth and Identity', p. 113).
2   R.R. Davies, *Conquest, Coexistence and Change: Wales 1065–1415* (Oxford, 1987), pp. 19–20; T. Charles-Edwards, 'Some Celtic Kinship Terms', *Bulletin of the Board of Celtic Studies*, xxiv (1970–2), pp. 117, 122.
3   Though, as Cowan points out, the Scottish *fir n'Alban* — '*the* men of Scotland' — has much the same sense: 'Myth and Identity', p. 113, and cf. Dauvit Broun's essay, above.
4   R.R Davies, 'Law and National Identity in Thirteenth-Century Wales', in *Welsh Society and Nationhood*, ed. R.R. Davies *et al.* (Cardiff, 1984); D.A. Binchy, 'Ancient Irish Law', *Irish Jurist*, new series, i (1966).

whatsoever. From the original Scoto-Pictish conglomerate (discussed above by Dauvit Broun), the kingdom expanded south of the Forth-Clyde line during the tenth and eleventh centuries to include Anglian Lothian in the east and Brythonic Strathclyde in the west. In addition, there was Galloway, which was probably more Gaelic than Brythonic, but was quite distinct from the Scottish-Gaelic kingdom north of Strathclyde; there were extensive Norse regions in the far north from Caithness to the Moray Firth and in the Western Isles; and finally, from the 1130s, there was the Anglo-French-Flemish penetration initially sponsored by David I and his 'Norman' followers.[1] The result was that in the twelfth century there were three main languages in Scotland, Gaelic, English and French — plus Latin for the Church and for administration, and Norse on the fringes — while behind the languages was an even greater variety of ethnic groups. Scotland was very much a hybrid kingdom[2] — in stark contrast to Wales and Ireland, where concepts of racial purity were more strongly maintained.

The striking hybridity of Scotland, and particularly the linguistic split, caused an acute problem for John Fordun when he wrote the first part of his *Chronica Gentis Scotorum* in the 1360s. There is a famous passage — normally misquoted from an unsatisfactory nineteenth-century translation — in which Fordun described the differences between Scottish Lowlanders and Highlanders.

> The customs and habits of the Scots differ according to the difference of language; for two languages are in use, the Scottish [by which Fordun meant Gaelic] and the Teutonic [by which he meant English]. The latter is the language of those living by the sea coast and in the plains, while the race of Scottish speech inhabits the highlands and outlying islands. The people of the coast [the Lowlanders, including Fordun himself] are home-loving, civilised, trustworthy, tolerant and polite, decently attired, affable and pacific, devout in their worship of God, yet always ready to resist an injury at the hands of their enemies. The highlanders and people of the islands, on the other hand, are a wild and untamed race, primitive and proud, given to plunder and the easy life, clever and quick to learn, handsome in appearance, though slovenly in dress, consistently hostile and cruel to the people and language of the English, and, when the speech is

---

1   See, in general, A.A.M. Duncan, *Scotland: The Making of the Kingdom* (Edinburgh, 1975), chapters 4, 5, 7.
2   Some of the political aspects of this hybridity are discussed in A. Grant, 'Scotland's "Celtic Fringe" in the Late Middle Ages: The Macdonald Lords of the Isles and the Kingdom of Scotland', in *The British Isles 1100–1500: Comparisons, Contrasts and Connections*, ed. R.R. Davies (Edinburgh, 1988).

National Consciousness in Medieval Scotland

different, even to their own nation. They are, however, loyal and obedient to their king and country, and provided they be well governed they are obedient and ready enough to respect the law.[1]

In the nineteenth century Fordun's words for race and nation — *gens* and *natio* — were translated simply as 'race', which destroyed much of the point of the passage. In fact, Fordun used the term *gens* for the linguistic races within Scotland: the Lowlanders were *gens maritima*, the Highlanders *gens montana*. But then he continued that the Highlanders were hostile to the people and language of the English (*populo quidem Anglorum et linguae*) and also, because their speech was different, to their own nation (*sed et propriae nationi*). Thus, when he was talking about the *populo Anglorum* he meant the people of England, not those living in Scotland who spoke what we would nowadays consider a form of the English language. And in Scotland, Fordun counted both the Lowland race (*gens*) and the Highland race as part of one Scottish nation (*natio*). He had to say that the Lowlanders spoke the Teutonic language, not the English, because he had to make the distinction with the English-speaking people of England. Fordun's choice of words shows him wrestling with the fact that the realities of fourteenth-century Scotland did not fit contemporary theories which equated language, race and nation.[2] In Scotland there were two races, speaking different languages, but both part of the same nation.

An earlier example of the gulf between theory and reality with respect to the languages of Scotland can be found, strikingly, in the charges made against William Wallace at his trial at Westminster in 1305. Among a long list of alleged atrocities was that he had refused to spare the lives of anyone who spoke the English language.[3] This echoed the anti-French propaganda of Edward I in 1295, when it was proclaimed that Philip IV of France intended to destroy the English language. Here, English language was equated with English nation.[4] It is easy to see how that could apply to war

---

1 *Chron. Fordun*, i, p. 24. The translation is based on that in G.W.S. Barrow, *The Anglo-Norman Era in Scottish History* (Oxford, 1980), p. 146; but there both *gens* and *populus* are translated as 'people', which also probably blurs Fordun's point.
2 Cf. Reynolds, *Kingdoms and Communities*, pp. 254–6; Guenée, *States and Rulers in Later Medieval Europe*, pp. 52–4. It is worth noting the very different belief of King Stephen of Hungary (d. 1038), that 'a kingdom of one language and one way of life would be weak and fragile.... Foreigners should be welcomed: their different languages and customs, their example and their arms, would ... enrich the kingdom and deter its enemies' (*ibid.*, p. 257). King David I of Scotland (d. 1153) surely thought the same; is it merely a coincidence that his mother, St Margaret, had been brought up in Hungary at the court of Stephen's successor?
3 *Annales Londonienses*, in *Chronicles of the Reigns of Edward I and Edward II*, ed. W. Stubbs (Rolls Series, 1882–3), i, p. 141.
4 M. Prestwich, *Edward I* (London, 1988), p. 383 (and note).

with France; less so to war with Scotland. In reality a form of English would have been spoken by many, perhaps most, of the men in Wallace's army; ninety years later, at the night-time battle of Otterburn in 1388, it was said that in the dark friend and foe could not be distinguished, because the speech was the same on both sides.[1] And Wallace himself almost certainly spoke English; the famous remark attributed to him before Falkirk, 'I have browghte 3owe to the ryng, hoppe 3ef 3e kunne', may be apocryphal, but it was recorded by a contemporary English chronicler, who saw no incongruity in Wallace's speaking English.[2] It is the accusation that Wallace was the enemy of the English language that is incongruous.

Earlier still, a more mundane illustration of the problem with which Fordun was grappling is illustrated by the fairly common Scottish place-name 'Ingliston' (and its variants). Ingliston means the village, or settlement, of the English, who were evidently seen as strangers or foreigners. But when the various forms of Ingliston are mapped, they almost all turn out to be close to the sites of 'Norman' mottes and castles, and can thus be associated with the twelfth-century 'Norman' penetration of Scotland. 'Ingliston' appears to denote foreign settlements, possibly of English peasants, which were established by the new lords who, though nowadays called 'Normans', had come into Scotland from England.[3] Now 'Ingliston' itself is an English-language word. The local Scots who, in the twelfth century, regarded incoming English settlers as foreigners did not use the Gaelic language — there is no Gaelic form of Ingliston — but a form of English itself. The place-name clearly denotes the separate concepts of Scots and English, but obviously the difference was not thought to be a linguistic one. It was based simply on geographical origins: people from south of the Border were English, and hence foreigners, irrespective of the fact that they spoke much the same language as the southern Scots. Here we have a geographical, not a linguistic, concept of the foreigner — as, in reality, with Wallace. It is paralleled in the notorious St Brice Day massacre of Danes in Anglo-Saxon England in 1002, when instructions were given to kill all the Danes present in England. That did not mean all those Danes who had been

---

1 *The Westminster Chronicle 1381–1394*, ed. L.C. Hector and B. Harvey (Oxford, 1982), p. 348.
2 *Chronica Willelmi Rishanger*, ed. H.T. Riley (Rolls Series, 1865), p. 187; cited by Barrow, *Robert Bruce*, p. 346.
3 I owe this point to G.W.S. Barrow, who made it publicly during discussion of R.R. Davies's Wiles Lectures in Belfast in May 1988; he informs me that his map and analysis of 'Inglistons' are to be published in due course. The conjunction of Inglistons and mottes is noted, though not entirely accurately, in W.C. Mackenzie, *Scottish Placenames* (London, 1931), p. 214. Cf. R.R. Davies, *Dominion and Conquest: The experience of Ireland, Scotland and Wales 1100–1300* (Cambridge, 1990), pp. 12–14, for the introduction of English peasants by 'Norman' lords in Wales and Ireland.

settled in Danish England — the 'Danelaw' — for over a century. It was the Danes who had come into England during the invasion of the previous decade who were targeted: the 'Danish Danes', rather than the 'English Danes', so to speak.[1]

*

If geographical rather than linguistic concepts are applied, what made someone a foreigner? How was Scotland defined? What made it coherent geographically? The only answer which is meaningful in practice is surely that Scotland was the area whose people were ruled by, or at any rate acknowledged the superiority of, the king of Scots — in contrast to the area to the south where superiority was exercised by the king of England. From the king's point of view, the Scottish people were most commonly described as *omnibus probis hominibus tocius terre sue* ('all the good men of his whole land'); that is the standard form of address in royal charters in Scotland and England. In the earlier twelfth century racial descriptions were often added, such as *Francis et Anglis, Scottis et Galwensibus* ('French and English, Scottish and Galwegian'), but these ceased to be employed after about 1180.[2] In the two countries, the change in the standard form of addressing royal charters reflects the development of concepts of Scottishness and, south of the Border, Englishness which transcended ethnic and linguistic origins. There is an obvious contrast with Wales and Ireland, where ethnic and linguistic concepts were much stronger — but where, instead of single kings who could refer to all the men of their land, there were numerous rival petty kingdoms and principalities, whose feuding and warfare gave the opportunity for piecemeal Anglo-Norman conquest.[3]

The importance of the king as a focal point in medieval Scotland is poignantly brought out by the earliest surviving piece of Scottish poetry — a ballad which can almost certainly be dated to the years shortly after 1286, when with the death of Alexander III a long period of relative peace and prosperity was replaced by the disastrous warfare with England. It runs,

Quhen Alysandyr our king wes dede,
That Scotland led in luwe and le,

---

1 S. Keynes, 'A Tale of Two Kings: Alfred the Great and Æthelred the Unready', *Transactions of the Royal Historical Society*, 5th series, xxxvi (1986), pp. 211–12.
2 *Regesta Regum Scottorum*, ed. G.W.S. Barrow *et al.* (Edinburgh, 1960–, in progress), i, pp. 73–4; ii, pp. 76–7.
3 Davies, *Conquest, Coexistence and Change*, part I; F.J. Byrne, 'The Trembling Sod: Ireland in 1169', in *A New History of Ireland*, ii: *Medieval Ireland, 1169–1534*, ed. A. Cosgrove (Oxford, 1987).

Away wes sons off ale and brede,
Off wyne and wax, off gamyng and glé:
Oure gold wes changyd in to lede.
Cryst, borne in to Vyrgynyte,
Succoure Scotland and remede,
That stad is in perplexyte.[1]

Here there is the idea of Alexander *our* king, who led Scotland in love and law, and after whose death *our* golden age ended; the relationship between king and people is clear. The jingle 'love and law' is an important concept in medieval English legal history, denoting the two ways of settling disputes, by 'love' or arbitration, and by 'law' through the formal law courts. Since arbitration in disputes was even more common in medieval Scotland than in England, it is no surprise to find the jingle in a Scottish context.[2] The ballad shows how the king's chief role was seen as being the head of the country's dispute-settling procedures, the fountain of justice, in both 'love' and 'law'. It echoes the imagery of medieval great seals, which depict kings seated in majesty, dispensing justice to their people. Several English ballads of roughly the same date contain the same idea, that the king was the person to turn to for good justice — but their main burden tended to be the defects of English justice caused by the failings and corruption of the king's legal officers.[3] Judging by this admittedly fragmentary piece of evidence, that is not how Alexander III's reign was remembered in Scotland.

The Alexander ballad is echoed at the beginning of John Barbour's long, chivalric poem *The Brus*, on Robert I and his main companions, which was written in about 1375:

---

1 'luwe and le' is generally translated as 'love/law and peace', but the alliterative jingle 'love and law' is almost certainly what is meant (see the following note); 'sons' = 'abundance'; 'remede' = 'aid'. Andrew Wyntoun, who preserved the ballad, implies that it was written shortly after Alexander's death (*Chron. Wyntoun* [Laing], ii, p. 266), and from the sense it would have to date from before 1314. N.H. Reid has recently commented that most of the early narrative sources give little justification for treating Alexander III's reign as a 'golden age', and that the concept was only introduced by Bower in the 1440s: 'Alexander III: The Historiography of a Myth', in *Scotland in the Reign of Alexander III, 1249–1286*, ed. N.H. Reid (Edinburgh, 1990), pp. 181, 193. But the 'golden age' is already there in the ballad.
2 M. Clanchy, 'Love and Lawe in the Middle Ages', and J. Wormald, 'The Blood Feud in Early Modern Scotland', both in *Disputes and Settlements*, ed. J. Bossy (Cambridge, 1983); Wormald's essay is also in *Past and Present*, 87 (1980).
3 R.W. Kaeuper, *War, Justice and Public Order: England and France in the Later Middle Ages* (Oxford, 1988), pp. 325–37.

Quhen Alexander ye king wes deid,
Yat Scotland had to steyr and leid.[1]

It was included in full in Wyntoun's early fifteenth-century *Orygynale Cronykil*, and later in the century was quoted by the greatest of all Scottish poets, Robert Henryson, in his *Taill of the Scheip and the Doig*. That gives at least some impression of its popularity. But while the works of Barbour, Wyntoun and Henryson can be considered to have been produced for the elites, the Alexander ballad looks more like a piece of popular verse, one of several lays or ballads which were used or echoed by Barbour, Fordun and Wyntoun.[2] As such, it shows how a focus on the king, his identification with the kingdom's well-being, and a realisation of its plight without him, may be found among the more ordinary people of Scotland, well beyond the level of the great men and the high political community. It is always extremely difficult for medieval historians to find evidence of how ordinary people thought on any matters; here, the Alexander ballad possibly provides a glimpse of their attitudes to the king, to the kingdom, and perhaps to the effects on them of the English invasions.

*

To explore further the issue of national consciousness among ordinary people, let us consider, for a start, some instances from England, where the documentation is so much better. One is a story, related by K.B. McFarlane, of how in 1338 the townsmen of Southampton, with help from the surrounding countryside, expelled a force of French privateers. One knight 'was clubbed to the ground by a rustic. Prostrate, he cried for quarter: "Rançon" (i.e. "ransom"). But, "Yes, I know you're a Françon", the man replied and killed him.'[3] Here a local English peasant failed to understand the culture of the chivalrous elites, and killed the knight because he was French. Ten years earlier, when, after the Anglo-Scottish Treaty of Edinburgh of 1328, the English government proposed to restore the 'Stone of Scone' — the ceremonial stone on which past Scottish kings had been inaugurated, seized by Edward I in 1296 — this was prevented by a London mob, which wanted to keep the symbol of Scottish defeat in Westminster Abbey. This is an example of ordinary Londoners taking action against what was generally

---

1 'steyr and lede' = 'steer and lead'. (John Barbour,) *Barbour's Bruce*, ed. M.P. McDiarmid and J.A.C. Stevenson (Scottish Text Society, 1980–5), ii, p. 2.
2 *Ibid.*, i, pp. 14–16 ('Introduction: Before Barbour'); Nicholson, *Later Middle Ages*, p. 275; M.P. McDiarmid, 'The Metrical Chroniclers and Non-Alliterative Romances', in *The History of Scottish Literature*, i: *Origins to 1660*, ed. R.D.S. Jack (Aberdeen, 1988), pp. 28–9; F. Riddy, 'The Alliterative Revival', in *ibid.*, p. 40.
3 K.B. McFarlane, *The Nobility of Later Medieval England* (Oxford, 1973), p. 19.

a highly unpopular peace process with Scotland.[1] A third example is one of the reactions to the 'Mise of Amiens' of 1264, the arbitration award by Louis IX of France in the Henry III/Simon de Montfort conflict, which entirely favoured Henry III: a London chronicler wrote, 'When this was known, almost the whole commune of the middling people of England (*veri omnis communa mediocris populus*), who had not agreed to abide by the arbitration, rejected it.'[2] While that no doubt referred more to the Londoners than to the population as a whole, it is a significant reference to the attitude of at least some middling, or 'mediocre', people, outside the high political processes. A consciousness of national politics was being displayed from levels fairly far down the social scale. And while that example, like the previous one, relates to London, even obscure villages were involved in the national conflicts: in 1265 the villagers of Peatling Magna, in Leicestershire, attacked a royalist force for being 'against the welfare of the community of the realm and against the barons'.[3] David Carpenter has recently demonstrated that 'there was nothing unusual or isolated about the actions of the villages of Peatling Magna', and that in many places 'peasants were caught up in the "common enterprise" which had begun in 1258'.[4] At the beginning of the crisis, in 1258, English versions of the reforming legislation and the king's undertaking to accept it were distributed throughout the counties for public consumption; and, earlier, Magna Carta was almost certainly proclaimed country-wide in English.[5] In thirteenth-century England, an awareness of, and even some involvement in, national politics was not restricted to the political elite, but percolated well down the social scale.[6]

For Scotland, the events of the early years of the Wars of Independence,

---

1 E.L.G. Stones, 'An Addition to the "Rotuli Scotiae"', *Scot. Hist. Rev.*, xxix (1950). The treaty was generally vilified in England, and instead of publicly proclaiming it, as was customary, the government tried to keep it a secret; one chronicler wrote, 'The kyng grauntied a chartour to the Scottis and the teneure of that chartoure is vnknowen to the Englissh menne yit': R. Nicholson, *Edward III and the Scots* (Oxford, 1965), p. 54.
2 Reynolds, *Kingdoms and Communities*, p. 272.
3 D.A. Carpenter, 'English Peasants in Politics 1258–1267', *Past and Present*, 136 (1992), p. 3; from *Select Cases of Procedure without Writ* (Selden Society, 1941), pp. 42–5.
4 Carpenter, 'English Peasants in Politics' (quotations from pp. 41–2). Carpenter's article has very important implications for Scottish students of popular participation in the Wars of Independence.
5 M. Clanchy, *From Memory to Written Record: England 1066–1307* (London, 1979), pp. 171–3, 213–14.
6 In addition to Carpenter, 'English peasants in politics', cf. J.R. Maddicott, 'The County Community and the Making of Public Opinion in Fourteenth-Century England', *Transactions of the Royal Historical Society*, 5th series, xxviii (1978).

between 1296 and 1298, lead to much the same conclusion. For instance, after overrunning Scotland in 1296, Edward I took homages from some 1,500−2,000 Scots, whose names were listed in what is known as the 'Ragman Roll'.[1] Admittedly most of those listed were landowners, but there were also lesser clergy and many townsmen; and, in general, it is a far cry from the fifty or so nobles who would have made up the political elite. It in fact takes us a long way down the Scottish social scale; bearing in mind that English historians generally reckon the English gentry in the late thirteenth century as totalling around 3,000, and allowing that the Scottish population as a whole was probably then only about one sixth of England's, it appears that the Ragman Roll dealt with many people of a rather lower status than English gentry.[2] They may have been landowners, but most of them were simply petty lairds, probably closer to ordinary freeholders than to members of the political elite. With their homages to Edward I's agents, they were brought within the scope of the political processes — if they were not there already.

The homages recorded in the Ragman Roll resulted, of course, from English action. But in the anti-English revolts which broke out across the country the following year, the initiative was obviously purely Scottish. The Scots leadership in 1297 is difficult to categorise. Sometimes it has been said that there was a spontaneous rising of the Scottish people, who had been deserted by the country's elite. But that is untrue: among those involved in the revolts were, for instance, James the Steward of Scotland, the young Robert Bruce, earl of Carrick (the future king), and Bishop Wishart of Glasgow. There were also representatives of great men, such as MacDuff of Fife, then head of the kindred of the earldom, and Andrew Murray of Petty, rebel leader in Moray, whose magnate father and uncle were both in English prisons. On the other hand, the leaders included much less prominent figures, such as Alexander Pilche, burgess of Inverness, who was a close colleague of Andrew Murray — and, of course, that younger son of a minor Renfrew landowner, William Wallace. English documentation of the early stages gives a strong impression of anonymous leadership and of guerilla activity; while when Bishop Wishart, the Steward and Bruce did act openly they soon sued for peace. In general, it is clear that the impetus behind the

---

1 *Calendar of Documents relating to Scotland in H.M. Public Record Office*, ed. J. Bain (Edinburgh, 1881−8), ii, no. 823; Barrow, *Robert Bruce*, pp. 76−8; Duncan, *Nation of Scots*, p. 12.
2 C. Given-Wilson, *The English Nobility in the Late Middle Ages* (London, 1987), pp. 14−16, 69−72; N. Denholm-Young, 'Feudal Society in the Thirteenth Century: The Knights', in his *Collected Papers on Medieval Subjects* (London, 1946), pp. 56−67; A. Grant, *Independence and Nationhood: Scotland 1306−1469* (London, 1984), pp. 72−3 (for the population ratio).

revolts did not come purely — or chiefly? — from members of the political elite; in fact, 'it would be absurd to deny that Stirling Bridge was a popular victory'.[1] The best analysis, indeed, is probably that of the well-informed Yorkshire chronicler Walter of Guisborough:

> The common folk of the land followed him [William Wallace] as their leader and ruler; the retainers of the great lords adhered to him; and even though the lords themselves were present with the English king in body, at heart they were on the opposite side.[2]

In other words, all kinds of Scotsmen (and Scotswomen: Mary Melville, widow of a Roxburghshire laird, was the joint leader of one cross-Border raid[3]) took part in the war in 1297 — but Guisborough believed that the elite were the least prominent.

For Guisborough, they revolted simply because they were Scots; he had no problems about a purely nationalistic analysis. Nowadays historians are rightly more cautious, and would probably prefer to think more in terms of specific grievances and motivations. If we ask why magnates were lukewarm in 1297, the answer is perhaps that they had a great deal to lose by rebellion: the conventions of the time were that if they submitted after an initial defeat they would keep their estates, but if they rebelled once more and were again defeated they risked suffering complete forfeiture. The fact that many Scottish nobles held lands in England (and *vice versa*) is also obviously significant.[4] Therefore, in 1297, many magnates no doubt preferred to wait and see whether the independence cause looked like winning. Lesser people, on the other hand, were perhaps in a different situation. Many of them, indeed, may well have believed they had as much to lose from submission to the English in 1296−97. A major threat to their livelihoods came from the proclamation by Hugh Cressingham, the head of the English administration in Scotland, that all the wool in Scotland was to be requisitioned for Edward I; the intention was to sell it in Flanders, use the proceeds to finance the Anglo-French war, and subsequently (in theory) repay the producers. In Scotland, as in England, wool (in many ways the medieval equivalent of oil) was by far the most important commodity in the economy; most of it came

---

1 Barrow, *Robert Bruce*, pp. 80−9 (quotation from p. 88); Duncan, *Nation of Scots*, pp. 12−16; E.M. Barron, *The Scottish War of Independence* (2nd edn, Inverness, 1934), pp. 32−57, for Murray and Pilche.
2 *The Chronicle of Walter of Guisborough*, ed. H. Rothwell (Camden Society, 1957) [hereafter *Chron. Guisborough*], p. 299; quoted by Barrow, *Robert Bruce*, p. 85.
3 *Ibid.*, p. 93.
4 The very considerable extent of cross-Border landownership in the 13th century is analysed in K.J. Stringer, *Earl David of Huntingdon, 1152−1219: A Study in Anglo-Scottish History* (Edinburgh, 1985), pp. 178−98.

from flocks belonging to lesser landowners and, in particular, to substantial peasantry.[1] Their livelihoods, and those of the townsmen who normally handled the exports to the looms of the Low Countries, would have been severely hit.

Secondly, it was believed that Edward was also going to take Scottish men for his war in France. Scots magnates stated in July 1297 that 'they were told for a certainty that the king would have seized all the middle people of Scotland [*tuz le menzane de Escoce*] to send them across the sea in his war, to their great damage and destruction'.[2] Following on the seizure of the wool, that was certainly a reasonable belief, for Edward, whose strategy generally depended on recruiting the largest armies possible, was desperate for troops in 1297.[3] Whether or not he did intend to conscript large numbers of Scots, it is easy to see why that was feared — by the same middling folk whose wool had been requisitioned. It is worth pointing, in passing, to a modern British parallel: the proposal to introduce conscription in Ireland in 1917–18 proved a major turning-point in the modern struggle for Irish independence.[4] In 1297, moreover, Edward's demands for taxes, wool, and manpower from the people of *England* had brought that country to the verge of rebellion;[5] they are unlikely to have done any less in Scotland. There were therefore other reasons beside national consciousness for the people of Scotland to revolt against Edward I in 1297; but the awareness that these demands were being made by a foreign conqueror surely heightened and focused the grievances.

The concept of the middling folk is particularly significant when placed in a military context. In medieval Scotland, as in England (where that was formalised by the late twelfth-century Assize of Arms), all adult males were supposed to possess arms for police and military purposes; the level of equipment depended on their income or possessions. In Robert I's legislation of 1318, one section, *De armaturis pro guerra,* laid down that everyone with goods worth £10 was required to have, 'for his body in the defence of the kingdom', a thick leather jacket, preferably with metal plates, a helmet or 'hat of iron', armour-plated gloves, a spear and a sword. Those who were less well off, with goods only to the value of a cow, were simply to have a good spear or a good bow with a sheaf of arrows. Failure to have the equipment would mean the forfeiture of all possessions. This legislation

---

1 *Memoranda de Parliamento, 1305,* ed. F.W. Maitland (Rolls Series, 1893), p. 184; Grant, *Independence and Nationhood,* pp. 62–3, 70–2.
2 *Documents illustrative of the History of Scotland, 1286–1306,* ed. J. Stevenson (Edinburgh, 1870), ii, no. 452.
3 Prestwich, *Edward I,* pp. 230, 513–14, 564.
4 R.F. Foster, *Modern Ireland, 1600–1972* (London, 1988), pp. 487–90.
5 Prestwich, *Edward I,* chapter 16.

dates from after the first Wars of Independence, but it was no doubt re-enacting or modifying existing rules. Judging by the similar English legislation, the £10 possessions level was that of the substantial peasantry: the middling folk, well above the poor but below the gentry (who, in arms legislation, generally had to be equipped as cavalry); it is the same social level as that which provided the famous English archers.[1] So far as Scottish infantry were concerned, those with body-armour and swords as well as spears would obviously have been much more valuable than those without; they would have been in the front ranks of the Scottish *schiltroms*, or massed bodies of spearmen, which repelled the charges of English knights in the defeat with Wallace at Falkirk in 1298 and in the victory with Robert I at Bannockburn in 1314.[2] This then tallies with the fears that Edward I wanted to conscript the middling folk of Scotland for warfare across the sea. What Edward would have wanted from Scotland would surely have been the better-quality, well-equipped troops; poorly armed Scots would have been little use to him. In the event, he was unable to recruit them to any extent; instead, they presumably formed the basis of the armies which resisted him.

Unfortunately, scarcely any details of the ordinary people who revolted in 1297−8 have survived. But Geoffrey Barrow has provided us with one delightful sketch.

> If we ask ourselves from what sources Wallace could draw on support we might consider the stories of Thomas of Edinburgh and William of Bolhope. As the victorious English army advanced upon Edinburgh in the summer of 1296, an obscure priest of the town named Thomas, duly equipped with bell and candle, solemnly pronounced sentence of excommunication against King Edward and his men in a spirit of hostile defiance. He and his assistant Richard Gulle who had rung the bell were both sent for punishment to the appropriate church court, which may well have dealt with them very leniently. William of Bolhope was a Scotsman (evidently from the Borders) who at the time war broke out in 1296 had been long resident in England, probably in Northumberland. He had hurried home to enlist with the Scottish army, only to see King Edward 'gain the upper hand in his country', as the record has it. Whereupon, undaunted, he armed himself with two swords and set off southward on a one-man expedition against England which took him as far as Alnmouth. There he was challenged by two local men, refused to

1 *Acts of the Parliaments of Scotland*, i, pp. 473−4; G.W.S. Barrow, 'The Army of Alexander III's Scotland', in *Alexander III*, ed. Reid, p. 134 and n. 13; M.R. Powicke, *Military Obligation in Medieval England* (Oxford, 1962), pp. 54−6, 118−22, 194−9.
2 Barrow, *Robert Bruce*, pp. 100−3, 218−30.

acknowledge fealty to King Edward, and was promptly put to death. We have no reason to suppose that this trio of Tom, Dick, and Willie, who happened to have found their way on to surviving record, were in any way untypical.[1]

Barrow has also pointed to a more general piece of evidence. After the Scottish victory at Stirling Bridge, Edward I mounted a huge invasion in 1298, and defeated Wallace's army at Falkirk. In the aftermath of that battle, when an English grip was being re-established over Scotland, those who had fought with Wallace were punished with the forfeiture of their lands and tenancies. Some details of that process come from the lands of Coldingham Priory (a daughter-house of Durham Cathedral Priory) in southeast Berwickshire. Forty-two individuals from the Coldingham estates are shown in Durham records as having been forfeited, while another forty-seven probably or possibly suffered that fate as well. In three instances there are specific references to the 'discomfiture' of Falkirk, and it is highly likely that all the forfeitures were for following Wallace in 1297−8.[2] The estate belonged to an English priory, not a Scottish lord, so it is not a case of the lord calling up his men to fight against the English. Perhaps the men went to fight *because* their landlord was English; if so, that would imply a grievance about English landownership in Scotland, which would also be significant. But the main point is that Coldingham was a smallish estate, some five miles across, and consisting of only a couple of parishes — yet it produced at least forty men, and possibly more than twice that number, to join the Scottish armies of 1297−8. Moreover, the Durham records show that it was mostly the substantial tenants who were forfeited: the middling folk, once again.

There were about a thousand parishes in medieval Scotland.[3] If, hypothetically, they all provided fighting men on the same scale as Coldingham — at least forty from two parishes, or twenty per parish — that would give a total of 20,000 men. In reality, recruitment would have been much more patchy, and the 1298 Scottish army was, presumably, nowhere near 20,000. On the other hand, for it to have resisted Edward I's forces for as long as it did indicates quite a substantial size, at a guess between 5,000 and 10,000 — and to raise that would have required recruitment on the Coldingham scale from a large number of parishes across much of the country. Something like that must have happened to provide the armies which fought at Falkirk or, later and much more successfully, at Bannockburn. And while at Bannock-

---

1 G.W.S. Barrow, *Kingship and Unity: Scotland 1000−1306* (London, 1981), p. 165.
2 G.W.S. Barrow, 'Lothian in the first War of Independence', *Scot. Hist. Rev.*, lv (1976), pp. 155−7, using *The Correspondence, Inventories ... of the Priory of Coldingham*, ed. J. Raine (Surtees Society, 1841), pp. lxxxv−civ.
3 I.B. Cowan, *The Parishes of Medieval Scotland* (Scottish Record Society, 1967).

burn it might be argued that the recruitment was done by the local landlords, it is harder to suggest that for Falkirk.

What the events of 1297−8 indicate, therefore, is a strong hostility to the English and willingness to take part in the Scottish cause among the middling folk of Scotland. Obviously fears of English lordship, government and administration were involved here — gruesomely expressed at Stirling Bridge, when the body of Hugh Cressingham, the English treasurer of Scotland, who had been killed in the battle, was flayed and pieces of his skin were distributed among the army.[1] As far as the peasants were concerned, they were perhaps also afraid of the imposition of English-style serfdom; later, in Barbour's *Brus*, English lordship was depicted as making a free man into a *thryll* or serf.[2] Also, the the Scottish peasantry did not have the same kind of divided loyalties that cross-Border estates caused for many of the magnates. Finally, as we have seen, the Scottish peasantry were hit in 1296−7 by the wool requisitioning, and were afraid of conscription into English armies. Each of these factors, on its own, cannot be said to have produced a widespread sense of Scottish national consciousness; but when they are all put together, that is what is quite likely to have emerged.

*

To conclude this essay, the issue of military recruitment will be considered further: one extreme expression of national consciousness, after all, is to die in warfare for one's country. As already said, in medieval Scotland all adult males were required to possess appropriate weapons and equipment. This was coupled to an equally general obligation of service in the armies when summoned. That was distinct from feudal landowners' knight-service; it applied comprehensively to all the men and all the land (with only a few exemptions for some ecclesiastical lords). Every unit of territory had to provide a certain number of fighting men, not on a feudal basis, but as something like the *fyrd* of Anglo-Saxon England. It was called 'common army service', or 'Scottish service', and had various gradations. In an absolute emergency, everybody was called out to defend the homeland; otherwise, lands were expected to send limited, selected numbers of men.

---

1 *Chron. Guisborough*, p. 303.
2 *Barbour's Bruce*, ii, pp. 9−10. Barbour possibly had landowners in mind; his famous 'Ah, fredome is a noble thing' is perhaps ambiguous. But it is significant that serfdom was fast disappearing in 14th-century Scotland; cf. Grant, *Independence and Nationhood*, pp. 66−7, 87−8, and also A. Grant, 'Late Medieval Rural Revolt: the anomalous case of Scotland', in *Dissent, Protest and Rebellion in Pre-Industrial Scotland*, ed. K. Brown (St Andrews, 1987). It should, however, be added that the *Memoranda de Parliamento, 1305*, p. 230, contains a petition from Scottish peasants on the royal demesne asking for the same security of tenure as their counterparts in England.

Common army service was organised on a provincial basis: the men of a particular province or region would turn out to fight under their local lords and the sheriffs, as part of the army of the province or, in much of the country, the 'army of the earldom'. From about the eleventh century until the mid-fifteenth, Scottish earldoms — unlike those of England — mostly consisted of large areas of territory, generally equivalent to provinces. These 'provincial' earldoms, and certain great 'provincial' lordships which were very similar, were the main regional divisions of Scotland; within them, the earl or lord led the regional armies.[1]

One illustration of this comes from a dispute between the earl and the bishop of Moray in 1389; among the points at issue was whether the earl was entitled to lead the bishop's tenants in war in the army of Moray (the argument probably arose out of the Otterburn campaign the previous year).[2] An earlier, well-known, illustration is from a letter of Robert Bruce, earl of Carrick (the future king), written in 1302 when he had just decided to submit to Edward I. He informed the monks of Melrose Abbey that

> whereas I have often vexed the abbey's tenants on their grange [farm] of Maybole [in Carrick] by leading them all over the country in my army of Carrick although there was no summons of the common army of the realm; now troubled in my conscience I shall never again demand any such army service, neither of many nor of few, unless the common army of the whole realm is raised for its defence, when all the inhabitants are bound to serve.[3]

That, then, was how the Scottish armies were generally recruited during the Wars of Independence — through the general obligation to serve in the common army of the realm. It was surely this institution that Andrew Murray and William Wallace employed in 1297: after Stirling Bridge, Murray and Wallace described themselves as 'commanders of the army of Scotland'.[4] In Fife, the earl's representative, whom we only know by the family name MacDuff,[5] presumably led out the army of the earldom of Fife. But other earls and provincial lords seem to have been sitting on the

---

1 Barrow, 'Army of Alexander III's Scotland'; Duncan, *Making of the Kingdom*, pp. 378–85; Grant, *Independence and Nationhood*, pp. 122–3, 136, 154–6.
2 *Registrum Episcopatus Moraviensis*, ed. C. Innes (Bannatyne Club, 1837), no. 48; Grant, *Independence and Nationhood*, pp. 41–2.
3 Barrow, *Robert Bruce*, p. 124; from *Liber Sancte Marie de Melros*, ed. C. Innes (Bannatyne Club, 1837), i, no. 351.
4 *Chron. Guisborough*, p. 306; *Documents illustrative of Sir William Wallace*, ed. J. Stevenson (Maitland Club, 1841), p. 159; J. Anderson, *Diplomata Scotiae* (Edinburgh, 1739), plate XLIII.
5 Cf. J. Bannerman, 'MacDuff of Fife', in *Medieval Scotland*, ed. Grant and Stringer.

fence, while some were working for the English. At best, they may have given their approval to the summons of the armies of their earldoms, but they did not lead them actively. On the eve of Stirling Bridge, James the Steward and Earl Malcolm of Lennox negotiated at Stirling with the English commanders, offering, if given time, to make the Scots disperse; but, as they reported the next day, they could not persuade any of their own men to desert Wallace. They may not have tried very hard; nevertheless they clearly had little control over the men of Lennox and the Stewart lordship.[1] Murray and Wallace appear to have raised 'the common army of the whole realm ... for its defence'; 'all the inhabitants [were] bound to serve'; and if the earls and great lords did not lead them, it looks as if a substantial number of Scotsmen were prepared to serve anyway.

This general obligation to perform military service surely helped to stimulate a sense of national identity in the most practical way possible; we are no longer talking about theories, we are talking about practical action. But the common army of Scotland was made up of local provincial armies, particularly the armies of the earldoms. Where, then, was the focus for the ordinary man? The army of the earldom is another of those important topics of Scottish medieval history which have yet to be fully researched, but it can be found long before the 1290s. One significant early reference is in the record of a lawsuit concerning lands in Fife, dating from *c.*1128. The case was determined before the men of the province of Fife, who were described as consisting of Earl Constantine of Fife and the army of Fife together with the army of the bishop of St Andrews, whose see was in Fife. In other words the concept of the men of the province of Fife did not have a geographical basis — all those living within a certain area — but a military one: the men of Fife were the men who served in the army of the earl and the army of the bishop.[2] That probably lay behind the geography of the Scottish provinces: they were, essentially, the areas within which the inhabitants were accustomed to serve in the armies of the local earls and bishops (and, in some areas where earldoms had not evolved, provincial lords).

The *c.*1128 lawsuit shows that the institution of the army of the earldom was already well established. Other evidence indicates that it originated many centuries before that — possibly, indeed, in the separate tribal lands of Dark Age and perhaps even pre-Roman Scotland. The actual rank of earl is not found then, of course. But at some stage in Scotland's early history, the local rulers, who were referred to as kings (*rí*) in the Irish Annals of the time, were replaced by men known as mormaers (the first reference to a

1 *Chron. Guisborough*, p. 300; Barrow, *Robert Bruce*, p. 87.
2 *Early Scottish Charters*, ed. A.C. Lawrie (Glasgow, 1905), no. 90; Duncan, *Making of the Kingdom*, pp. 167–8.

mormaer is with respect to the year 918); then during the eleventh century mormaers apparently changed into earls. Thus the distant origins of the army of the earldom may well lie in the armies of the local Dark Age petty kingdoms.[1]

But these, it might be suggested, were more likely to have been instruments of local particularism than forces making for cohesion across the whole of Scotland. Certainly, the history of early medieval Scotland is full of wars, in which the provincial armies fought against each other and against the kings — most of whom perished at the hands of their rivals. Nevertheless, so far as we can tell, the internal warfare that persisted in early medieval Scotland was not waged by provincial rulers, mormaers and earls in order to break away from rule by the Scottish king — as is characteristic of Welsh and Irish medieval history — but was aimed at gaining the crown itself.[2] The great northern province of Moray might be an exception here; in practice, for much of the time it was probably independent under its mormaers, who are called kings in Norse and Irish sources. Yet the most famous mormaer of Moray was MacBeth — immortalised by William Shakespeare. When MacBeth challenged and killed King Duncan in 1040, he did not then split Moray off from Scotland south of the Grampians, but, instead, took over the southern region and the Scottish crown itself, reigning as king from 1040 to 1058.[3] MacBeth's career provides a striking illustration of the unitary nature, not the divisions, of the kingdom of the Scots. His revolt is a reflection, actually, of the *unity* in the kingdom.

That point is reinforced by the term mormaer: it is a Gaelic word meaning 'great steward' (*mór* = 'great', *maer* = 'steward').[4] The concept of a steward, however great, automatically implies subordination to some superior authority, in this case, obviously, the king. Since mormaer is not an Irish Gaelic term — Ireland's provincial rulers were themselves called kings — it looks as if it was specially coined at a time when the Scottish provinces were brought under some degree of central royal authority. Thus even as early as the tenth century, there was a notion of the provinces being subordinated to the kingdom. And that would tally with the long-established

---

1 *Ibid.*, pp. 43, 108−11, 164−6; A.P. Smyth, *Warlords and Holy Men: Scotland AD 80−1000* (London, 1984), pp. 219−20; and see Dauvit Broun's essay, above.
2 Compare Duncan, *Making of the Kingdom*, chapters 4, 5, and Smyth, *Warlords and Holy Men*, chapters 6, 7, with, e.g., Davies, *Conquest, Coexistence and Change*, chapters 2−4; D. Ó Corráin, *Ireland before the Normans* (Dublin, 1972); or Byrne, 'Ireland in 1169', *New History of Ireland*, ii.
3 Duncan, *Making of the Kingdom*, pp. 99−100; E.J. Cowan, 'The Historical MacBeth', in *Moray in the Middle Ages*, ed. W.D.H. Sellar (Edinburgh, 1993).
4 K. Jackson, *The Gaelic Notes in the Book of Deer* (Cambridge, 1972), pp. 102−10.

system of military recruitment; as Robert Bruce's letter to Melrose Abbey stated, the men of the province were not obliged to obey the summons of the earl (or previously, presumably) mormaer, unless the king had summoned the whole army of Scotland. Strictly speaking, mormaers and earls could not lead out the men of their provinces — and, equally importantly, could not lawfully punish those who did not turn out[1] — without the king's authority.

In that way, it may be suggested, the mormaers and earls, through their provincial armies, acted as links between the provinces and the kingdom; they were the middle men, so to speak, providing a national focus for local affairs. Even if they fought against particular kings, they did so to support rival claimants to the crown. Much the same point, incidentally, emerges from a study of Gaelic poetry and literature from the later medieval Highlands. Despite all the Highland revolts against the kings of Scots, there is never any suggestion in Gaelic poetry and other literature 'that the Gaels do not owe allegiance to the true line of the Scottish monarchs, no matter how much their loyalty might be obscured in the turbulence of history or hostility to policies of an individual monarch and attitudes of central authority'.[2] The Gaels — the Highlanders — would fight against the central government, yet be absolutely loyal to the concept of the king and the kingdom at the same time. This can probably be taken back to the earlier Middle Ages. It is, in a sense, a unifying concept — giving Scotland a strikingly different political history to that of medieval Wales and Ireland, but one which is very like that of Anglo-Saxon England.

The unitary nature of pre-Norman Scotland and England may have had the same stimulus: the Viking invasions of the ninth and tenth centuries. But also, in Scotland, the remarkable upsurge of Scottish kingship which appears to have taken place in the aftermath of the Viking attacks involved dealing with a more ethnically diverse kingdom than in England;[3] so the kings of Scots probably had to be particularly conscious of and careful about fostering loyalty to the Scottish crown. The kings seem to have taken over different regions by assimilating them rather than by conquering them outright (hence the hybridity of the medieval kingdom of Scotland). Moreover, while there was no primogeniture in Gaelic society, it was the

---

1 A glimpse of how the system worked may be had from the statement of the scales of forfeitures for failure to perform common army service, due to earls and to the king, which was recorded for Alexander II in 1220: *Acts of the Parliaments of Scotland*, i, p. 398.
2 J. MacInnes, 'Gaelic Poetry and Historical Tradition', in *The Middle Ages in the Highlands*, ed. L. Maclean (Inverness, 1981), p. 147.
3 Duncan, *Making of the Kingdom*, chapters 4, 5, especially p. 111; Smyth, *Warlords and Holy Men*, chapters 6, 7; Cowan, 'Myth and Identity'; cf. Dauvit Broun's essay, above.

rule that only members of the royal kindred could become king. Therefore when provincial revolts led to the replacement of one king by another, the leaders had to have belonged to the royal kindred — which they could only have done if their forbears had been established in the provinces (as mormaers?) by previous kings. This, again, gives an idea of ties between centre and localities operating through the mormaers. And, finally, for a provincial ruler like MacBeth, taking over the kingdom rather than breaking away from it was essential because to the north he was engaged in conflict with the Norse rulers of the far north of Scotland; Moray could not have stood alone both against the earl of Orkney/Caithness (whose power probably stretched southwards into Ross) to the north, and against the kings of Scots to the south.[1] In these kinds of circumstances the binding together of local loyalties into provincial ones, which were expressed through the armies of the provinces led by the mormaers and earls, must also have promoted a certain sense of national consciousness among those liable to be summoned for the army: not only before the Wars of Independence but even before the Norman conquest of England.

The relative unity of eleventh-century Scotland is probably the main reason why, unlike Wales and Ireland, it was not conquered either wholly or in part by the Normans in the period after 1066. Whether or not the Scots could have withstood an all-out attack led by William the Conqueror or one of his successors is uncertain; but the English crown never attempted that, presumably because (until the time of Edward I) the English kings' interests focused much more on France. And whereas in Wales and Ireland individual Anglo-Norman barons could exploit local feuding to conquer territory for themselves, that was not possible in Scotland; indeed for much of the later eleventh and the twelfth centuries pressure on the Anglo-Scottish Border came more from Scotland than from England. When the 'Normans' did come into Scotland, it was not as conquerors but as friends and agents of the Scottish kings, David I and his successors Malcolm IV and William I.[2] They provided these monarchs with vital support against internal rebellions, especially from Moray and Ross in the north, in favour of rival candidates to the throne. The difference in 'Norman' activities in Scotland, where they acted as agents of the Scottish crown — in contrast to Wales and Ireland, where ultimately they were agents of the *English* crown[3] — was to be of the greatest importance during the Wars of Independence.

1   Duncan, *Making of the Kingdom*, p. 100; B.E. Crawford, *Scandinavian Scotland* (Leicester, 1987), pp. 71–8.
2   Barrow, *Anglo-Norman Era*; R.L.G. Ritchie, *The Normans in Scotland* (Edinburgh, 1954).
3   Davies, *Domination and Conquest*, chapter 4; R. Frame, *The Political Development of the British Isles 1100–1400* (Oxford, 1990), chapters 3, 4.

But it is not simply a matter of the Scottish 'Normans' (or many of them) taking the Scottish side during the Wars of Independence. As was argued above, these wars were fought by the ordinary people of Scotland too; not just the aristocracy, especially not in 1297−98. What there was, it may be suggested, was a community of interest between both the Normanised land-owners and the substantial peasantry: together producing the sense of community in the realm. We began with the political theory of the Declaration of Arbroath, ostensibly written on behalf of the earls, the barons and the rest of the community of the realm. Now, having considered the Scottish military system and its operation during the Wars of Independence, the case may be made that members of that community of the realm, including not only landowners but also, and vitally, many of the middling folk of Scotland, actually fought side by side in the struggle for Scottish independence.[1]

*

One last comment should be added. Much the same sense of unity can be found in medieval England, especially during the Hundred Years War against France; and there, as in Scotland, the peasantry were armed and took a leading part in the war, providing the kings with their vital archery weapon.[2] But in France, in contrast, although the Hundred Years War did stimulate French nationalism in the fourteenth and the fifteenth centuries,[3] it was not in quite the same way as in Scotland and England. One illuminating incident was a local French revolt in English-occupied Normandy in 1435. According to the French chronicler Thomas Basin, 'a great crowd of peasants took up arms in Normandy and turned them against the English, for whom they possessed a natural hatred'. Here we have French peasants, like the Scottish ones in 1297−8, trying to drive out the English. But, although the revolt was initially led by a few French captains and local nobles, these refused to attack an English-held strong point; instead they deserted their peasant followers, who were subsequently cut to pieces by two or three hundred English horsemen. Basin wrote bitterly:

> The people of Rouen and the inhabitants of the other towns did not desire it [i.e. liberation from the English] less than the inhabitants of

---

1 That is, of course, to take 'the community of the realm' at its widest, as in Barrow, *Robert Bruce*, pp. 88−9; in normal political circumstances, it — or more exactly its dominant part — was essentially aristocratic, as is stressed by A.A.M. Duncan, e.g. in *Nation of Scots*, p. 16. See, in general, Reynolds, *Kingdoms and Communities*, chapter 8, 'The community of the realm'.
2 Powicke, *Military Obligation in Medieval England*, chapters 10, 11.
3 C. Allmand, *The Hundred Years War* (Cambridge, 1988), chapter 6.

the countryside, and they waited each day for the arrival of this people's army in order to have the opportunity of ridding themselves of the English. But neither this desire nor this concern entered the mind of the French captains or the lords of the country who flocked into these districts. They were jealous of the people for having initiated the undertaking so well, falsely and criminally professing that this would be a great danger for themselves and for the kingdom of France if these people were fortunate enough to drive the English from the country by their own efforts and only with their own weapons.[1]

That passage makes it abundantly clear that the French peasantry were not considered to be part of the French war effort. In medieval France the peasantry was not armed, and did not make up the bulk of the French armies. The French principle was that peasants paid taxes, while nobles fought in the army.[2] The military system therefore operated on a class basis — which probably means that there was not the same consolidation of national consciousness during France's wars that, it is argued here, took place in Scotland (and England). Thus when, for later periods, French historians state that there is little evidence for any national consciousness among the people of France (see Ralph Gibson's essay, below), it is worth asking whether that might reflect the very different operations of the military system in France as opposed to England and Scotland. In the two medieval kingdoms of the British Isles, the people were involved along with the elites in their countries' wars; in France, they were not.

---

1 Thomas Basin, *Histoire de Charles VIII*, ed. C. Samaran (Société de l'Histoire de France, 1933−45), i, pp. 226−7; quoted in G. Bois, *The Crisis of Feudalism* (Cambridge and Paris, 1984), p. 338.
2 P. Contamine, 'The French Nobility and the War', in *The Hundred Years War*, ed. K. Fowler (London, 1971). The extent of French peasant 'resistance' to the English is, however, a very complicated issue; see M. Evans, 'Brigandage and Resistance in Lancastrian Normandy: A Study of the remission evidence', *Reading Medieval Studies*, xviii (1992).

Nationalism and Language in England, c.1300–1500

Stanley Hussey

Before the Norman Conquest, English had been the official language of all classes of people in England, and an important literature had already been written in it. During the period c.1100–1250, when a form of French (Norman French, or better, Anglo-Norman) was the language of the upper classes, English was the language of a subject lower class. The Normans, perhaps only one in eight or nine of the population, rapidly took over the top positions in both Church and state, and so could influence education and language in England out of all proportion to their numbers. French became the tongue of civil and polite conversation, English the language in which one addressed inferiors. Then, during the thirteenth century, with the gradual loss of English possessions in France (Normandy was lost in 1204) and following the decree of Henry III and King Louis in 1244 that nobles could not hold lands in both countries, English began to make a comeback. There was something of a hiccup as a result of the marriage of Henry III and Eleanor of Provence, who was accompanied by followers speaking Central French (*francien*), which was eventually to become the basis of standard French. But by the later fourteenth century English was triumphant: the language of Chaucer, Gower, Langland, the *Gawain*-poet and Wyclif.

That is how the story goes, canonised in the standard histories of the English language. Bowdlerised versions regularly surface in examination papers up and down the land. And the story is not, in the main, untrue. It is simply a good deal too pat. In the first place, are we talking of spoken or written English? Obviously written English is all we have, but even here the extent of French influence varies from region to region — it was greatest in London and the east Midlands — and also according to the subject-matter. French supplied English with much of the language of chivalry and the gentler arts, such as courtly love, music and fashion, but a few areas, agriculture for instance, remained relatively untouched:

> acre, field, hedge, furrow, sow, till, reap, harvest, plough, sickle, scythe, spade, rake, seed, wheat, barley, oats, grass, hay, fodder, ox, horse, cow, swine, sheep, hen, goose, duck, sty, pen, barn, fold.[1]

---

1 C.M. Millward, *A Biography of the English Language* (New York, 1988), p. 173.

All these words come from Old English. French contributed almost exclusively lexical (content) words. Grammatical (function) words, the 'small change' of language, remained almost completely English in origin. Since the Normans came as administrators rather than as founders of new settlements, there are few French place-names either. The resulting English language can be a mish-mash of English, French and Scandinavian: a *knight* (English) is called *sir* (French), his wife *lady* (English), but compare *Madam* (French); an *earl's* (English-Scandinavian) wife is a *countess* (French). *King* and *queen* are English, but *royalty, sovereign, rule, reign, court, govern, parliament* are all French.

Latin survived as the ecclesiastical language and was also used in more formal documents; less formal — but still legal — ones were apt to be written in French. Because French itself is derived from Vulgar Latin, it is not always easy to tell which words in Middle English were borrowed directly from Latin, as opposed to the hundreds more which had originally been Latin but were borrowed from French. Sometimes the Middle English spelling will help us to decide. Any serious study of Middle English has to consider all three languages. It is worth remembering that Gower, in the late fourteenth century, wrote his three major works: one in English, one in French and one in Latin. Presumably he had an audience for each of them.

What we need to know in rather more detail than the standard histories provide is which classes spoke and read what, and, if we can find out, how French and Latin were regarded in later medieval England. We might expect to find some evidence from the books read by the monarch and his court. But there is, unfortunately, no catalogue of a royal library until 1535, and probably such a library did not exist before the end of the fifteenth century. We think of a library as a *building*, containing books. For most of the Middle Ages, however, a royal 'library' may well have been scattered around several residences with books transported in chests. We are hampered, too, by the loss of the royal chamber accounts, in which the purchase of many books would probably have been recorded.[1] Henry II (1154−89) was evidently addicted to romances in French. Isabella, wife of Edward II (1307−27) apparently owned several books in French; she, of course, was the daughter of a king of France, but it is worth noting her friendship with Richard de Bury, author of *Philobiblon* and picker-up of unconsidered literary trifles on his journeys abroad. For both Henry and Isabella, that is what we might expect from the linguistic climate of their times. Matters become a good deal more interesting in the reigns of Richard II, Henry IV and Henry V, by which time English was making (had even

---

1   R.F. Green, *Poets and Princepleasers: Literature and the English Court in the Late Middle Ages* (Toronto, 1980), pp. 91−9.

made) its comeback. Richard II clearly loved books, but perhaps as much for their bindings as for their contents. Froissart presented him with an anthology of all his works of love and morality, 'illuminated, bound in red velvet and decorated with buttons and clasps of silver and gilt'. Gower originally dedicated *Confessio Amantis* to Richard who, according to the author, summoned him into the royal barge:

> And whan I was with him at large,
> Amonges othre thinges seid
> He hath this charge upon me leid,
> And bad me doo my besynesse
> That to his hihe worthinesse
> Som newe thing I scholde boke,
> That he himself it mihte loke
> After the forme of my writynge.[1]

However, he later changed his mind, and in 1393 rededicated the work — in English, but with Latin marginal summaries — to Henry of Lancaster, the future King Henry IV. 'A bok for king Richardes sake' is changed to 'A book for Engelondes sake'. One wonders, with Jeanne Krochalis, whether Richard ever got a presentation copy.[2] Chaucer probably wrote his *Legend of Good Women* for Richard's queen, Anne of Bohemia, and perhaps also the earlier *ABC to the Virgin* for Blanche, Duchess of Lancaster. Hoccleve, in the next century, composed the lengthy *Regimen of Princes* and Lydgate the even longer *Troy Book* for Henry V. Lydgate's *Life of Our Lady* is also dedicated to him in several manuscripts. While Henry was still prince of Wales, his father's cousin, Edward, duke of York, had translated *Le Livre de la Chasse* into English for him under the title *The Master of the Game*. So perhaps Henry was actually a *reader* of books in English rather than a mere collector of presentation copies for the royal coffee tables. Henry's brother, Humphrey, duke of Gloucester, the 'Duke Humphrey' of the library in the Bodleian, owned a copy of *Confessio Amantis* and three English books were dedicated to him: John Russell's *The Book of Nurture*,

---

1 Gower, *Confessio Amantis* (*The Works of John Gower*, ed. G.C. Macaulay [Early English Text Society, 1900−1]), Prologue, lines 46−53.
2 I am indebted to J.T. Rosenthal, 'Aristocratic Cultural Patronage and Book Bequests, 1350−1500', *Bulletin of the John Rylands Library*, lxiv (1981−2); and to J.E. Krochalis, 'The Books and Reading of Henry V and his Circle', *Chaucer Review*, xxiii (1988). See also J. Coleman, *English Literature in History, 1350−1400: Medieval Readers and Writers* (London, 1981), chapter 2, especially pp. 18−26. Dr Carol Meale shows how difficult it is to be sure where Malory obtained the French books he used: 'Manuscripts, Readers and Patrons in Fifteenth-century England: Sir Thomas Malory and Arthurian Romance', *Arthurian Literature*, iv (1985).

Lydgate's *Fall of Princes*, and the anonymous translation of Palladius on husbandry.

If this suggests a growth of books in English in the late fourteenth and the fifteenth centuries, we should remember that they are still in a minority and that there are several more in French and Latin — at least in royal circles. For the likely reading of the court as a whole, I cannot do better than quote John Scattergood:

> ...the available lists of books suggest that the culture of the court was still overwhelmingly Latin and French, and French of a somewhat old-fashioned sort too; most of the French books are romances evidently of some antiquity; apart from *Le Roman de la Rose*, the newer sort of love poetry as written by Machaut and Deschamps is not represented and the only book of Froissart's is the one presented to Richard II. There are no Italian books. And of all the books so far mentioned as appearing in lists, only four were certainly in English. English evidently had far to go before it acquired any sort of prestige — despite, for example, legislation in 1326 which made it (theoretically if not actually) the language of pleading in the law-courts.[1]

In recent years we have become much more aware of the 'new men' at court — career diplomats, civil servants, administrators of various kinds — amongst whom Chaucer most probably found his friends. These men were the most likely audience for the serious-minded works on philosophy, ethics and love, and the poems, delightfully fresh (for England at least) but sober in their conclusions, which were written in the vernacular. John Burrow called the poetry of the second half of the fourteenth century 'Ricardian' poetry, Anne Middleton more recently described it as 'public' poetry.[2] It is easier to define it by its content and its audience than by its style. *Piers Plowman* does not have much in common with *Sir Gawain and the Green Knight*, except that they are both in the alliterative long line (functional, even colloquial, in the first and courtly and decorative in the second). Chaucer and Gower, of course, wrote in the newer French-derived metres. J. H. Fisher has very properly reminded us of Chaucer's European dimension:

---

1 V.J. Scattergood, 'Literary Culture at the Court of Richard II', in *English Court Culture in the Later Middle Ages*, ed. V.J. Scattergood and J.W. Sherborne (London, 1983).
2 J.A. Burrow, *Ricardian Poetry: Chaucer, Gower, Langland and the Gawain Poet* (Yale, 1971); A. Middleton, 'The Idea of Public Poetry in the Reign of Richard II', *Speculum*, liii (1978).

Born into a family with a French name, married to the daughter of a Flemish knight, living in an Anglo-French court, serving in capacities that required him to write daily in French and Latin, Chaucer was bicultural and bilingual to a degree that it is hard for us to comprehend.[1]

If we descend the social ladder, the class division often corresponds with the language division. By the fourteenth century there are several books in English for the *lewed*, the unlearned (although *lewed* may sometimes simply mean lacking Latin). They usually make a point of saying that this is the reason why they were written in English. They include popular history (in verse) and books of religious instruction for the laity — or sometimes for their parish priests — in verse and prose. One of the most quoted passages on the language divide is these lines from the chronicle of 'Robert of Gloucester', looking back from the standpoint of 1300 or earlier:

þus com lo engelond in to normandies hond.
& þe normans ne couþe speke þo bote hor owe speche
& speke french as hii dude atom, & hor children dude also teche;
So þat heiemen of þis lond þat of hor blod come
Holdeþ alle þulke spreche þat hii of hom nome.
Vor bote a man conne frenns me telþ of him lute.
Ac lowe men holdeþ to engliss & to hor owe speche ʒute.
I wene þer ne beþ in al þe world contreyes none
Þat ne holdeþ to hor owe speche bote engelond one.
Ac wel ne wot uor to conne boþe wel it is,
Vor þe more þat a mon can, þe more wurþe he is.[2]

Vor bote a man conne frenns me telþ of him lute: 'Unless a man knows French, nobody thinks much of him' — in other words, 'On yer bike; get some French!' But this, and the compromise final line, must mean that there was more bilingualism than is commonly admitted, certainly if we define bilingualism as the ability to understand the non-native language and to be understood, in the main, when using it. In the fourteenth century the language of instruction in schools was French, if we believe Higden's *Polychronicon* (in John Trevisa's translation):

Þis apeyryng of þe burþtonge ys bycause of twey þinges. On ys for chyldern in scole, aʒenes þe vsage and manere of al oþer nacions,

---

1   J.H. Fisher, 'Chaucer and the French Influence', in *New Perspectives in Chaucer Criticism*, ed. D.M. Rose (Norman, Oklahoma, 1981), p. 191.
2   *The Metrical Chronicle of Robert of Gloucester*, ed. W.A. Wright (Rolls Series, 1887), ii, lines 7537–47.

buþ compelled for to leue here oune longage, and for to construe here lessons and here þinges a Freynsch, and habbeþ suþthe þe Normans come furst into Engelond. Also gentil men children buþ ytau3t for to speke Freynsch fram tyme þat a buþ yrokked in here cradel, and conneþ speke and playe wiþ a child hys brouch; and oplondysch men wol lykne hamsylf to gentil men, and fondeþ wiþ gret bysynes for to speke Freynsch, for to be more ytold of.

For to be more ytold of is taken almost verbatim from 'Robert of Gloucester'. But Trevisa, translating and updating Higden, adds:

Þys manere was moche y-vsed tofore þe furste moreyn, and ys seþthe somdel ychaunged. For Iohan Cornwal, a mayster of gramere, chayngede þe lore in gramerscole and construccion of Freynsch into Englysch; and Richard Pencrych lurnede þat manere techyng of hym, and oþer men of Pencrych, so þat now, þe 3er of oure Lord a þousand þre hondred foure score and fyue, of þe secunde kyng Richard after þe Conquest nyne, in al þe gramerscoles of Engelond childern leue Frensch, and construeþ and lurneþ an Englysch, and habbeþ þerby avauntage in on syde, and desavauntage yn anoþer. Here avauntage ys þat a lurneþ here gramer yn lasse tyme þan childern wer ywoned to do. Disavauntage ys þat now childern of gramerscole conneþ no more Frensch þan can here lift heele, and þat ys harm for ham and a scholle passe þe se and trauayle in strange londes, and in meny caas also. Also gentil men habbeþ now moche yleft for to teche here childern Frensch.[1]

Another factor in the growing use of English, at least by the middle classes (if that concept is accepted), is the later fourteenth-century desire to end the war with France in which the English were coming off decidedly second best. The gentry, Church, and substantial citizens were being taxed more and more to support the war effort, and, not surprisingly, they did not like it. They were not quite the 'poor condemned English' of Shakespeare's *Henry V*, perhaps, but, in the popular imagination, the enemy were certainly the vain, licentious French aristocrats of that same play. The French even appeared to have appropriated Arthur, the great English hero who (if Geoffrey de Monmouth and his literary descendants were to be believed) would one day return from Avalon to help the English out of their troubles. Here is Robert Mannyng of Bourne, Lincolnshire, in 1388:

In Fraunce men wrot, & 3it men wryte,
But herd haue we of hym but lyte;

---

1 *Fourteenth-Century Verse and Prose*, ed. K. Sisam (Oxford, 1921), pp. 148-9.

Þerefore of hym more men fynde
In farre bokes, als ys kynde,
Þan we haue in þys lond.
. . .
Þer haue men bokes of al his lyf,
Þer are his merueilles red ful ryf;
Þat we of hym here alle rede,
Þere were þey writen ilka dede.
Þyse grete bokes so faire langage,
Writen & spoken of Fraunces vsage,
Þat neuere was writen þorow Englischemen,
Swilk stile to speke, kynde ne can,
But Frensche men wryten hit in prose,
Right as he dide, hym for to alose.[1]

'And in *prose*, too'! I owe this reference to Dr Thorlac Turville-Petre, who, in an excellent recent article,[2] has shown how easy it was to portray the English as 'Nature's aristocrats, unjustly and unnaturally dominated by an alien race', and to project this fourteenth-century nationalism backwards into the earlier Middle Ages. And there is another point: was not the language of the law Frenchified so that decent Englishmen could be condemned in a language they did not know?

Almost certainly, by the second half of the fourteenth century at the latest, French in England had become a cultivated second language rather than the real language of men, or at least of gentlemen. But all educated people could read it and almost certainly speak it, too. The decline of French as the language of official business went hand in hand with the growing emergence of 'Chancery Standard' English (chancery comprised almost all the national bureaucracy, except for the exchequer). This type of English won out against two other possible contenders in the late fourteenth century, 'London' English, as used by Chaucer, and the Wycliffite language of north Midland counties like Leicestershire, Northamptonshire and Bedfordshire, spread around the country by itinerant Lollard preachers. What seems to have happened is that the Chancery clerks, 120 or so of them with a rigid apprenticeship system, copied official documents into their own reasonably consistent language, sent them out to different areas of England, and gradually began to receive replies in which the regional dialect started to

---

1 *The Story of England by Robert Manning of Brunne*, ed. F.J. Furnivall (Rolls Series, 1887), i, lines 10607–11, 10967–76.
2 T. Turville-Petre, 'Politics and Poetry in the Early Fourteenth Century: The Case of Robert Manning's Chronicle', *Review of English Studies*, xxxix (1988).

accommodate itself to Chancery Standard. Dr David Burnley has argued that this coincided with some degree of social approval for a 'curial' style.[1] Chaucer was admired and imitated in the fifteenth century not for his language but for his style. Chancery Standard was where the future lay. And that is a moral for our own times, perhaps: however creative we may be, the administrators get us in the end.

So where does this leave French in popular regard at the close of the Middle Ages in England? The peak of borrowing had certainly passed by 1400, but French words still stuck out in English because French is a Romance language whereas English is a Germanic one. In Chaucer a French loan-word will usually require another French loan-word to rhyme with it: *Maistrie/jalousie*; *resoun/consolacioun*; *purveiaunce/governaunce*; *conclusioun/disputisioun*. These examples happen to come from *The Franklin's Tale*. Incidentally, the last word in the description of the Franklin in the *General Prologue* is *vavasour*, 'an old-fashioned word, even at the time, with resonances about it of chivalric romance, hospitality, and assistance to knights errant'.[2] The impression of a rather old-fashioned country gentleman, who will later tell a Breton *lai*, a possibly old-fashioned type of story, is crystallised by finally calling him a *vavasour*. It is worth noting that some of the above abstract words are among the most difficult to translate properly into Modern English. French had provided English with an abstract vocabulary — God's *governaunce* over man and the lady's *ordinaunce* over her lover. Rhymes between French loans and native English words do occur, but less often: two examples from *The Wife of Bath's Tale* are *lymytacioun/ up and doun*, and *hous/dangerous*.[3] Or French words may be contrasted with those of English derivation. In the short, and perhaps early, *Complaint to his Lady*, the poet, savouring the exquisite pains of love ('The more I love, the more she doth me smerte') calls himself '*unconnyng* and *unmete*' ['unskilful and unsuitable'], whereas his beloved is characterized by the French *pitee ... gentilesse ... debonairtee*,[4] even though she is not, at that moment, demonstrating these qualities to him.

In a less aristocratic vein, however, fun can be had with what was obviously not the French true Frenchmen really used (or Englishmen at

---

1   J.D. Burnley, 'Sources of Standardisation in Later Middle English', in *Standardising English: Essays in the History of Language Change*, ed. J.B. Trahern (Tennessee Studies in Literature, 1989).
2   H. Cooper, *Oxford Guides to Chaucer: The Canterbury Tales* (Oxford, 1989), p. 45; and earlier, R.J. Pearcy, 'Chaucer's Franklin and the Literary Vavasour', *Chaucer Review*, viii (1973).
3   *The Canterbury Tales: Wife of Bath's Tale*, lines 877−8, 1089−90. (References to Chaucer are to *The Riverside Chaucer*, ed. L.D. Benson [London, 1988].)
4   *Complaint to his Lady*, lines 69, 101−2.

court, for that matter). Chaucer says that his Prioress's French, although spoken *ful faire and fetisly* ['most beautifully and elegantly'], was

> After the scole of Stratford atte Bowe
> For Frennsh of Parys was to hire unknowe'.[1]

Rather worse was Langland's Avarice who, when commanded by Repentance to make restitution for his ill-gotten gains, states (or pretends) that

> 'I wende riflynge were restitucion', quod he, 'for I lerned nevere
> rede on boke,
> And I kan no Frenssh in feith, but of the ferthest ende of
> Northfolk'.[2]

Or there is the uneducated character, a plain man who knows what's what but who cannot get his tongue round those outlandish foreign words. Chaucer's Host, near apoplectic at the terrible death of Virginia in *The Physician's Tale* which he has just listened to, believes he is in danger of having a *cardynacle* (for *cardiacle*, 'heart attack'). Old John the carpenter, in *The Miller's Tale* twice talks of *astromye*.[3] Rather more subtle than this is the Wife of Bath, a great one for euphemisms:

> For if I wolde selle my *bele chose*
> I koude walke as fressh as is a rose;
> But I wol kepe it for youre owne tooth.

Or, switching to Latin for a change:

> And trewely, as myne housbondes tolde me,
> I hadde the beste *quoniam* myghte be.[4]

In the darkness of the Miller's cottage in *The Reeve's Tale*, husband and wife out-snore each other and their lumpish daughter joins in, 'The wenche rowteth eek, *par compaignye*' ['just to be sociable']. No wonder the *clerkes*, Aleyn and John, can't get to sleep and find other ways of passing the night. The same phrase, obviously popular with a fabliau audience, occurs at the

---

1 *Canterbury Tales: General Prologue*, lines 124–6. But perhaps this was not so provincial after all: see W. Rothwell, 'Stratford atte Bowe and Paris', *Modern Language Review*, lxxx (1985).
2 *Vision of Piers the Plowman*, B text (ed. A.V.C. Schmidt [London, 1978]), passus V, lines 235–6.
3 *Miller's Tale*, lines 3451, 3457.
4 *Wife of Bath's Tale*, lines 447–9, 607–8.

end of *The Miller's Tale*, in Nicholas and Alison's cruel exposure of old John, the carpenter husband:

> He hadde yboght hym knedyng tubbes thre,
> And hadde hem hanged in the roof above;
> And that he preyed hem, for Goddes love,
> To sitten in the roof, *par compaignye*.[1]

These extracts, however, are actually *using* French loan-words to make a point. A good dictionary will state from which language the word came and approximately when it was borrowed into English. What is much more interesting is what English did with the word once it had acquired it. My last few examples of French borrowings all come from *The Miller's Tale*. The Miller *can* get his tongue round a polysyllabic French word, even though it may be a struggle:

> But first I make a *protestacioun*
> That I am dronke; I knowe it by my soun.

— that over-careful articulation we have all heard from the man the worse for drink. (The same word is used 'straight' in the *Parson's Prologue*, line 59.) Miller and Reeve, in the ensuing conversation, are adamant that nobody is calling anybody else a cuckold, although the Miller adds that there may be some things it is better not to know, especially, perhaps if you were to know them in French:

> An housbonde shal nat been inquisityf
> Of Goddes *pryvetee*, nor of his wyf.

God's hidden secrets, perhaps something terrible — but, *nor of his wyf*, his wife's 'private parts'? He continues:

> So he may fynde Goddes *foyson* there
> Of the remenant nedeth nat enquere.

'God's plenty', perhaps a phrase used at harvest-time, is here turned into a dirty joke. Alison, in the Tale proper, pretends to rebuff the over-eager Nicholas: 'Do wey youre handes, for your *curteisye*' [l. 3287]. A courtly word, genteel even, for this sexy, eighteen-year old country girl. 'Kindly have the manners to take your hands away!' She knows what she ought to say, and she says it. But equally she knows what she wants to *do*, and a couple of lines later is busy making an assignation with Nicholas. The same word, *curteisie*, is used of Nicholas's rival, the parish clerk Absolon, who is not taking the collection because he is eyeing the local talent, especially

---

1 *Miller's Tale*, lines 3836−9.

Alison: 'For *curteisie*, he seide, he wolde noon.' The description of that same Absolon ends:

> But sooth to seyn, he was somdeel squaymous
> Of fartyng, and of speche *daungerous*.[1]

That becomes all too evident at the climax of the story. *Daungerous*, however, was usually used of courtly ladies who were advised to keep the young man at arm's length. Absolon is not only fastidious but distinctly effeminate too.

Latin appears largely to escape this sort of exploitation, possibly because it was confined to a much more limited register. Chaucer's Constance, in *The Man of Law's Tale*, speaks *A maner Latyn corrupt* which is nevertheless understood in Northumbria, but this is clearly not meant to be funny in the way Langland's Avarice was. Holy Church, in *Piers Plowman*, upbraids the Dreamer:

> 'Thow doted daffe!' quod she, 'dulle are thi wittes.
> To litel Latyn thow lernedest, leode, in thi youthe:
> *Heu michi quia sterilem duxi vitam iuvenilem!*[2]

where the gist of the Latin proverb is given in the preceding line. Elsewhere he seems to need no translation. As part of her attack on clerical ignorance, Anima complains:

> Grammer, the ground of al, bigileth now children:
> For is noon of thise newe clerkes — whoso nymeth hede —
> That kan versifye faire ne formaliche enditen,
> Ne naught oon among an hundred that an auctour kan construwe,
> Ne rede a lettre in any langage but in Latyn or in Englissh.[3]

Inability to compose, or even to translate, properly is what we might expect in this context, yet the last line seems to suggest some competence in Latin and English — but not in French? One of the few deliberately mocking references to Latin occurs in the play of *Mankind* (c.1470) where there is an exchange between New Guise, Nowadays and Mercy, who has just made a long speech on the benefits of Christ's crucifixion in which she uses words like *indygnacyon, obsequyouse, revyuyde, redempcyon, veryfyede, rectyfye, remocyon, partycypable, retribucyon, restytucyon, preemmynence, medyacyon, perseuerante*:

---

1 *Ibid.*, lines 3137−8, 3163−4, 3165−6, 3287, 3351, 3337−8.
2 *Piers Plowman*, B, I, lines 140−1.
3 *Ibid.*, B, XV, lines 370−4.

NEW GYSE. But of yowr name, ser, I yow prey,
That we may yow ken.

MERCY. Mercy ys my name by denomynacyon.
I conseyue 3e haue but a lytyll fauour in my communycacyon.

NEW GYSE. Ey, ey! yowr body ys full of Englysch Laten.
I am aferde yt wyll brest.
'Prauo te', quod þe bocher onto me
When I stale a leg a motun.
3e are a stronge cunnyng clerke.

NOWADAYS. I prey yow hertyly, worschyppull clerke,
To haue þis Englysch mad in Laten:

'I haue etun a dyschfull of curdys,
Ande I haue schetun yowr mowth full of turdys.'
Now opyn yowr sachell wyth Laten wordys
Ande sey me þis in clerycall manere! [1]

The function of New Guise and Nowadays is, of course, to cock a snook at Christian teaching, but Mankind, with or without Latin, will, as in all morality plays, be saved at the end. However, the Carmelite Richard Maidstone was deadly serious when he complained that John Ashwardby, his opponent in the running debate on mendicant poverty, had set out his views *in lingua materna*, whilst he himself had properly conducted his case 'in scolis et coram clericis *in lingua latina*'.[2] Lydgate, according to Lois Ebin,[3] created from Latin and French 'a new critical language for poetry', *aureate* poetry; it is a word he introduced into English, meaning not only 'golden', but 'inspired', 'eloquent', 'appropriate', to take its place with *adourne*, *enbellissche* and *sugrid*. The high style naturally accompanies the frequent amplification. Noble deeds deserve a noble style: in a word, decorum.

Deschamps, praising Chaucer extravagantly for his translation of the *Roman de la Rose*, said he has greatly benefited 'Aux ignorans de la langue pandras' — has enlightened those ignorant of French. But let us not forget that it was a Frenchman who said this, and of course the original poem was extant, an original created by two Frenchmen. In English, and surprisingly

---

1 *Mankind*, lines 120-34, from *The Macro Plays*, ed. M. Eccles (Early English Text Society, 1969).
2 Quoted by W. Scase, *Piers Plowman and the New Anticlericalism* (Cambridge, 1989), p. 65.
3 L. Ebin, 'Lydgate's Views on Poetry', *Annuale Mediævale*, xviii (1977).

late, a good deal of linguistic chauvinism remained. And the jokes still do. When, in an early episode of *Yes, Minister*, the senior civil servant, Sir Humphrey, suggests that a certain course of action will only benefit 'our traditional enemies', the minister, Jim Hacker, agrees: 'Yes, I suppose that would help the Russians'. To which a very pained Sir Humphrey replies, 'No, Minister, the *French*!'

National Identity in Ireland and Scotland, 1500–1640

Michael Lynch

In the course of what is sometimes called the 'long sixteenth century', between 1500 and 1640, both Scotland and England came to acquire a more sharply etched sense of national identity. For some historians, this had much to do with the parallel processes by which the Scottish and English crowns acquired a tighter grip over their subjects and their borderlands, found in the case of England in Ireland and Wales as well as in its troublesome north. In 1493 James IV of Scotland (1488–1513) annexed the Lordship of the Isles, the vital instrument for the aggrandisement of the MacDonald regional warlords in the west during the fourteenth and early fifteenth centuries; James's son and heir was significantly termed 'Prince of Scotland and the Isles'.[1] The fall in 1534 of the Fitzgeralds of Kildare, the greatest of the local magnates in the late medieval lordship of Ireland, was the prelude to the claiming by Henry VIII of England (1509–47) of the crown of Ireland in 1541 and the first act in the story of the conquest of Ireland, which reached its climax in 1601. Only two years later these two royal dynasties, of Tudor and Stewart, would be joined, in the person of James VI of Scotland, and the three kingdoms — of England, Ireland and Scotland — would be united. The vehicle of union was kingship itself: James was styled on his coinage after 1604 as *Jacobus/Carolus DG Mag. Brit. Fra. et Hib. Rex*. Dual monarchy — now of Britain and Ireland — was reinforced by a novel *patria*, the 'blessed Ile' of 'Great Britain'.[2]

Or so it seemed. The sixteenth-century history of the British Isles is all too easily sketched as the victory of nation-states over the dark corners of their lands. That process was riddled with ambiguities and reverses. In 1138, at the battle of the Standard, English chroniclers recounted their shock at being confronted by the motley assembly of 'Normans, Germans,

---

1 A. Dunbar, *Scottish Kings* (Edinburgh, 1906), p. 219; also J.W.M. Bannerman, 'The Lordship of the Isles', in *Scottish Society in the Fifteenth Century*, ed. J.M. Brown (London, 1977).
2 B. Galloway, *The Union of England and Scotland, 1603–1608* (Edinburgh, 1986), p. 60; *The Jacobean Union*, ed. B. Galloway and B.P. Levack (Scottish History Society, 1985), pp. xxx–xxxv.

English, Northumbrians and Cumbrians ... Galwegians and Scots' which made up the army of the king of Scots, drawn from the various *nationes* which owed allegiance to him.[1] In 1513, the army raised by Henry VIII of England was hardly less diverse, being made up of 'French, English, Northern [English], Welsh or Irysh'. In 1544, Henry raised over 1,000 'kerne' from his Irish kingdom to prosecute his claim to suzerainty over Scotland during the 'Rough Wooing'.[2] The growing sense of 'true born Englishmen' and an English *patria*, which gathered pace in the sixteenth century, ironically depended greatly on the military resources provided by the king's lieges from the borderlands of the Tudor state. The English military revolution of the sixteenth century depended as much on massive numbers made possible only by recruitment from the Tudor borderlands as on new weaponry and sophisticated military architecture; the battle of Pinkie in 1547 was fought by probably the largest English army ever to invade Scotland.[3] The inevitable result was a new level of ruthlessness, seen in Scotland in the 1540s but, more notably, during the Elizabethan conquest of Ireland.[4]

The sixteenth century, however, was only in part the story of the 'iron century'[5] and the growth of state power, often in the guise of colonialist regimes. From another perspective, paradoxically, it also saw the *consolidation*, in both Ireland and Scotland, by regional warlords of power in their own localities, aided (as in the fourteenth century) by access to new military resources.[6] If the fall of the Fitzgeralds can be made to seem like the victory of a new, more assertive monarchy, it can also be viewed as a disaster for royal power, which did not as yet possess the resources to

---

1   *Scottish Annals from English Chroniclers*, ed. A.O. Anderson (London, 1908), p. 181.
2   Quoted in S.G. Ellis, 'Nationalist historiography and the English and Gaelic worlds in the late middle ages', *Irish Historical Studies*, xxv (1986), p. 15; see also S.G Ellis, 'Representations of the past in Ireland: whose past and whose present?', *Irish Hist. Stud.*, xxvii (1991), p. 306; D.G. White, 'Henry VIII's Irish kerne in France and Scotland, 1544–1545', *Irish Sword*, iii (1957–8).
3   I am grateful to Dr Marcus Merriman for this point.
4   B. Bradshaw, 'Nationalism and historical scholarship in modern Ireland', *Irish Hist. Stud.*, xxvi (1989), pp. 338–9.
5   H. Kamen, *The Iron Century: Social Change in Europe, 1550–1660* (2nd edn, London, 1976), pp. 57, 60.
6   K. Simms, *From Kings to Warlords: The Changing Political Structure of Gaelic Ireland in the Later Middle Ages* (Woodbridge, 1987), pp. 147–50; H. Morgan, 'The end of Gaelic Ulster: a thematic interpretation of events between 1534 and 1610', *Irish Hist. Stud.*, xxvi (1988), pp. 8, 13–22. For a similar process in Scotland (that of the Campbells of Glenorchy), see M.D.W. MacGregor, 'A political history of the MacGregors before 1571' (Edinburgh University Ph.D. thesis, 1989), chapter 5.

National Identity in Ireland and Scotland, 1500-1640

sustain direct rule in any part of Ireland outside the Pale.[1] Much of the history of subsequent Tudor rule in Ireland underlined the weaknesses of royal power rather than its strengths. In Scotland, the eclipse of the MacDonald Lordship of the Isles similarly produced not a new order but seven separate rebellions in the course of the next fifty-two years, brought to a halt only by the death of the last 'pretender', Donald Dubh, in 1546. Every reign between those of James IV and James VI (1567–1625) saw a rebellion in the west. Although James IV, V and VI each repeatedly tried to 'daunt' the Isles, the 'problem' of the king's 'barbarous subjects' was arguably no nearer resolution in 1625 than it had been in 1500.[2] Royal policy, ever inconsistent, did much in both Ireland and Scotland to foster the very 'problem' it so frequently decried.

A paradox underlies the sixteenth-century history of the British Isles. The familiar story of the consolidation of the Tudor and Stewart monarchies and their unification after 1603 in a new 'dual monarchy',[3] focused on a novel *terra* of 'Great Britain', needs to be set against the recrudescence of a pan-Celtic world. Far from being exposed as defunct or anachronistic amidst the confusing changes of the period, Gaelic culture and lordship proved both resilient and flexible.[4] In Ireland (and, to an extent, in the Scottish *Gaidhealtachd* too) the processes of administration and criminal justice within individual lordships were being overhauled and rationalised. Marriage alliances and artillery were the two chief weapons in the armoury of Gaelic lords; the administrations in Dublin and Edinburgh proved incapable of demilitarising Gaelic society. In both Ireland and Scotland the main lordships, it seems likely, were growing in strength and resources as the sixteenth century progressed, often at the expense of less successful

---

1 See Ellis, 'Nationalist historiography', pp. 17–18.
2 K.A. Steer and J.W.M. Bannerman, *Late Medieval Monumental Sculpture in the West Highlands* (London, 1977), pp. 209–13; M. Lynch, *Scotland: a New History* (London, 1991), pp. 167–8, 241–2.
3 The phrase is much used by Jenny Wormald: see her 'James VI and I: two kings or one?', *History*, lxviii (1983), and 'The first King of Britain', in *The Making of Britain: The Age of Expansion*, ed. L.M. Smith (London, 1986).
4 For Scottish bardic poetry, see J. MacInnes, 'Gaelic poetry and historical tradition', *The Middle Ages in the Highlands*, ed. L. Maclean (Inverness, 1981); D.S. Thomson, *An Introduction to Gaelic Poetry* (London, 1977), especially pp. 99–115, for what bards called 'the age of the forays'; V. E. Durcacz, *The Decline of the Celtic Languages* (Edinburgh, 1983), chapter 1. For Irish bardic poetry, cf. B. Bradshaw, 'Native reaction to the Westward Enterprise: a case study in Gaelic ideology', in *The Westward Enterprise: English Activities in Ireland, the Atlantic and America, 1480–1650*, ed. K.R. Andrews, N.P. Canny and P.E.H. Hair (Liverpool, 1978); N. Canny, 'The formation of the Irish mind: religion, politics and Gaelic Irish literature, 1580–1750', *Past and Present*, 95 (1982); T.J. Dunne, 'The Gaelic response to conquest and colonisation: the evidence of the poetry', *Studia Hibernica*, xx (1980).

branches of their own family or of former client septs: this was the background to the rise in Tyrone and Tirconnell of the dominant O'Neill lineages to the status of regional overlords by the 1580s.[1] The rise of the main branch of the Campbells, based in Argyll, to claim the 'headship of the Gael' had benefited from the misfortunes of the MacDonalds after the forfeiture of the Lordship of the Isles, but it also depended on the calculated restriction of marrying Campbell heiresses only within the clan and the legitimation lent to their acquisition of new fire-power by being made king's lieutenant in the west. The expansion eastwards into Perthshire of the Campbells of Glenorchy also depended on their ruthless shedding of client clans such as the MacGregors.[2]

The reorganisation and consolidation of Gaelic lordship in the sixteenth century lies behind the growing chorus of abuse heaped on the 'barbarous' customs of Gaeldom by governments in London, Dublin and Edinburgh in the period. The process was all the more difficult to arrest because the links between the two branches of the Gaelic world were significantly increasing. The annexation of the Lordship of the Isles had accelerated a process of migration by MacDonalds and other clans across the North Channel which had been notable since the fourteenth century; by the 1530s the scale of migration had begun to alarm the Dublin authorities, who saw the expulsion of these 'Scots Irish' settlers as an essential precondition of the extension of Tudor rule in Ireland.[3] Diplomats began as a result to think in international terms, of the interwoven problem of the three kingdoms, at least a century before the appalling reality of a 'War of the Three Kingdoms' broke out in the 1640s.[4]

Despite the efforts of the English and Scottish crowns, every decade of the sixteenth century from the 1520s onwards saw the use made by Irish regional lords of Scots mercenaries from the Isles or western Highlands, either in their own dynastic wars or in those provoked by the Tudor state. The employment of Scots 'gallowglasses' by Irish lords had a long and chequered history going back to the fourteenth century, but the mercenaries of the sixteenth century, now called 'redshanks' or 'bonnaghts' and usually hired on three-month contracts, were often specialists in the new warfare;

[1] Morgan, 'End of Gaelic Ulster', pp. 9, 13−19; Simms, *Kings to Warlords*, pp. 126−8, 148−9. For Gaelic lords' use of mercenaries from the Isles, see G.A. Hayes-McCoy, *Scots Mercenary Forces in Ireland, 1565−1603* (Dublin, 1937); G. Hill, *An Historical Account of the MacDonnells of Antrim* (Belfast, 1873), pp. 37, 186−7.

[2] MacInnes, 'Gaelic poetry', p. 149; J. Dawson, 'Two kingdoms or three?: Ireland in Anglo-Scottish relations in the middle of the sixteenth century', in *Scotland and England*, ed. R.A. Mason (Edinburgh, 1987), pp. 120, 122, 128−9; MacGregor, 'Political History of MacGregors', chapter 6.

[3] Hill, *MacDonnells of Antrim*, p. 37; Morgan, 'End of Gaelic Ulster', pp. 14−15.

[4] Dawson, 'Two kingdoms or three?', pp. 129−31.

the MacDonald redshanks employed regularly by O'Neill in Ulster between the 1560s and 1590s provided him with 'shot and pikemen' as well as traditional heavy infantry.[1] In Scotland too, a minor military revolution transformed the terms of feud and clan warfare: a quarter of the force of 6,000 men raised by the earl of Argyll in 1594 to pursue a rival regional overlord, the earl of Huntly, was made up of musketeers and hagbutters.[2] With the redshanks there often went smiths and masons from the Lowlands; features of the distinctive Scots tower-house went with them. Alongside the guns which Scottish merchants imported from the Baltic or the Netherlands and re-exported to Ulster during the Nine Years' War (1592–1601) went other continental influences to satisfy an aristocratic society which was no less Renaissance in its tastes for being Gaelic.[3] It seems likely that the result was increased trade in the opposite direction of cattle, linen, oats or timber to pay for munitions.[4] The volume of this trade is unquantifiable because it was not monitored by government and thus evaded written record in the *Exchequer Rolls*. It is, however, a mistake — of which Scottish historians have been more guilty than most — to suppose that order imposed by central government is a necessary precondition for the growth of trade. The backcloth to the union of the crowns in 1603 was half a century or more of the reforging of a pan-Celtic world across the North Channel; it had many aspects.

It was small wonder that the new construct of Great Britain should feel threatened by this prospect or that the reign of 'Great Britain's Solomon',[5] James VI and I, would see a concerted attempt at military conquest, plantation and reformation of its two Achilles' heels. The results

---

1 Hayes-McCoy, *Scots Mercenary Forces*, especially pp. 24–76; Morgan, 'End of Gaelic Ulster', p. 19; Simms, *Kings to Warlords*, p. 139.
2 *Historie and Life of King James the Sext* (Bannatyne Club, 1825), p. 338. In one sense, Argyll's force raised in 1594 was a royal army, authorised by parliament to act against a rebel earl. It was also a clash of rival regional magnates, each of whom had for a century often acted as king's lieutenant in the Highlands. It was, in effect, a war for the Lordship of the Isles which threatened to become embroiled with the Nine Years' War in Ulster; as such, it would be resumed in 1640: D. Gregory, *The History of the Western Highlands and Isles of Scotland, 1493–1625* (2nd edn, London, 1881), pp. 257–62; K. Brown, *Bloodfeud in Scotland, 1573–1625* (Edinburgh, 1986), pp. 144–82; Lynch, *Scotland*, pp. 271–2.
3 B. Bradshaw, 'Manus "the Magnificent": O'Donnell as Renaissance prince', in *Studies in Irish History presented to R. Dudley Edwards*, ed. A. Cosgrove and D. McCartney (Dublin, 1979); Morgan, 'End of Gaelic Ulster', p. 26.
4 M. Perceval-Maxwell, *The Scottish Migration to Ulster in the Reign of James I* (London, 1973), pp. 290–1.
5 See M. Lee, *Great Britain's Solomon: James VI and I in His Three Kingdoms* (Chicago, 1990), chapter 7.

of that campaign were paradoxical. In Scotland the king's Highland policy, although it drew on Lowland nostrums of the barbarous nature of Gaeldom which were some two centuries old, became costly and increasingly unpopular, with the Estates showing a marked reluctance to sanction taxation to finance expeditions to the Isles; it came to be seen as another example of absentee kingship making novel demands of his realm, quickening in his subjects a sense of alienation and promoting a heightened sense of Scottish identity.[1]

Nowhere was James's administration more British in complexion than in his other kingdom, of Ireland. There, the impact of an increasingly foreign, alien regime, in both Church and State,[2] provoked amongst the various communities in Irish society a sharper sense of their own identity. In the process, a distinctive sense of Irish nationality came of age. Though no less Gaelic than before, it drew on an Irish Gaeldom rather than any sense of a pan-Celtic society. Although James's successor, Charles I (1625–49), reined in much of his father's multi-fold pursuit of a British *patria*, he would nevertheless be confronted by a crisis of the three kingdoms which fed on the newly sharpened sense of distinctive national identity felt by his subjects in Ireland and Scotland.[3] A counter-culture emerged, in both Ireland and Scotland, to challenge the threat of the new Britain. It roots were tangled; what follows is a preliminary attempt to disentangle some of them.

*

The distance travelled by James VI after 1603 to claim the crowns of England and Ireland was not simply a matter of geography, although the gulf between London and Edinburgh, which the king had promised to visit once every three years, increased over the fourteen years which it took for him to revisit his Scottish kingdom. The very essence of Scottish kingship was transformed by the union of the crowns. In 1529, in a letter to the pope

---

1 *The Register of the Privy Council of Scotland* (Edinburgh, 1877–), vi, pp. 112–13, 130; *The Acts of the Parliaments of Scotland* (Edinburgh, 1814–75), iv, p. 404; Lee, *Great Britain's Solomon*, pp. 201, 215; Gregory, *History of Western Highlands*, pp. 292–3, 320. Two royal taxes raised in 1596 and 1598 for expeditions to the southwest had already cost £28,000 Scots: J. Goodare, 'Parliamentary taxation in Scotland, 1560–1603', *Scottish Historical Review*, lxviii (1989), p. 51. The blunt instrument of commissions of lieutenandry, relying on private armies of great (and often feuding) nobles, was the other recourse of a monarchy usually teetering on the edge of insolvency.
2 A. Ford, *The Protestant Reformation in Ireland, 1590–1641* (Frankfurt-am-Main, 1987), chapters 7, 9.
3 C. Russell, 'The British background to the Irish rebellion of 1641', *Historical Research*, lxi (1988); A.I. MacInnes, *Charles I and the Making of the Covenanting Movement* (Edinburgh, 1991), especially chapter 1.

National Identity in Ireland and Scotland, 1500-1640

about the appointment of the bishop of Argyll and the Isles, his grandfather James V (1513–42) had described the far west as 'the greatest part of the Scottish kingdom at the first'.[1] By that he meant that the long line of kings of Scots (in which he counted himself the 105th) stretching into prehistory was firmly based in the kingdom of Dalriada, situated in modern-day Argyll and Kintyre, which had been colonised by migrant Scots from the north of Ireland in the sixth century. The official mythology of the Scottish crown in his reign insisted that it traced its origins to a pan-Gaelic society; kingship was still at least notionally 'hybrid' — with two faces, Celtic and feudal.[2] His grandson was not only an absentee king after 1603 but also one who, despite relying on officially inspired propaganda that he was 107th of his line to bolster his status amongst his English subjects, did much to separate himself from Gaeldom, before 1603 as well as after.[3] In 1541, when Henry VIII of England accepted the crown of Ireland, he did so not as a deliberate act of statecraft, but as a result of pressure from the descendants of the thirteenth-century conquest, a group usually known as the Anglo-Irish or the Old English. The assertion made by the Irish parliament in 1541 that Henry and his predecessors had enjoyed unrivalled suzerainty over the whole of Ireland for 400 years past was scant camouflage.[4] Direct rule by the English crown was a new departure and its novelty does much to explain the difficulties it faced in Ireland over the rest of the century. The crowns of Ireland and Scotland had already seen sovereignty stretched as never before — *before* they were united in 1603. The double vision of a new kingship and a new *patria* was built on foundations that had scarcely had time to set firm.

In reality, the three kingdoms were *not* united, except in the person of the monarch. James's schemes for what he called a 'perfect union' were rebuffed by the English parliament in 1607; in the same year his privy council in Edinburgh objected that they had not intended union to mean that Scotland became 'a conquered and slavish province'.[5] It was Ireland, ironically the kingdom James never visited, that saw the most concerted effort to impose a British solution, in both Church and State. Yet, despite more than thirty years of 'conquest' before 1601 and forty years of

1 *Letters of James V*, ed. R.K. Hannay and D. Hay (Edinburgh, 1954), p. 162.
2 A. Grant, 'Scotland's "Celtic fringe" in the late Middle Ages: The MacDonald Lords of the Isles and the kingdom of Scotland', in *The British Isles 1100–1500*, ed. R.R. Davies (Edinburgh, 1988), p. 119; Lynch, *Scotland*, pp. 79–83, 91–2.
3 R.A. Mason, 'Scotching the Brut: politics, history and national myth in sixteenth-century Britain', in *Scotland and England*, ed. Mason, pp. 75–6; Lee, *Great Britain's Solomon*, pp. 114, 196–202.
4 *Early Modern Ireland, 1534–1691*, ed. T.W. Moody, F.X. Martin and F.J. Byrne (New History of Ireland, iii, 1976), pp. 47–8.
5 *Reg. Privy Council Scot.*, vii, p. 536.

aggressive Protestant plantation after it, there would be massive disaffection of the Old English colonists, who joined Gaelic culture and politics in droves, leaving behind them a vacuum which the 'new English', the planters, administrators and churchmen, were unable to fill. The first four decades of the seventeenth century witnessed the failure of the first British state. Its fault-lines were nowhere more evident than in the British mission in Ireland, which took on the dual guise of a colonial reformation and a plantation. The Stuart British state was a multi-national corporation which had sought to erect a new cultural identity — of Great Britain — which had many aspects, including a new history, new emblems like flags and coinage, an apocalyptic vision of king and kingdom, and an attempt to forge a common religion out of three previously separate Protestant state Churches.[1] Initiatives and failures in one sphere of operations of this early modern multi-national, however, would provoke a crisis of confidence in the others; that, in brief, proved to be the history of the ten years after 1633.

The literature of British union, of the new *terra* of a blessed Protestant isle, which was hailed as a new British Israel, helps draw back the veil on the existing visions of national identity which predated it and with which it came into direct competition.[2] There was a clash of new identities and old — which, in societies where horizons were limited to the *pays* or local dynasty, were usually of *communitates*. In Ireland the identities of both Old English and Gaeldom clashed with a new British cultural and colonial mission; the single success of the more determinedly Calvinist Jacobean Church was ironically the crystallisation of a Protestant community with a sharp sense of its own separate identity amongst the new settlers.[3] The Church of Ireland, as a result, was by the 1630s a refuge for the new English rather than a missionary Church seriously intent on the conversion of the whole of Irish society; coercion had replaced comprehension as its rationale. Scotland, still in the early seventeenth century a highly

---

1 Galloway, *Union of England and Scotland*, pp. 30–55, 59–62, 82–4: B.P. Levack, *The Formation of the British State: England, Scotland, and the Union, 1603–1707* (Oxford, 1987), especially pp. 179–97; C. Russell, 'The British problem and the English Civil War', *History*, lxxii (1987), pp. 395–401.

2 One example of the notion of a British Israel is Robert Pont's tract 'Of the Union of Britayne' (1604), reprinted in *Jacobean Union*, ed. Galloway and Levack, pp. 1-38. In his *Apology* of 1609, King James referred only to the 'Ile', not to his three kingdoms: see A.H. Williamson, *Scottish National Consciousness in the Age of James VI* (Edinburgh, 1979), pp. 39–47. Some English settler clergy in Ireland also wrote of 'our English-Irish Israel', but only to emphasise the godliness of their mission in a sinful land; others, in a more straightforwardly colonialist vein, referred to Ireland as 'West Britain': Ford, *Reformation in Ireland*, pp. 245–6; T. Barnard, 'Crises of identity among Irish Protestants, 1641–1685', *Past and Present*, 127 (1990), p. 42.

3 Ford, *Reformation in Ireland*, p. 291; cf. Barnard, 'Crises of identity', p. 48.

decentralised collection of *pays* largely held together by lordship and kindred (some of them also belonging to a pan-Gaelic world), depended on kingship as the keystone to hold together a feudal realm undergoing rapid and bewildering change. It was offered instead an apocalyptic, centralising Greater Britain. The counter culture which emerged, in both Ireland and Scotland, emanated largely from a Church which increasingly took on the role of incubator and guarantor of national identity. Counter-Reformation and Tridentine in Ireland, Presbyterian, neo-Calvinist and no less uncompromising in Scotland, the two Churches acted out remarkably similar roles: each claimed to be the re-embodiment of a primitive Celtic Church; both saw themselves as the mouthpiece of the Israelites threatened by a hostile world around them. The essence of a new *patria*, which had emerged in both Catholic Ireland and Presbyterian Scotland by the 1630s, was the notion of the nation as a new Israel.

*

The distinctiveness of both Irish and Scottish history in the early modern period is a matter of considerable dispute. The debate has been sharper in the case of Ireland. Two distinguished Irish historians have recently made different and seemingly conflicting claims. Nicholas Canny has stated that 'Ireland remained much more localised than other western-European countries. While it is true that the majority of the population everywhere in Europe remained close to their place of origin, in Ireland the same held true for the ruling element.'[1] Thus in Ireland there were (until 1591) no universities; the Irish parliament was largely an assembly of the Pale, the small arc of territory around the administrative centre of Dublin; there were as yet few towns outside the Pale; the great lords outside the Pale, whether Anglo-Irish or Gaelic, were largely cut off from Dublin, content to exercise power in their own lordships. By contrast, Steven Ellis has argued that Ireland was divided in the late medieval and early modern periods between the English and Gaelic worlds, with the north and west more in touch with a pan-Celtic world which stretched across the Irish Sea to the west of Scotland, and with the lowland parts of Leinster and Munster, the areas of English lordship, gravitating towards Dublin and London. Ireland's history was, as a result, largely 'one of conflict and interaction between two separate civilizations', pan-Celtic and pan-English, and Irish history was consequently much *less* 'self-contained' than that of major European nation-states.[2]

1   N.P. Canny, *The Elizabethan Conquest of Ireland: A Pattern Established, 1565−76* (Hassocks, 1976), p. 2.
2   S.G. Ellis, *Tudor Ireland: Crown, Community and the Conflict of Cultures, 1470−1603* (London, 1985), p. 12.

The juxtaposition of these two theses gives something of the flavour of the working paradox of cultural identity of sixteenth-century Ireland — but also, it could well be claimed, of contemporary Scotland as well.[1] There too was a society which was politically highly localised, with its focus in lordship and lineage, but also, because of the similarity of local customs and institutions throughout the country, with a strong sense of cultural unity, rooted in the mythology of a Gaelic past. Scottish society was also pulled after 1603 between the local community (which might be Scots or pan-Celtic in ethos) and a pan-British world, centred in the court in London.[2] A successful regional magnate such as the earl of Argyll increasingly operated in the different, overlapping worlds of his own 'country' and the national stage. Because in his case his own locality was located in Gaeldom, Argyll, like the earl of Tyrone, had different personae; he was Gaelic patron, hailed by the bards as 'king of the Gaels', as well as Renaissance prince.[3] The real contrasts between Irish and Scottish society came with the different configuration of *communitates* which made each up and their interaction.

In sixteenth-century Ireland there were four competing interests — the Old English, the English crown, the new English planters and adventurers still largely confined to Munster, and the traditional Gaelic lords. Each had an ambivalent and shifting attitude towards its own identity and those of the others. Much of the confusion stemmed from the incompleteness of the previous English conquest, of the thirteenth century. English authority was steadily shrinking: by 1520 it reached only a third of Ireland, in the Pale and a vague buffer zone around it. A concept of two cultures persisted; the English crown still talked of 'two nations' — 'the king's lieges' (the Old English or Anglo-Irish lords) and the 'king's Irish enemies' or the 'wild Irish' (Gaelic society) — but slippage of royal authority and the assimilation of the two elites into each other had largely undermined the distinction. By the 1530s the English crown was beginning to take a more realistic view of the complex situation in which there were two separate cultures with a growing series of bridges built between them; in 1536 the king's council reported that 'the English blood of the English conquest is worn out in this

---

1 The analogy between Ireland and Scotland is recognised in Ellis, 'Nationalist historiography', pp. 5–10, but largely in terms of Gaelic Ireland and Gaelic Scotland being 'borderlands' of a London polity. If the view is taken, however, that the 'Gaelic resurgence' in Scotland *survived* the forfeiture of the Lordship of the Isles in 1493, comparisons between it and the much disputed 'Gaelic revival' in Ireland become more meaningful.
2 K.M. Brown, 'Courtiers and cavaliers: service, anglicisation and loyalty among the royalist nobility', in *The Scottish National Covenant in its British Context*, ed. J. Morrill (Edinburgh, 1990).
3 MacInnes, 'Gaelic poetry', p. 149.

land'.[1] Already two sets of solutions had begun to crystallise: conquest or reformation. English policy would waver between the two for the next forty years, until the mid-1570s when it opted for conquest. But the fluctuations in English attitudes towards the Irish problem, the agonising whether or not the Gaelic Irish could be civilised, Protestantised, and anglicised (or any combination of the three) underlines the fact that the eventual English stance, self-consciously akin to that of *conquistadores* against the Incas, of condemning the Irish as a barbarians who had first to be conquered, came only after forty years of failure of policy and vast expense.[2]

The road to English disillusionment with Ireland had two key stages. It was, ironically, the new English adventurers of the 1570s and 1580s who first conceived of an Irish national identity, which transcended and obscured distinctions between the Anglo-Irish of the Pale, the Old English outside the Pale and the Gaelic Irish. By the mid-1570s, after five rebellions by Old English lords against the drift of English policy towards plantation and conquest, English paranoia had conceived a Romish conspiracy against Protestant England; the Irish had begun to intrigue 'with all the papisticall princes of Christendom'. By 1576 Sir Henry Sidney, who had earlier promoted a humanist reformation of the Irish to bring them to civility in a well-ordered Christian commonwealth, argued it was 'preposterous to begin reformation of the politique part and to neglect the religious'.[3] The spectre was born premature: Counter-Reformation Catholicism would be the dynamic which harnessed (albeit unsatisfactorily) the disparate visions of Anglo-Irish and Gaelic Irish, but it would not do so for another thirty years, and then only in exile on the continent of Europe. Ironically English fears helped to foster the appalling prospect they imagined in the 1570s and 1580s.[4]

By the 1580s a new rationale for English conquest had appeared. The Irish began to be condemned not as papists but as 'atheists or infidels'. The English were the new Romans, civilisers by conquest of a barbarian people who stubbornly refused to accept the benefits of a commonwealth. It helped justify a policy of total war. So widely accepted was the propaganda of the conquest that Sir Thomas Smith, who helped found an Irish plantation but never visited Ireland, could confidently compare the Irish to 'Tartarians' and 'Arabians'. The circle of stigmatisation was completed by English experience in the Americas: the Irish were also likened to red Indians, who

---

1 See, e.g., 'State of Ireland and a plan for its reformation' (1515), in *State Papers, Henry VIII*, ii, pp. 1–31, which had strong echoes of the Statutes of Kilkenny of 1366; *ibid.*, p. 338 (1536); also Ellis, *Tudor Ireland*, pp. 22–3, 121, 137.
2 Canny, *Elizabethan Conquest*, pp. 34, 117–36.
3 *Ibid.*, pp. 122–5, 156.
4 *Ibid.*, pp. 147, 153, 156; Canny, 'Formation of Irish mind', pp. 94–5.

had first to be civilised before they could be Christianised. Edmund Spenser's *A View of the State of Ireland*, published in 1596 in the form of a Platonic dialogue, neatly demonstrated the two English views of Ireland: one was eirenic, stressing (like the clergy of the Elizabethan Church of Ireland) the long and distinctive heritage of Irish Protestantism and the ability of the Old English to civilise the Gaels; the other, confronted by a barbarian people 'altogether stubborn and untamed' and able to understand only force, was uncompromising. A cameo of past and future English policy, Spenser's work signalled the eclipse of commonwealth humanism and the absolute victory of a neo-Renaissance ideology.[1]

Many of the ambiguities of English policy in Ireland over the first three quarters of the sixteenth century can be explained by the conflicting advice it received, from both English administrators and Anglo-Irish lords. The confusions also arose because the Anglo-Irish community was itself divided and offered conflicting advice. The identity of that community has been the subject of a fierce debate amongst Irish historians. Various terms were used by contemporaries — Anglo-Irish, Anglo-Hiberni, and English-Irish — even if the community itself usually preferred to be described as English or the 'English of Ireland'. As might be expected in a group which still in 1640 owned fully a third of the land in Ireland, it was not a single unifocal community but one which held within it various strains of Anglo-Irish identity.[2] An important, if untypical, attitude can be illustrated by Richard Stanihurst, son of a speaker of the Irish parliament, who was often patronising about the Gaelic community and fond of arrogant assumptions about the superiority of English civility. For Stanihurst, the late 1570s were a process of disillusionment and self-discovery. In 1577 he was commissioned to join the editorial team which produced Holinshed's *Chronicles of England, Scotland and Ireland*. There he gave vent to a colonialist mentality which resented Gaelic lords like Shane O'Neill who refused 'to writhe his tongue around clattering English'; if the 'respublica' of the Anglo-Irish community was to survive (and it was Stanihurst who coined the phrase 'Anglo-Hiberni' in 1584) it had to practise apartheid to survive, by shunning the Gaelic Irish 'like rocky crags'. His was a colonial establishment's view of itself, which stressed the aristocratic basis of Anglo-Irish society and the political

---

1 Canny, *Elizabethan Conquest*, pp. 125–36; K.S. Bottigheimer, 'Kingdom and colony: Ireland in the Westland Enterprise, 1536–1660', in *Westward Enterprise*, ed. Andrews *et al.*, pp. 52–5.
2 Cf. *Early Modern Ireland*, ed. Moody *et al.*, pp. xlii, 39; Ellis, 'Nationalist historiography', p. 3; R. Foster, *Modern Ireland, 1600–1972* (London, 1988), pp. 11–13. The crisis of 1641 underlined the fault lines in the composite identity of the Old English: see Russell, 'British background', pp. 167–8.

maturity of its citizens. By 1584, however, when he was in exile, Stanihurst withdrew his earlier claims that the Gaelic Irish ate meat 'half-raw' and were a nomadic people who 'had cast off all humanity':

> There is a certain widespread opinion in many minds that the Irish have cast off all humanity, that they wander scattered and dispersed through very dense woods, and generally that they live unrestrainedly in a rough and uncivilised fashion. But those who defame them are manifestly wrong.

Less affected by his Catholicism than by his exile, Stanihurst's tract of 1584 is the first important example of a literature of exile which would begin by trying to identify the heritage and identity of an Anglo-Irish community and end up making common cause with a broader Irish patriotism.[1]

Stanihurst was hardly typical. The claim that there was a mainstream tradition, best seen in an anonymous treatise written about 1555, which addressed the two communities, Anglo-Irish and Gaelic lords, as 'dear countrymen', who were integrated into a greater community held together by a notion of *patria* rather than by religion, is also a matter of considerable dispute. Both groups, it has been argued, owed love and loyalty to the same native land, their 'own mother'. This was a concept which thus embraced three elements: Christian commonwealth, sovereign kingdom and *patria*, bringing together the old medieval *nationes* who both had a 'natural affection' for their 'native country'. It has some analogies with the emergence in Scotland in the 1530s and after of the idea of a 'commonweal', which would be used by both parties during the Reformation crisis of 1559−60 and would find mature form in the last quarter of the century.[2] Each was prophetic of a more mature sense of *patria* which would materialise, with heavy religious overtones, in the early seventeenth century.

The 1570s brought about a crisis of Anglo-Irish identity. Gradually the Old English arguments that they alone could bring the Gaelic lords to civility were discounted by London. The Anglo-Irish were forced into a

1 C. Lennon, 'Richard Stanihurst (1547−1618) and Old English identity', *Irish Hist. Stud.*, xxi (1978−9).
2 B. Bradshaw, *The Irish Constitutional Revolution of the Sixteenth Century* (Cambridge, 1979), pp. 276−82. Cf. R.A. Mason, 'Covenant and commonweal: the language of politics in Reformation Scotland', in *Church, Politics and Society: Scotland 1408−1929*, ed. N. Macdougall (Edinburgh, 1983); as in Ireland, the Scots' notion of a 'commonweal' had a distinctive national flavour, distinguishing it from contemporary English commonwealth attitudes. Religion was not necessarily a barrier: in 1559 the Catholic Lord Sempill was urged to join the revolt of the Protestant Lords of the Congregation 'for the commoun wealth and libertie of this youre native cuntray': *Scottish Correspondence of Mary of Lorraine* (Scottish History Society, 1927), p. 429.

series of rebellions, in which they adopted the stance of loyal rebels. But the rebel earls also began to take on a new Gaelicised posture. Some abandoned their English titles in favour of Irish ones; others donned the dress of Gaelic chieftains; and some even banned English dress from their lordships. This new Gaelicisation of the earls gave to the Anglo-Irish community a more distinct, less ambivalent identity than before. But ironically it did not move them closer to the Gaelic lords whom they were aping. The Old English of the Lordship were now set apart from both the English crown and the Old English of the Pale, but they had yet to make common cause with the Gaelic community. The merging of the Gaelic community and the ersatz Gaeldom of the Anglo-Irish community would take at least another half century to complete, and the first steps would be taken, not in the form of a common revolt against English conquest, but in the special climate of exile.[1]

The history of the Gaelic community in the sixteenth century has a basic irony about it. As has been seen, the pace towards the emergence of an Irish cultural identity was forced not by Gaelic society but by an English crown which was fearful of it, and by a colonial elite which, deprived of its role as the agent of English rule, chose to assert its particularist privileges and culture. Only vague and mostly poetic concepts of a separate Irish identity existed in 1500: concepts of Ireland existed, such as *Inis Banba* or *Inis Fail*, but they reflected a Gaelic ethnic consciousness rather than an distinct Gaelic identity. Politics, it is true, was seen as a struggle between *Gael* and *Gall* (Celts and foreigners), but this embraced the wider Gaelic world, including Scotland.[2] The Gaelic lords proved highly responsive to Henrician policy in the 1540s: the policy of surrender and regrant was designed to induce Gaelic lords to surrender their Irish lordships which were then regranted as English earldoms. It had considerable success. Gaelic lords like Con O'Neill took up with apparent enthusiasm the English policy of uniformity; he bound himself and his heirs to speak the English language and adopt English dress, housebuilding and forms of tillage. Some even hired genealogists who managed to find descent of 'English blood' in their veins to help them along the way. It was only a century later that a mythology of loss grew up, bemoaning that 'the sovereignty of every Gaelic lord was lowered' by surrender and regrant.[3]

The bards and poets, most Irish historians agree, did not provide a literature of Gaelic complaint either. Concerned more about the threat to

[1] Canny, *Elizabethan Conquest*, pp. 142–3, 150–2; Ellis, *Tudor Ireland*, pp. 287, 319–20.
[2] Dunne, 'Gaelic response', pp. 12–13; Ellis, *Tudor Ireland*, pp. 46–7; Bradshaw, 'Native reaction', p. 73; Foster, *Modern Ireland*, pp. 39–43.
[3] *Early Modern Ireland*, ed. Moody *et al.*, pp. 50–1; Foster, *Modern Ireland*, pp. 37–45.

National Identity in Ireland and Scotland, 1500-1640

their own patrons than the attack on Gaelic society, worried more about the next polished phrase than a crisis of Gaelic identity, the poets did not — with few exceptions — provide a new notion of patriotism before the seventeenth century. Most poetry did not rise above defence of the local or the individual lord. Even when it did, it was still concerned with the class of Gaelic lords rather than Gaelic society as a whole. This was, at best, O'Neillism rather than nationalism proper; pragmatic, fatalistic, escapist and apolitical. Only in retrospect, fifty years after, did the war of the 1590s become a religious struggle of a chosen people, the Irish Israelites.[1]

As a final irony, the seventeenth-century development of a new patriotism took place at the very time when both the bards and their patrons, the Gaelic lords, were becoming casualties of conquest and colonisation. It was in exile after 1610 that Old English and Gaelic Irish began to find common cause — in the homesick literature of a diaspora, now explicitly Irish rather than pan-Celtic. The seal of the Catholic Confederacy, as proclaimed in 1642, was *pro deo, rege et patria Hiberni*, and its emblems were the crown, cross, holy dove, flaming heart and the harp, which ironically had first been gifted to Ireland by Henry VIII. Accompanying the novel symbols of Counter-Reformation Catholicism were a new Gaelic literature and freshly retouched origins legends. The Franciscans had plans for a full-scale ecclesiastical history of Ireland; old Gaelic texts were rediscovered, copied and, where necessary, rephrased to fall in with the new party line. In Ireland, argued the secular priest and influential historian, Geoffrey Keating, the old Celtic moral code had made the early acceptance of Christianity easier — John Lesley, Catholic bishop of Ross, had claimed much the same in his *History of Scotland*, written sixty years earlier. New post-Tridentine practices, like penance, were represented as falling in line with traditional Irish custom — changed days from those of the Jesuits who had briefly visited the Irish in 1539 and dismissed them as barbarous! The notion of a Celtic golden age was polished, when the moral code was in complete conformity with current Counter-Reformation practice.[2]

The myth of a rediscovered, primitive Celtic Church served Counter-Reformation Irish Catholicism, and it would benefit Scottish Calvinism as well. If Patrick was made a Jesuit who lived before his time, Columba was given the identity of a Presbyterian, resistant to the blandishments of Rome, eleven centuries before his time.[3] Increasingly in the 1630s and 1640s the

---

1 Dunne, 'Gaelic response', pp. 12–16; Foster, *Modern Ireland*, pp. 28, 42–3.
2 *Early Modern Ireland*, ed. Moody *et al.*, pp. xliii, 67, 530–41, 568–9; Canny, 'Formation of Irish mind', pp. 94–9.
3 See Ford, *Reformation in Ireland*, pp. 221–2, for Archbishop Ussher's efforts to claim the Church of Ireland as the true heir of Patrick; it was an argument anticipated by

Irish were compared with the Israelites, for their hour of deliverance from their oppressors was at hand. In the process the traditional view of the Gaelic lord was subtly changed: still heroes of a Celtic past, they were now also made biblical and classical heroes as well. The 'job-description' of a noble now included not only being a defender of the Catholic faith but also being an exemplar of the true Christian way of life.[1] The same moving frontier of expectations of the nobility would mark the Protestant Church in Scotland; in lieu of a godly prince, the 'little nursing fathers' of the Kirk were in 1637 given the role of the leaders of what contemporaries called the 'second reformation'.[2]

By the 1640s, a composite Irish identity was being formed, backed by a reawakened interest in Gaelic sources and a history which reinterpreted events since 1560 in stark confessional terms.[3] The new identity, such as it was, was the achievement of a siege mentality viewed by an exilic diaspora, not of nobles or bards but of a new Church. A new Gaelic literature would follow, in the second half of the century, when the plight of Ireland would be transmitted in a personification of 'mother Ireland' — a woman in captivity or in mourning. Though new, it was also in part traditional, a variant of the theme which had emerged in the 1590s of the leading Gaelic lord as the spouse of Ireland.[4] In the Nine Years' War, when the focus remained fixed on the magnate, dynasty and locality, it had still at best been an ethnic nationalism. By the 1640s a broader patriotism had emerged, whose dynamic was provided not by secular lords but by a new and highly disciplined Tridentine missionary Church.

The failure of the Reformation in Ireland was predictable, but it has been

---

some Anglo-Irish Protestants in the 1570s: see N. Canny, 'Rowland White's "The Dysorders of the Irisshery"', 1571', *Studia Hibernica*, xix (1979), pp. 151–2. See David Calderwood, *History of the Kirk of Scotland* (Wodrow Society, 1842–9), i, pp. 39–42, for his description of the 'Culdees' and of Columba as 'a presbyter not a bishop'. This neo-Calvinist interpretation of the Culdees had been anticipated by George Buchanan (see his *History*, ed. J. Aikman [Glasgow, 1827–9], i, p. 203), and that of Columba by the unionist Protestant exile, John Elder, who in the 1540s had eccentrically claimed Columba as a Pict even though he preached 'Goddis worde syncerly in Eyrish' (*Collectanea de Rebus Albanacis* [Iona Club, 1833], pp. 23–32).

1 Canny, 'Formation of Irish mind', pp. 104, 109; Morgan, 'End of Gaelic Ulster', pp. 28–9.
2 *Letters of Samuel Rutherford*, ed. A.A. Bonar (Edinburgh, 1891), p. 458; Lynch, *Scotland*, pp. 250–1.
3 H.A. Jefferies, 'The Irish parliament of 1560: the anglican reforms authorised', *Irish Hist. Stud.*, xxvi (1988), p. 136.
4 Dunne, 'Gaelic response', pp. 16–20; Bradshaw, 'Native reactions', pp. 72–3.

National Identity in Ireland and Scotland, 1500-1640

variously dated.[1] If the view is taken that ecclesiastical change was thwarted by the huge size of parishes and the poverty of livings, the Elizabethan settlement was as foredoomed to failure as the colonial reformation which took its place after 1603.[2] From another perspective, the sixteenth-century reformation fell prey to the same confusions which afflicted crown policy in other spheres. The Church in Ireland had long had a split identity: in 1500, twenty of its bishops were Old English, and fourteen were Gaelic. Only nominal conformity was sought from those Gaelic bishops by Henry VIII's reformation in the 1530s. In practice the Protestant campaign was confined to the Pale and the Lordship during the reigns of Henry VIII and Edward VI (1547 – 53). Little effort was made to convert the far west before 1603. The special concessions made to the Irish Church continued into the reign of Elizabeth (1558 – 1603): in 1542 and 1559 use of a Latin prayer book was conceded because of the widespread ignorance of the English language; and in 1551 the council grudgingly allowed services in Gaelic for the same reason.[3] Despite its internal divisions on the matter, the Church of Ireland deserves some credit for taking the initiative in providing Protestant literature in Gaelic. Following the publication in Edinburgh of a Gaelic translation of the Genevan *Book of Common Order* by John Carswell, bishop of the Isles, in 1567, attempts were made to recruit Gaelic-speaking clergy from Scotland; they, however, bore little fruit. The first book to be printed in Ireland, in 1571, was a Protestant catechism; and a translation of the Bible into Gaelic had been authorised in 1561, although it would take until 1613 for an Irish New Testament to appear. But in Ireland, unlike in Scotland or Wales, Protestantism lacked private patrons in non-English-speaking areas.[4] The Church of Ireland had, as a result, a colonialist image

1 Cf. B. Bradshaw, 'The Edwardian reformation in Ireland', *Archivum Hibernicum*, xxxiv (1976 – 7); K. Bottigheimer, 'The failure of the Reformation in Ireland: une question bien posée', *Journal of Ecclesiastical History*, xxxvi (1985); Ford, *Reformation in Ireland*, especially chapters 1, 3; H.C. Walshe, 'Enforcing the Elizabethan settlement: the vicissitudes of Hugh Brady, bishop of Meath, 1563 – 84', *Irish Hist. Stud.*, xxvi (1989); S.G. Ellis, 'Economic problems of the Church: why the Reformation failed in Ireland', *Journ. Eccles. Hist.*, xli (1990). The balance of opinion, if from differing perspectives, has swung towards a 'second reformation' of the 1590s and the following half century. The mirror image, the problem of the timing of the *success* of a Protestant reformation in Scotland, has as yet only lightly touched the psyche of most Scottish historians.
2 Ellis, 'Economic problems of the Church', pp. 248 – 57; Ford, *Reformation in Ireland*, p. 64.
3 *Early Modern Ireland*, ed. Moody *et al.*, pp. 511 – 12; Ellis, *Tudor Ireland*, pp. 202 – 12.
4 Jefferies, 'Irish parliament of 1560', pp. 133 – 4; Ellis, 'Economic problems of the Church', pp. 257 – 8. Carswell's liturgy, *Foirm na n-Urrnuidheadh*, addressed to the

even before 1603.

There were two ironical aspects of Protestantism's promotion of the Gaelic vernacular. It anticipated Catholic use of the printing press by forty years: it was not until 1611 that the first Counter-Reformation product in Irish was printed, a catechism which appeared in Antwerp. Also, the siting of a printing press in Dublin helped to encourage its growth in the 1570s as a Gaelic literary centre. English policy was as ambivalent towards the Gaelic language and the evangelisation of the native population as elsewhere. Much the same shift towards a hard-line attitude took place here in the late 1580s. By the time Edmund Spenser, Renaissance poet and secretary to the Deputy, Lord Grey de Wilton, was writing his *View of the State of Ireland* in 1596, the humanist interest in the vernacular had disappeared: 'it hath ever been the use of the conqueror to despise the language of the conquered, and to force him by all means to learn his own ... The speech being Irish, the heart must needs be Irish.'[1] With it there also disappeared the prospect of a mass evangelisation of the Irish people.

The seventeenth-century Church in Ireland abandoned all pretence of being anything other than a colonial mission. All but one of the Elizabethan prelates were succeeded by Scots or Englishmen. It was an avowedly British Church, which, like the government, saw the forcible establishment of 'civility' as an essential precondition of religious reformation. The most hard-working civil servants of the British Stuart state were the bishops who cut their teeth in its papist borderlands, in Ulster and the fringes of the Scottish Highlands. Amongst the first of the breed in Ireland were George Montgomery, a Scot who had held an English benefice since 1584 and was given no fewer than three dioceses in Ulster, and Andrew Knox, bishop of the Isles and one of James VI's key advisers in Scotland, who succeeded Montgomery in Raphoe in 1610. Both were convinced coercionists and anglicisers. The Scottish clergy whom they imported in significant numbers were not Gaelic-speakers (as Sidney had advocated in the 1570s) but English-speaking colonialists, as convinced as their English colleagues of their mission to civilise a people 'as barbarous as the Indians and Moors'.[2] It

---

'men of *Alban* [Scotland] and of *Eireand* [Ireland]', is available in Gaelic (Scottish Gaelic Texts Society, 1970), and also in English translation as *The Book of Common Order*, ed. T. McLauchlan (Edinburgh, 1873).

1   Edmund Spenser, *A View of the State of Ireland*, ed. W.L. Renwick (Oxford, 1970), pp. 67–8.
2   Ford, *Reformation in Ireland*, pp. 33, 123, 142, 159–68; Lee, *Great Britain's Solomon*, p. 126, note; Lynch, *Scotland*, pp. 268–9; D.G. Mullan, *Episcopacy in Scotland: the History of an Idea, 1560–1638* (Edinburgh, 1986), pp. 122–3.

was small wonder that Scots became alarmed at the prospect of a British Church.

*

Nothing did more to shape and mould Scottish identity than kingship. As late as the seventeenth century it was said that 'the king of Scots is king of men, because he is not entitled efter the countrie as other kings, but efter the nations'.[1] There was still a residue of the sense in which royal charters of the twelfth or thirteenth centuries addressed the various *nationes* amongst the king's subjects — French, English, Scots and others. The sixteenth, however, was the last century in which 'hybrid kingship', in the sense of being both feudal and Celtic, operated in any real sense. That century saw increasing distance being put between the Lowlands and Gaeldom: it reflected changes in the attitude of the crown and Lowlanders towards the *Gaidhealtachd* more than any new lawlessness in the Highlands. None the less, the mythology of the Scottish national identity remained stubbornly invested in its Celtic past.

Two myths underpinned Scottish kingship (and in turn national identity) in the sixteenth century. They were potent enough as late as 1633 to figure as the centrepieces of the official entry organised for Charles I (1625–49) when he first visited his Scottish capital.[2] An 'Arch of the Kings' Genealogy' presented portraits of the 107 kings of Scots stretching back to Fergus mac Erc, who also materialised to Charles in person — incongruously in Latin! Although the notion of a long line of kings reached its apogee in the *History of Scotland* written by Hector Boece in 1520s, it was still a potent force more than a century later. That myth had been given a fresh twist by George Buchanan in his *History of Scotland*, eventually published in 1582 but written to justify the deposing of Mary, Queen of Scots (1542–67) in favour of her young son, James VI, in 1567. In it Buchanan had heaped example upon example of how for centuries the Scottish nobility had acted as guardians of the commonweal, censuring and correcting the faults of innumerable kings of Scots — making Mary only the last in a long line of

---

1 Patrick Gordon of Ruthven, *A Short Abridgement of Britane's Distemper from 1639 to 1645* (Spalding Club, 1844), p. 220.
2 The best original account is William Drummond of Hawthornden, *The Entertainment of the High and Mighty Monarch Charles* (Edinburgh, 1633), reprinted in *The Poetical Works of William Drummond of Hawthornden*, ed. L.E. Kastner (Scottish Text Society, 1913). See also E. McGrath, 'Local heroes: the Scottish humanist Parnassus for Charles I', in *England and the Continental Renaissance: Essays in Honour of J.B. Trapp*, ed. E. Chaney and P. Mack (London, 1990). I am grateful to Mr J.A. Martin for access to his 'A study of the entertainments for the state entry of Charles I, 1633' (Edinburgh University M.A. dissertation, 1990).

royal defaulters. By the 1590s, with the imminent prospect of James VI succeeding to the throne of England once Elizabeth died, two versions of the origins myth of kings were being polished — an official royalist one, and a Presbyterian rival. The royalist propaganda was, for the moment, more polished and more successful. One example of it was the propaganda tract written by John Monipenny in 1603, a *Who's Who* not only of James's 107 illustrious ancestors since 'Fergus I' in 330 BC but also of his contemporary nobles. A Presbyterian minister, John Johnston, published in 1602 a similar work with engravings of each and every one of the 107, but also with Latin verses pointing out their virtues and the vices; that work had a preface written by no less than Andrew Melville, doyen of the Presbyterian establishment.[1] Both king and Presbyterian Kirk invested heavily in the mythical kings of Scots. The union of the crowns of Scotland and England in 1603 was a battle of the books, a contest between two versions of Scottish history and rival sets of origins legends. Within a generation — by the 1630s — it would give birth to two alternative cultural identities.

The second underpinning myth, of the origins of the Scottish royal line, was also represented in the triumphal entry of 1633, but was more ambiguous. On an 'Arch of Caledonia', a painting depicted the flight of both Roman soldiers and Picts from Scotland; the Latin inscription below it, 'Broken in war and repelled by destiny', hailed Charles I as the heir of kings of Scots and conqueror of the Picts.[2] The idea that the Scottish crown traced its own origins to the Gaelic west — mirrored in the pages of the *History* of Hector Boece, a pensioner of James V — was still commonplace, even though Buchanan had since attacked the notion of a Celtic conquest of the Picts. A second version of the idea was current amongst the Gaelic bards, amongst whom persisted a strong sense of a pan-Celtic community — which could grip imaginations on both sides of the Irish Sea. Although it was usually an undercurrent, it was potent enough for James V, king of Scots, to be offered the high kingship of Ireland in 1540. It was strong enough in Scotland's Gaeldom to be given vivid expression in a Gaelic poem written on the eve of the battle of Flodden in 1513, a battle between James IV and Henry VIII's England portrayed as a clash between rival cultures:

> Meet it is to rise against Saxons ... ere they have taken our country from us. Let us not yield up our native country, let us make no gentle warfare. Let us after the pattern of the Gael of *Banbha* [Ireland] watch over our fatherland ... Against Saxons I say to you, lest they rule our country too, fight roughly; like the Irish Gael, we

1   Mason, 'Scotching the Brut', p. 75; Lynch, *Scotland*, p. 260.
2   Martin, 'Entertainments for Charles I', pp. 19–20.

will have no English Pale. Send thy summons east and west, let
Ireland come at your behest, drive the Saxons westward over the
high sea, that Scotland [Alba] may suffer no division.[1]

This, a poem which fed on the myths of Irish history and which, like much
Irish verse, separated *Gael* from *Gall*, Highlander from Lowlander, is nevertheless one of the most remarkable examples of Scottish nationalism in the
period. There can be no doubt that a cultural pan-Gaeldom still existed
throughout the sixteenth century, even if it rarely found political expression.
Even so, the prospect of a Gaelic international was the nightmare scenario of
many English diplomats throughout the reign of Elizabeth.

Until at least the reign of James IV, specific place had been reserved at
the Scottish court for Gaelic culture. It may be significant that in the
Renaissance triumph organised at Stirling to mark the baptism of Mary
Stewart's son in 1566 'wild Highlanders' were, like the Moors, one of the
marauding bands whose assaults on the enchanted castle representing the
Stewart monarchy were repulsed.[2] By the 1580s, Gaelic culture was the butt
of court satire. Alexander Montgomerie, elegant poet at the court of James
VI, made fun of the Irish origin legends: 'How the first Helandman, of God
was maid, of an horse turd, in Argyle, as is said.'[3] By the second half of the
1590s, there had begun to emerge a counter-culture — of a British identity,
given expression in a rival set of historical origins legends, in new emblems
of Britishness, and a new notion of civility which, like Montgomerie, would
look askance at Gaelic culture.[4]

Ever since the late fourteenth century, the Gaelic language had been on
the retreat, into the Highlands and the west. But even then Gaelic was
referred to as 'Scottish' speech, and what we now know as vernacular
Scots was called 'Teutonic'. The chronicler John Fordun, writing in the
1380s, had first made explicit the notion of a division between Highlands
and Lowlands,[5] and James VI in his *Basilikon Doron*, written in 1598,
brought a fresh refinement to this strain of thought. In it, he, like
some English commentators on Ireland in the 1580s and 1590s, contrasted
two populations, one which was utterly barbarous and the other possibly

1 *Scottish Verse from the Book of the Dean of Lismore*, ed. W.J. Watson (Scottish Gaelic Texts Society, 1978), p. 161.
2 J.W.M. Bannerman, 'The king's poet and the inauguration of Alexander III', *Scot. Hist. Rev.*, lxviii (1989), pp. 135–6; M. Lynch, 'Queen Mary's triumph: the baptismal celebrations at Stirling in December 1566', *Scot. Hist. Rev.*, lxix (1990), p. 9.
3 *Poems of Alexander Montgomerie* (Scottish Text Society, 1887), pp. 280–1; C.W.J. Withers, *Gaelic in Scotland, 1698–1981* (Edinburgh, 1984), pp. 24–5, 28.
4 Lynch, *Scotland*, p. 241; Lee, *Great Britain's Solomon*, pp. 197–200.
5 John Fordun, *Chronica Gentis Scotorum*, ed. W.F. Skene (Edinburgh, 1871–2), i, p. 24; Withers, *Gaelic in Scotland*, p. 22.

redeemable, reclaimable to civility:

> ... [those] that dwelleth in our mainland, that are barbarous for the most part, and yet mixed with some show of civility; the other, that dwelleth in the Isles, and are utterly barbarous, without any sort or show of civility.[1]

Just as English policy in Ireland had wavered, between believing that the Irish could be civilised and holding that they would have to be conquered first, so the government of James VI was caught in two minds between 1587 and 1607. Its dilemma was made more difficult by the fact that George Buchanan, tutor of the young King James and author of what was now the standard work on Scottish history, had taken a highly sympathetic view of the Highlands and Isles: these were the parts of Scotland, he had argued, which were most in touch with the old values of civility, kindliness, and discipline.[2] Buchanan, in common with other historians of the first three quarters of sixteenth century, looked to an ancient Scottish culture, expressed partly in its long line of kings and partly in the interaction of *Gael* and *Gall*. They urged that Scotland should be seen as a self-contained unity, that the link and interaction between Highlanders and Lowlanders had been the key to Scotland's survival as an independent nation.

By 1608, however, the Scottish state had made up its mind. The clearest indication of this came in the Statutes of Iona of the following year. This legislation, masterminded by Bishop Knox of the Isles, unequivocally stigmatised what it referred to as 'Irish' manners, dress, customs and violence; it forced clan chiefs to have their eldest sons or daughters educated on the mainland, safely removed from these barbarous influences and taught to 'speak, read and write in English'.[3] The Statutes were subscribed by nine clan chiefs who had been forcibly kidnapped for the purpose — by Knox himself. Although it is sometimes argued that Knox advocated a policy of reconciliation rather than confrontation with Gaeldom,[4] it is difficult to see him as having a different persona from the coercionist he undoubtedly was in Ulster. James's policy had had a potential military arm ever since 1596 when he first threatened to lead an expedition to the Isles himself — emulating his grandfather in 1540. After 1603 plantation and joint military

---

1 *The Basilikon Doron of James VI*, ed. J. Craigie (Scottish Text Society, 1944–50), i, p. 71. Both James and the English privy council thought that the remote west of Ireland and Ulster, because they were the 'least civil', would be more easily won over to a godly reformation: see Ford, *Reformation in Ireland*, pp. 158–9.
2 Williamson, *Scottish National Consciousness*, pp. 118–19.
3 *Reg. Privy Council Scot.*, ix, pp. 26–30.
4 M. Lee, *Government by Pen: Scotland under James VI and I* (Chicago, 1980), pp. 77–80.

action to subdue the worst pockets of Gaeldom in both Ireland and Scotland were the twin instruments of royal policy, which was now cast in a new British dimension. In 1608, plans were already being laid for English expeditionary forces to be sent to reduce the Isles to obedience; in effect the new king of Great Britain was planning a conquest of the Isles. And the king's privy councillors in Edinburgh found themselves cast in the role which the Old English had long adopted in Ireland, of arguing that they, along with the bishop of the Isles, were the natural agents of crown policy in Gaeldom.[1]

Amidst the confusions and abrupt changes of tactics in James's policy towards the western Highlands and the Isles, the traditional policy of the Scottish crown since the reign of James IV jostled with the experience of the English conquest of Ireland. Nowhere were there so many bewildering shifts of royal policy than in its plans for Lewis: after the prospects of a personal expedition by the king foundered, the traditional instruments of royal policy, commissions of lieutenandry, were tried in what was avowedly a 'conquest of Lewis' but were also found wanting; private adventurers from Lowland Fife proved as unable to organise a plantation.[2] Towns, described by an Elizabethan diplomat in Ireland as 'sheet anchors of the state', were planned to provide a nucleus of English speakers, but it was a policy which took more than a century to come to fruition.[3] Frontier clans, with a foot in both Lowland and Highland society, were used by the government as Trojan horses for undermining Gaelic society. Efforts were made to bring Highland landowners under the same legal obligations as elsewhere. This was, in effect, a surrender and regrant policy such as Henry VIII had attempted; in 1597 charters were demanded as proof of ownership of land; a flourishing cottage industry in the forging of charters started up and an even more flourishing trade for fake genealogies.[4] What happened in Scotland between 1590 and 1609 was a history in miniature of the varied English experience in Ireland in the second half of sixteenth century. Despite the joint resources

---

1 Gregory, *History of Western Highlands*, pp. 318, 322; Lee, *Great Britain's Solomon*, p. 214; cf. Ford, *Reformation in Ireland*, pp. 166–7.
2 Gregory, *History of Western Highlands*, pp. 278–80, 286–7, 290–2, 297–9, 304, 309–10; Lee, *Great Britain's Solomon*, pp. 200–1, 213, 217.
3 Quoted in J.F. Lydon, *The Lordship of Ireland in the Middle Ages* (Dublin, 1972), p. 241. Apart from Inverness, the only established towns in the Highlands before 1600 were Dingwall and Inveraray. There were few immediate, tangible results of an act of the Scottish parliament of 1597 to encourage the establishment of burghs with colonies of English speakers; with the exception of Stornoway (1607), none of the private burghs, of barony or regality — Inverara in Sutherland (1601), Cromdale in Moray (1609), Laggan in Islay (1614) and Campbelltown in Inverness-shire (1623) — was much more than a parchment foundation.
4 Gregory, *History of Western Highlands*, pp. 275–9, 281–2, 319.

of the British state, it had only patchy success.

It is difficult to believe that the increasing royal interference in Gaeldom was a direct response to an escalating problem of violence there. Crown policy itself often exacerbated troubles in the Highlands: royal lieutenants, most often in the shape of the earls of Argyll in the south and the earls of Huntly in the north, were prone to use commissions of lieutenandry as a blunt instrument to settle their personal disputes. Royal minorities, such a feature of sixteenth-century Scottish politics, were liable to lead to abrupt changes of patronage in the Highlands, as was the case after the fall of Angus in 1528. The feuds of national politics more frequently spilled over into the Highlands than in the opposite direction, as was the case when the 'bonnie' earl of Moray was murdered by Huntly in 1592 and Argyll, a rival royal lieutenant, was given *carte blanche* by the crown to organise a clan war against him. It was usually the case that internal disruption within Highland society stemmed from a fragmentation of the different septs of a clan, as was the case with the MacGregors from the 1550s on. The clans which fared best were those, as in Ireland, which, like the Campbells, had a foot in both Highland and Lowland society; so successful was the campaign of vilification pursued by the Campbells of Glenorchy against their former clients that the MacGregors headed the list of lawless clans drawn up by parliament in 1587.[1] The crown's motives, especially in the 1590s, were clear enough: the Highlands and Isles, which were claimed to be 'of auld the maist constant ... rent and patrimonie' of the crown, provided a last opportunity for a debt-ridden administration to increase its ordinary income.[2]

The focal point of the new Britain was kingship itself. Various personae were used to convey its different aspects. The image of David, leader of a new people of Israel, promised to lead the Scots into the sunset of a Calvinist Greater Britain. The recreation of the legendary empire of Arthur, ancient king of the Britons, demanded an alternative version of Scottish history, not of Scots or Picts but of Britons. It can also be detected in the change in the design of the king's Great Seal, which conjoined not only the English and Scottish arms but also those of Cadwallader and Edward the Confessor, respectively the last undisputed kings of Celtic Britain and Anglo-Saxon England.[3] Some this was not new — the myth of Arthur had

---

1 *Ibid.*, pp. 129–32, 254; Brown, *Bloodfeud*, pp. 144–82; MacGregor, 'Political history of MacGregors', pp. 133, 408–12.
2 *Reg. Privy Council Scot.*, vi, pp. 255–6; A.L. Murray, 'Sir John Skene and the exchequer, 1594–1612', *Stair Society Miscellany*, i (1971), p. 129; J. Goodare, 'Parliament and society in Scotland, 1560–1603' (Edinburgh University Ph.D. thesis, 1989), pp. 459–60.
3 Lee, *Great Britain's Solomon*, p. 153; Galloway, *Union of England and Scotland*, p. 16.

been regularly used by James IV and V, who both had sons named after Arthur (though both died in infancy). James IV had had constructed a round table, like Arthur's, and was fond of embarrassing English ambassadors by seating them at it. Another round table was used by Mary in 1566 at the royal baptism of 1566, when the court bards had sung of her son fulfilling the prophecy of Merlin and uniting the two kingdoms.[1] James, as it happened, did precisely that. But for him the vital image was that of Constantine — for Constantine combined a new Erastianism with James the godly prince, the unifying force behind a blessed Protestant isle, a British Israel, demanding loyalty from the troublesome Scottish Presbyterian Church. The notion of Roman emperor and civiliser neatly brought together Henrician ideas of England as an empire, the Elizabethan propaganda of Irish conquest and Stewart propaganda of how the west was won. And stigmatised in royal propaganda as enemies of the new British kingship were papists, Irish, Borderers and Highlanders.[2]

New emblems of a new British identity were created — in the form of a wave of British histories, flags, seals, Renaissance fêtes and coinage. The history of the new union flag can conveniently be used as a summary for the whole pan-British project. Before 1603, the Scots, significantly, had not one flag but two, the diagonal white cross of St Andrew on a blue ground and the king's banner, of a red lion rampant on a yellow ground — twin symbols of the diversity of the Scots and the role of the monarch as their unifier. At least eight attempts were made to merge the St Andrews cross and the English cross of St George, a vertical red cross on a white ground, and convey equal place to each. The ingenuity of the eventual design cut little ice. It proved highly unpopular, in both Scotland and England, and fell into disuse after 1625. It returned in 1654, at the time of the Cromwellian union of England, Scotland and Ireland with a new centrepiece, the harp, ironically Henry VIII's emblem for his Irish kingdom. After 1660 the flag continued, but without the harp, until 1801, when (in a further irony) the red diagonal cross of St Patrick was added to it — ironic because here was the emblem of a Protestant Church of Ireland which had in defeat claimed an origin legend for itself, finding it some eleven centuries before its foundation in Patrick.[3]

The claims made for the new British unionism and for James VI and I as the new Constantine provoked a direct riposte from Scottish Presbyterianism. The two leaders of the assault on a British Constantine were David

---

1 N. Macdougall, *James IV* (Edinburgh, 1989), p. 295; Lynch, 'Queen Mary's Triumph', pp. 12, 13.
2 Williamson, *Scottish National Consciousness*, pp. 5, 21; see *Jacobean Union*, ed. Galloway and Levack, pp. 18, 22.
3 Galloway, *Union of England and Scotland*, pp. 82–4.

Hume of Godscroft, son of a laird, poet and historian, and John Napier of Merchiston, another son from a gentry family, mathematician and inventor of logarithms. For Napier, James's claims for a new empire of Constantine demanded the recalculation both of the precise time from the fall of Rome and of the date of the millennium: the first neatly worked out 1,260 years later in 1560, the year of the Scottish Reformation, and the second as 1638. Here was an exposé of the original Constantine, who had, he argued, surrendered his authority to the Pope. The notion of a 'good' emperor was bogus, as was that of the godly prince which depended on it. The route taken by David Hume of Godscroft lay less in the pursuit of the millennium than a new prospect of Scotland's past — in a neo-Calvinist humanism to combat the neo-Renaissance humanism of royal propaganda. It was Hume who first identified the danger faced by a Presbyterian polity as a threat to Scotland itself, which would ultimately lead to England 'tyrannising' over it. The guarantor of Scottish identity had become the Kirk.[1]

By the 1630s the idea had gained a positive format: Scotland was the latter-day Israel; it and Israel were the 'only two sworn nations of the Lord'.[2] The idea of a covenanted nation gave a new, mature expression of Scots identity — 'We are the people' is still the cry from certain football terraces. The new ideology based itself not on customary law but on the new codification of Scots law which had been going on since 1580. It also drew on a popular national consciousness which in the later sixteenth century had cultivated a taste for the reading of histories of Scotland and the patriotic masterpieces of the later medieval period; the vogue began with the printing in 1570 of Blind Harry's *Wallace*, and Barbour's *The Brus* followed in 1571.[3] A patriotic age which contemplated Scotland's Wars of Independence against England was the foundation on which the Kirk built its new Israel in the 1630s. Along with the jettisoning of customary law went the abandonment of a notion of Gaeldom as the repository of the ancient laws, freedoms and disciplines. It would take Sir Walter Scott and Queen Victoria in the nineteenth century and music hall balladeers and the tourist industry in the twentieth to recapture the Highlands as the essence of Scottish identity.

In the late sixteenth century, the Kirk embellished one of John Knox's two key ideas, of a perfect Church, and jettisoned the other, of an imperial

---

1 Williamson, *Scottish National Consciousness*, pp. 21–30, 89; Lynch, *Scotland*, p. 243.
2 S.A. Burrell, 'The covenant idea as a revolutionary symbol: Scotland, 1596–1637', *Church History*, xxvii (1958), pp. 345–50. For Samuel Rutherford, the Gaelic-speaking 'Islesmen' were also included in the 'great Charter'.
3 Lynch, *Scotland*, p. 260; M. Lynch, 'The age of Renaissance and Reformation', in *Why Scottish History Matters*, ed. R. Mitchison (Edinburgh, 1991), pp. 30–3.

Britain. The Kirk also took one of George Buchanan's two key ideas — of a long line of kings of Scots corrected by their nobles — and shed the other, of the civility of Gaeldom (and, implicitly with it, the notion of a pan-Celtic Gaeldom).[1] It was a calculated and highly selective rearrangement of the legacy of the historians and the Protestant Reformation. It developed as a direct reaction to the new Britain of James VI and I. With the backlash came a new history and a new set of origins legends, this time not for kings but for the Protestant Church. The first to challenge the standard royal version of a Scottish past had been Buchanan. He found the origins not so much in the Scots of Dalriada as in the Picts. The transfer of origins legends was not accomplished quickly, but it was secure by the middle years of the seventeenth century. So widely accepted did it become that the leading Scottish Catholic historian of eighteenth century, Thomas Innes, accepted the Pictish history unreservedly; the case which he mounted on behalf of Jacobite pretenders was that they were directly descended from the long line Pictish kings.[2]

*

The failure of the Reformation in Ireland exemplifies, it has been argued, the failure of a king to mould a society to his will.[3] The Counter-Reformation which the English conquest of Ireland provoked and into whose arms it drove most of the Old English, was the major factor in the crystallisation of a new notion of Irish national identity — based not, as before, on lordship or kindred, nor on the symbols of a foreign king (despite some success in inventing new emblems such as the harp), but on Catholicism and on a notion of the *patria* and of 'mother Ireland'. By contrast, the very success of the Reformation in Scotland, which came not as is conventionally argued in the generation of John Knox, but in the third and fourth generations after 1560, between the 1590s and the 1630s, and saw the rapid Calvinisation of Scottish society, also reflected the failure of a king to mould society to his will. An absentee king intent on his own brand of an apocalyptic Calvinism was rejected, no less decisively. By the 1630s the Kirk had become a metaphor, both for the distresses of a commonweal under assault from foreign pressures and for Scottish identity itself — it was 'the bride of

---

1 *John Knox's History of the Reformation in Scotland*, ed. W.C. Dickinson (Edinburgh, 1949), ii, p. 3 (Preface to Book IV); cf. Williamson, *Scottish National Consciousness*, pp. 19−20, 109−11, 118−19.
2 Mason, 'Scotching the Brut', p. 77. The view, elaborated by Hector Boece, that the kings of Scots had exterminated the Picts had still, however, held sway in the official celebrations of 1633.
3 Bottigheimer, 'Failure of the Reformation', pp. 203−5.

Christ' or the 'tent of Israel'.[1] In the process, as two distinctive, 'born-again' identities for Ireland and Scotland emerged, the notion of a pan-Celtic society stretching across the North Channel waned. The invasion of Ireland by Covenanting armies from 1642 onwards and the expedition made by Alasdair MacColla to Scotland on behalf of the Catholic Confederacy in 1644−5 in the 'War of the Three Kingdoms' confirmed the growing distance between Irish Gaeldom and the Scots *Gaidhealtachd*.

The crystallisation of both Irish and Scottish national identity stemmed directly from the failure of the first British state. Its débacle was already complete by 1625. The collapse of the notion of a British *patria* had two effects: in both Ireland and Scotland it overtook and deflected attention from older, often ambiguous or competing notions of national identity; it also gave birth to sharply defined visions of national identity, not British but explicitly Irish and Scots. When union came again, under the Cromwellian regime of the 1650s, it took the form of the 'Commonwealth of England, Scotland and Ireland' rather than a union of Great Britain, which remained an uncomfortable reminder of Stuart absolutism.[2] The Cromwellian union did not pretend a British nation-state. It was an avowedly English empire, whose first battle was fought by 'God's Englishman', Oliver Cromwell, at Drogheda in 1649, and its last at Culloden almost a century later.[3]

1 Rutherford, *Letters*, pp. 457, 519.
2 *Into Another Mould: Aspects of the Interregnum*, ed. I. Roots (London, 1981), pp. 10−12; Lynch, *Scotland*, pp. 283−4.
3 H. Kearney, *The British Isles* (Cambridge, 1989), pp. 121−7, 145.

National Identity in Eighteenth-Century Denmark

Ole Feldbæk

During the eighteenth century, there was a most striking development in the national identity of Denmark.[1] It was a remarkably fast process, taking place during a period of no more than thirty years: starting in the 1740s and reaching its apogee in 1776. In that year the absolute king, Christian VII, issued an amendment to the constitution, namely the Law of Indigenous Rights. According to this, only those born in the country were eligible to hold offices in the civil and military service and in the Church. Clearly, therefore, a Danish national identity had already passed through its formative stages and was well established in at least parts of society before the outbreak of the French Revolution.[2]

Denmark in the mid-eighteenth century was a conglomerate state consisting of the kingdoms of Denmark and Norway with the North Atlantic possessions of Iceland, Greenland and the Faeroe Islands, and the duchies of Schleswig and Holstein. Formally, the constitution — the *Lex Regia* from 1665 — made the Danish king the most absolute ruler in Christendom. His subjects held no political rights whatsoever and the king was responsible only to God. The political reality, however, was that the king based his power on the great landowners and a rising bourgeoisie. Public opinion could express itself fairly freely and the king's ministers exercised the absolute power in an enlightened manner.

Danish was the language in Denmark and in the administration of Norway, whose population spoke a language close to Danish. In the two duchies the language was German except in northern Schleswig where the peasants spoke Danish. The actual lingual and cultural situation, however, was much more complicated than appears at first sight. In the first half of the eighteenth century the language of the ruling class was to a great extent

---

1 This essay presents some of the findings of the Research Group on the History of Danish Identity now published in *Dansk Identitetshistorie*, i–iv, ed. O. Feldbæk (Copenhagen, 1991–2), with a summary in English. It has previously been printed in *Info 21*, October 1990, published by the Swiss *Programme National de Recherche 21: Pluralisme Culturel et Identité Nationale*.
2 O. Feldbæk, 'Denmark', in *Nationalism in the Age of the French Revolution*, ed. O. Dann and J. Dinwiddy (London, 1988).

German and French. A Danish gentleman — it was sarcastically said — would study Latin, speak French to the ladies, use German to his dog, and condescend to use Danish only while speaking to his servant. The capital of the conglomerate state, Copenhagen, was in fact a bilingual metropolis where both Danish and German were spoken.[1]

A tension between different languages, cultures and social layers therefore existed, as did a potential conflict between 'us' and 'them'. Hitherto, tensions between the Danes and the foreigners had been kept under the surface. But what would happen when a new social group was formed, whose members were Danish-born, Danish-speaking and well qualified for the positions and the honours which were traditionally given to foreigners? Would they simply acquiesce? Or would they claim rights on the grounds that they were born in the country, spoke its language and shared its past? Such claims were in fact presented in the 1740s by a group of young Danes of bourgeois origin and with a university education.[2] They had found no natural place in a feudal society based on land and lineage and were not satisfied, as their fathers had been, just to live as loyal subjects, useful citizens and sinners before God. Rather they had developed a particular Danish identity which not only reflected their worldly ambitions and aspirations but also filled an emotional void.

*

As Professor Dahlerup's essay earlier in this volume reminds us, a Danish identity was not a new phenomenon in the 1740s. In fact it goes as far back as the written historical sources take us. Denmark as a kingdom and the Danes as a people are expressly referred to on the great runic stone in Jelling of about 980. In the *Gesta Danorum* written by Saxo Grammaticus around 1200 the *leitmotifs* are *amor patriae* and the struggle against the Germans. And throughout the Middle Ages and the Renaissance we frequently meet with references to a specific Danish identity and to a love of the fatherland.[3] Should this not, however, be interpreted as a political ideology fostered by the rulers and propagated by those who served them with the pen and the sword? They had an obvious political interest in a national ideology. Whatever the case, what we are concerned with here is the remarkable phenomenon of the development of a Danish identity *outside* that political elite. This is what was actually happening in the mid-1740s.

1   V. Winge, 'Dansk og tysk i 1700-tallet', in *Dansk Identitetshistorie*, i.
2   Where nothing else is indicated, this essay is based upon O. Feldbæk, 'Fædreland og Indfødsret: 1700-tallets danske identitet', in *ibid*.
3   H. Ilsøe, 'Danskerne og deres fædreland: Holdninger og opfatteleser *c*.1550−1700', in *ibid*.; cf. also I. Skovgaard-Petersen, 'Saxo, Historian of the Patria', *Medieval Scandinavia*, ii (1969).

One condition, however, for the development of a Danish identity was a Danish public able and willing to pay for being informed, enlightened and entertained, and who could be won over to the new national ideas and feelings. Around 1700 such a *Bildungsbürgertum* did not yet exist. The few who took an interest in Danish language and in Danish history did so within limited and mostly academic circles. But around 1720 we encounter a gradually growing market for newspapers and periodicals which introduced the Enlightenment to a Danish public. In 1722 the first theatre was opened to the public. The study of Danish history, which had until then been almost entirely the preserve of official royal historiographers whose job it was to glorify the kings, developed into a preoccupation with the national past — where, incidentally, it was shown how the non-noble groups of society had also played an important role. Academics started to make the Danish language a medium fit for a national literature and for introducing the Enlightenment to broader social circles. And the apogee of these cultural endeavours was the performance in 1756 of the first opera in Danish, based on a story demonstrably taken from the *Gesta Danorum*.

This cultural modernisation, which also enhanced the king's *gloire* and the country's prestige abroad, enjoyed the support of the king and his enlightened ministers. But how did a regime which relied so heavily upon foreigners at court, in the administration, in the armed forces and in cultural and economic life react to the rise of a particular national identity? This in fact posed serious problems. In itself it was a natural thing for the men in power to patronise the initiative taken by a group of young bourgeois academics in 1745 to erect a 'Danish Society for the Improvement of the History and the Language of the Fatherland', and to give economic support to its publications. But how were the men in power to interpret expressions like 'It is praiseworthy that the Danish people at long last begins to love itself and to acquire a taste for its own'? Or to understand the constant underlining of 'our language', 'our history', 'our countrymen' and 'our fatherland'? The publications of the young Society expressed deep loyalty towards the king. But they did not place the king above the fatherland: they juxtaposed these two central concepts, and that was something entirely new.

The new preoccupation with one's fatherland and the preference of one's countrymen to foreigners went completely against the Christian teachings of love of one's neighbour, and also against the spirit of the Enlightenment where talent and tolerance were paramount virtues. The central figure in Danish cultural life around 1750, Ludvig Holberg, therefore earnestly warned against these new ideas and feelings which might easily lead to contempt and even hatred towards other nations and other peoples. In fact two worlds, the old one and the new, stood against each another — and they did not speak the same language.

Ole Feldbæk

To a man like Ludvig Holberg love of the fatherland posed a problem of philosophy. To the men in power the new ideas and emotions posed a very real political problem. They knew very well the critical attitude of the Danes towards the foreigners — predominately Germans — who were serving the king and the state. And in an absolutist state any criticism was in the final analysis a criticism against the king and his dispositions. Nor could it possibly be ignored that the tensions between Danish and German constituted a threat against the cohesion of the conglomerate state with its Danish and German populations.

How, then, were the new Danish ideas and feelings to be interpreted? Were they demands? And if so, demands for what? For equal opportunities with the foreigners? Or was it that the Danes should be preferred to foreigners? And last but not least, how was the central concept of fatherland to be interpreted? Was it the cosmopolitic concept of the Age of Enlightenment: the land where you chose to live? Or was it the land where you were born, whose language you spoke, and whose past you shared? These, indeed, were vital questions for a political system such as Danish absolutism and for a state such as the conglomerate Danish state.

*

During the entire reign of Frederik V — from 1746 to 1766 — there was only one official interpretation of the concept of fatherland. It was *patria ubicunque bene* — 'my fatherland is wherever I live well'. This official interpretation was clearly expressed in the book *Reflections of the Love of the Fatherland*, written by Tyge Rothe and published in 1759. The author was a young Danish client of the German-born foreign minister J. H. E. Bernstorff, who had travelled on a stipend from the king, and who had stayed half a year in Geneva, where Bernstorff's former secretary, André Roger, had reported back favourably about the progress of the book. After his return to Copenhagen, Rothe had been appointed tutor to the king's younger son, and he had formally dedicated his book to the king.

In his book Tyge Rothe set out to prove three theses: that the fatherland was where you chose to live, not where you were born; that love of the fatherland could and should be disseminated to all classes of society; and that Denmark needed foreigners in order to bring the country on to a cultural par with the leading countries of Europe. Naturally, the book proved to be a very welcome one to the ruling elite, given that the government, the central administration and the cultural and economic life of the capital were all dominated by foreigners. And Danes travelling abroad were unlikely to meet with diplomatic representatives of their king who were able — or willing — to speak their language.

But it was obvious that there was an alternative definition of fatherland:

that is, the land where one was born and brought up. In fact Tyge Rothe explicitly argued against it in his book. This was the definition that probably prevailed with the Danish public, but their loyalty to the king and fear of reprisals from the men in power kept it under the surface as long as Frederik V reigned. In 1766, however, Frederik V died, and the sixteen-year-old Christian VII ascended the throne. As his official device he proclaimed *gloria ex amore patriae* — 'I shall seek my glory in love of my fatherland'. The ministers of the old reign were now attacked because of their foreign extraction, their foreign language and their alleged contempt for everything Danish, and some of them were ousted from power. There was an aggressive national reaction, and as early as 1767 the alternative definition of fatherland was publicly acclaimed. In a pamphlet a young and ambitious academic, Eiler Hagerup, set out to defeat Tyge Rothe's three theses. He claimed that your fatherland was where you were born; he rejected the idea that the lower classes could love their fatherland; and he explicitly stated that Denmark no longer stood in need of foreigners. Now, Eiler Hagerup was probably just voicing attitudes which had dominated Danish public opinion since around 1750. But in 1767 he went even further. For the first time in the history of Danish absolutism the monarch was presented with clear-cut demands, and even in a threatening form. As Hagerup put it, if the Danes were to love their fatherland, then the king must return their love; and Danes should in every respect be preferred to foreigners.

*

The development of Danish identity in the eighteenth century cannot be separated from the political history of the period. Until 1766 national tensions had been kept below the surface. But the change of government brought a strengthening of national ideas and emotions and an aggressive attitude towards foreigners, who were increasingly identified with Germans. And the political disturbances following in the wake of the young king's growing insanity came to accelerate the formation of a Danish identity and to hasten the chain of events leading up to the Law of Indigenous Rights in 1776.

In the autumn of 1770 the German-born physician Johann Friedrich Struensee took over complete control of the state by isolating the king and becoming the lover of the young queen. He ruled in the name of the king and he began his sixteen months in power by abolishing censorship and permitting a free press. This overt political gesture — which earned the king of Denmark a complimentary letter from the old Voltaire at Ferney — was meant to give the public an opportunity to attack his predecessors. In reality, however, the public soon turned against Struensee and his overhasty reforms, and in their attacks on him his German extraction and language and his alleged contempt for Danish customs and traditions played a prominent role.

His dictatorship was short lived, for in 1772 he was deposed by a palace revolution, condemned for *lèse-majesté* and publicly executed. But the Struensee interlude was nevertheless very important in the history of Danish identity. The members of the royal family who subsequently took power in the name of the hapless king were very much aware that this episode had demonstrated serious weaknesses in the fabric of Danish absolutism. They therefore found it expedient to identify themselves with a demonstrative Danishness. Less than a month after the fall of Struensee they insisted that in future the government and the administration in Denmark and Norway should be Danish. And shortly after that, they ordered that the language of command in the army — which had until then been German — should be Danish. (The language of the navy had always been Danish.) In 1775 Danish language and Danish history were made subjects in their own right in the grammar schools, and school books aiming at inspiring the pupils with loyalty towards the absolute king and love of their fatherland were written under official supervision. Finally, on the king's birthday in January 1776, this national policy reached its apogee with the solemn proclamation of the Law of Indigenous Rights. This Law — which was explicitly made part of the constitution and is still valid despite the spirit and laws of the European Community — is unique in the history of the *Ancien Régime* in giving those born in a particular country exclusive rights to hold offices in that state.

*

The Law of Indigenous Rights of 1776 was in fact many things to many people. To those in power it was basically a political device which was aimed at bolstering absolutism and safeguarding the conglomerate state. After the Struensee interlude, they were very much aware of the need to strengthen loyalty towards the king. They were likewise aware of the tensions between Danish and German — and that the Danes could not be relied on to distinguish between the king's German-speaking subjects from Schleswig and Holstein and Germans from the south of the Elbe.[1] They also followed with apprehension the growing expressions of a particular Norwegian identity.[2] And both these issues constituted a clear threat to the

---

[1] O. Feldbæk and V. Winge, 'Tyskerfejden 1789–1790: Den første nationale konfrontation', in *Dansk Identitetshistorie*, ii; and V. Winge, 'Dansk og tysk, 1790–1848', in *ibid*. Cf. also O. Feldbæk, 'Clash of Cultures in a Conglomerate State: Danes and Germans in 18th-Century Denmark', in *Clashes of Cultures: Essays in Honour of Niels Steensgaard*, ed. J.C.V. Johansen *et al.* (Odense, 1992).

[2] On early Norwegian national identity, see K. Lunden, *Norsk grålysning: Norsk nasjonalisme 1770–1814 på allmen bakgrunn* (Oslo, 1992).

cohesion of the conglomerate state. In response, the Law of Indigenous Rights was in fact a remarkably ingenious political construction. By transforming the love of the fatherland of the Danish bourgeoisie into love of king and fatherland, and by defining the fatherland not as Denmark but as the entire state, those in power endeavoured to safeguard both the absolute state and the conglomerate state.

To the cosmopolitan elite and to the believers in Enlightenment and in the brotherhood of all men, the Law was a political and cultural set-back — and was seen as such. On the other hand, to the middle and upper-class layers in the towns — and particularly in Copenhagen and the Danish provincial towns — the Law of Indigenous Rights was something entirely different. They reacted enthusiastically, with spontaneous festivities, church services, processions, dinners, balls and gun salutes, because they saw the Law as a victory. These urban groups greeted it as such because it fulfilled a strong emotional demand, a demand for a confirmation of an identity which had developed in their own lifetime with the land where they were born, whose language they spoke and whose past was their past, but where foreigners had been preferred. They had experienced the growth of this identity in their daily life and also in public debate. Their spontaneous reaction was probably also due to the fact that they saw the Law as a gift from above, sanctioned by constitution and religion, and not as a forced concession. They thus expressed relief at seeing their national identity merge so apparently harmoniously with their traditional loyalty to the king and their conception of society.

On the other hand, nothing indicates that the new national identity had by then reached the lower social strata of the capital and the provincial towns. And the few peasant diaries preserved from these years show that the new ideas and emotions had not reached the agrarian population either.[1] In 1776 the new national identity was entrenched within a numerically small but dynamic urban section of the Danish society which saw itself as the interpreter of the people, the nation.

*

There is no evidence that the development of this early national identity was directly influenced from abroad. The Danish participants in the public debate did not point to literary inspiration or to similar developments in other countries. The most obvious inspiration would, of course, be German. But until the beginning of the 1770s the German concept of the fatherland

---

1   O. Feldbæk, 'Skole og identitet 1789–1848: Lovgivning og lærebøger', in *Dansk Identitetshistorie*, ii; and L. Rerup, 'Folkestyre og danskhed: Massenationalisme og politik 1848–1866', in *ibid.*, iii.

seems to have been the traditional concept of the Enlightenment: *patria ubicunque bene*. And the new trends stimulated by Möser, Klopstock, Goethe and Herder apparently came too late to influence the early Danish developments leading up to the Law of Indigenous Rights in 1776.[1]

The preconditions for a particular Danish development of an early national identity — a Danish *Sonderweg*, so to speak — do seem on the other hand to be there. Some of these conditions are of course of a general European nature. These included the rise of a *Bildungsbürgertum* unable to find a natural place in the old predominantly feudal society, and whose concept of a fatherland which denied tensions between estates and classes formed the ideal solution to its problems — one offering at one and the same time a realisation of its worldly aspirations and a fulfilment of its emotional needs. Another general phenomenon was gradual secularisation, whereby the authority of the Church and the power of religion over minds were waning, which invited the development of a non-religious identity.

Other preconditions, however, seem to be of a particular Danish origin. The advocates for a Danish identity had, for instance, no need to construe arguments and invent historical reasons. The main components of a nation-state were already there: a state with a common language, a common creed and a common past. Moreover, a tension did exist between two cultures: an elite with a foreign language and a foreign culture, and an indigenous population. Or, to put it more bluntly, a state existed whose own population was looked upon as underdeveloped. And last but not least, this cultural and social tension developed into open conflict, where the advocates for a Danish identity could make use of a Danish language, history and culture in their struggle for realising their concrete ambitions and fulfilling their emotional needs. Furthermore, this was a conflict where a powerful Danish public opinion could be persuaded to support their views.

---

1 C. Prignitz, *Vaterlandsliebe und Freiheit: Deutscher Patriotismus von 1750 bis 1850* (Wiesbaden, 1981).

National Consciousness? The Ambivalences of English Identity in the Eighteenth Century

Eric Evans

Twentieth-century discussion about national identity in the United Kingdom turns on different perceptions about nationhood held in its four constituent elements: England, Scotland, Wales and Northern Ireland. The sense of national identity in both Scotland and Wales substantially reflects changing perceptions of the relationship with the larger partner in the Union. A sense of nationhood in these countries is reinforced by the widespread misuse of 'English' for 'British', not only in the United States — whose own citizens conventionally and complacently apply the adjective 'American' to denote far less than their Continent and have seen no need to devise a more precise neologism — but even in England itself. Scottish and, to a lesser extent, Welsh resentment is fuelled by an attenuated English consciousness of national identity that lazily 'incorporates' their own nations, so that England as Britain becomes, almost by default, *the* national identity.

Distinctive 'Englishness' has always been difficult to identify but the eighteenth century does offer some routes into an elusive phenomenon. Although the constitutional relationship between England and Wales had been settled in the sixteenth century, the first decade of the eighteenth century witnessed the merging of the English and Scottish parliaments. The symbolic representation of this development was the creation of what is properly termed the 'Union Flag' but whose universally recognised name, 'Union Jack', is not only more colloquial but also more personal and involving.[1]

The Act of Union of 1707 was a controversial measure, heatedly opposed by many Scots and provoking riots in Edinburgh. Two factors made the loss of a separate Scottish parliament politically feasible. Firstly, dominant Lowland Scots magnate families like the Hamiltons and Argylls had extensive English connections; secondly, the Scottish commercial access

---

1 T.C. Smout, 'The Road to Union', in *Britain after the Glorious Revolution*, ed. G. Holmes (London, 1969); G.S. Pryde, *The Treaty of Union of Scotland and England* (London, 1950); W. Ferguson, *Scotland, 1689 to the Present* (Edinburgh, 1968). See also D. Williams, *A History of Modern Wales* (London, 1977), and E.D. Evans, *A History of Wales, 1660–1815* (Cardiff, 1976).

to a much larger market both in Britain and overseas which union alone could secure. The Union proved less controversial in early eighteenth-century England, not least because it seemed to secure England's 'Glorious Revolution' of 1688. A united Britain could more effectively resist Jacobite-Catholic counter-revolution. The Stuarts after 1714 found it difficult to rouse the Scottish nation to wholehearted rebellion from a basis of largely tribal support in the Scottish Highlands. Union thus buttressed England's Protestant Succession.[1]

Not that the English exactly warmed to the Scots, whose more egalitarian and effective education system provided a steady stream of aspirant professionals into richer England in search of power, wealth and advancement. James Boswell had to endure from Dr Samuel Johnson hardly good-humoured jibes about allegedly coarser diets and inferior roads north of the Border. The image of Scottish 'backwardness' was frequently invoked in England, where wits in coffee-houses asserted their Englishness negatively in sardonic comment against Caledonian immigrants. Success was easier for those who became anglicised. Elocution lessons to eliminate the Scottish accent were available in London and, though such evidence may suggest specifically metropolitan rather than wider English dominance, there was much which pointed to the unequal nature of the relationship within the Union.[2] Only towards the end of the century, for example, did Scottish agriculture begin generally to catch up with the initiatives of English landowners and tenant farmers. Not surprisingly, the leading improvers were Anglo-Scots who spent much of their time in England and who embraced there the new ethic which stressed the importance of experiment and productive agricultural investment. Much Scottish farming remained peasant-based and subsistence oriented. Living standards in Scotland were substantially lower than in England.[3]

---

1   J.R. Jones, *Country and Court: England 1658–1714* (London, 1978), p. 329. See also T.I. Rae, *The Union of 1707: Its impact on Scotland* (Glasgow, 1974).
2   R. Porter, *English Society in the Eighteenth Century* (London, 1982), p. 50; K. Robbins, *Nineteenth-Century Britain. England, Scotland and Wales: The Making of a Nation* (Oxford, 1989), pp. 38–40; P.K. Monod, *Jacobitism and the English People, 1688–1788* (Cambridge, 1989); B. Lenman, 'A Client Society: Scotland between the '15 and the '45', in *Britain in the Age of Walpole*, ed. J. Black (London, 1985); D. Szechi and D. Hayton, 'John Bull's other Kingdoms: The English Government of Scotland and Ireland', in *Britain in the First Age of Party, 1680–1750*, ed. C. Jones (London, 1987).
3   T.C. Smout, *A History of the Scottish People, 1560–1830* (London, 1969); *Scotland in the Age of Improvement: Essays in Scottish History in the Eighteenth Century*, ed. N.T. Phillipson and R. Mitchison (Edinburgh, 1970); *People and Society in Scotland*, i, *1760–1830*, ed. T.M. Devine and R. Mitchison (Edinburgh, 1988); *Scottish Society, 1500–1800*, ed. R.A. Houston and I.D. Whyte (Cambridge, 1989).

Ambivalences of English Identity in the Eighteenth Century

English reservations about the Scots were exacerbated in the early years of George III's reign by the young king's reliance on the intelligent and well-educated but politically naive Scottish peer, the earl of Bute. Thanks almost exclusively to royal patronage, Bute achieved rapid promotion in 1760−1 and was prime minister from May 1762 to April 1763. Bute stood outside the narrow circle of politically influential English aristocrats. This was his main attraction for a monarch determined to cleanse his country of corruption which he naively attributed to the machinations of party politicians whose patriotism had been warped by the search for place, office and profit. George wished to be 'monarch of the British Islands, not King of a despicable party'.[1]

The story of Bute's brief and unsuccessful administration need not be told here, but the reaction to it is relevant. In June 1762 John Wilkes, MP for Aylesbury and a political maverick whose talent for lacing self-publicity with principle amounted to genius, launched a new opposition magazine, *North Briton*. The title was a satirical riposte to the pro-government journal *The Briton*, and derived from the official title of Scotland under the Act of Union as 'North Britain'. English historians have concentrated their attention on the final issue of this journal, No. 45, which prompted the next government to arrest the authors, printers and publishers on charges of seditious libel under a 'general warrant', thus precipitating a *cause célèbre* over the legality of such proceedings.[2]

The other forty-four issues, however, were all published during the prime ministership of Bute and were notable for the nature of their attacks. Not only was Bute lambasted, but Wilkes took the opportunity to attack Scotland and all things Scottish with a potent blend of wit and vulgarity. In July 1762, for example, he invoked John Bull, a figure who was increasingly being represented as a well-fed, but overburdened, Englishman. Bute was alleged to have been the death of John Bull, 'choked by inadvertently swallowing a thistle, which he had placed by way of adornment on the top of his salad. For many years he had enjoyed a remarkable state of health.' The conceit of Scotland as a mere 'adornment' was intended to be specially wounding. The irony was that John Bull himself had been the creation of a Scot, John Arbuthnot, half a century earlier.[3]

Wilkes was by no means alone in his anti-Scottish attacks. As has been

---

1 J. Brewer, *Party Ideology and Popular Politics at the Accession of George III* (Cambridge, 1976), p. 47.
2 G.F. Rudé, *Wilkes and Liberty* (Oxford, 1962), pp. 20−4; I.R. Christie, *Wars and Revolutions: Britain, 1760−1815* (London, 1982), pp. 63−6.
3 *North Briton*, 17 July 1762, quoted in M. Taylor, 'John Bull and the Iconography of Public Opinion in England, c.1712−1929', *Past and Present*, 134 (1992), p. 103.

noted by Drs Brewer and Rogers, antipathy to Bute in London was intense. He was hissed at in the streets, 'abused in a gross manner, and a little pelted'. Pamphlets and ballads embellished the general theme of unwarrantable Scottish influence in English politics. Bute was a particularly inviting target for 'nationalist' hostility because he linked 'foreign influence' with standard 'country' rhetoric about excessive Court powers which diminished the stock of English liberties. Opposition journalists in the early 1760s were not slow to alert their readers to the possibilities of a renewal of the 'Auld Alliance' between France and Scotland. France, by the middle of the eighteenth century, was firmly re-established as the national enemy.[1] Although any threat that Catholic absolutism might return to England *via* a Jacobite invasion had disappeared at Culloden (1746) and in the brutal suppressions of the Highland clan system thereafter, atavistic 'Catholicism and slavery' imagery remained potent.[2]

Journalism of the Wilkes variety alarmed opposition politicians from the Whig oligarchy who believed its populism dangerously inciting and ill-judged. As his subsequent career would amply demonstrate, however, Wilkes's strength lay in his appeal to those outside the elite whose political consciousness was being raised by just the kind of direct appeal in which he specialised. What John Brewer has termed 'popular politics' was an increasingly important factor in eighteenth-century England and *North Briton* undoubtedly located that xenophobic patriotism characteristic of a certain kind of 'Englishness' in the middle years of the eighteenth century.[3]

Although the specific target in the London of the early 1760s was an unpopular Scottish prime minister, the attitudes to which Wilkes was appealing were broader. English popular opinion, like most popular opinion, could readily be roused to dislike of the foreigner particularly if the foreigner threatened jobs and security. Wilkes appealed to popular opinion by suggesting that those who opposed Bute also stood for honesty, for plain dealing and for the interests of ordinary folk against the wiles of politicians seeking their own advancement. The message was deployed cynically by an arch-manipulator and it was not without irony, especially in view of George III's own purist and anti-party political objectives. It did, however, strike

---

1 N. Rogers, *Whigs and the Cities: Popular Politics in the Age of Walpole and Pitt* (Cambridge, 1989), p. 124. See also J. Brewer, 'The Misfortunes of Lord Bute: A Case Study in Eighteenth-Century Political Argument and Public Opinion', *Historical Journal*, xvi (1973).

2 Smout, *History of the Scottish People*, pp. 343–60; B. Lenman, *An Economic History of Modern Scotland* (London, 1977); B. Lenman, *The Jacobite Risings in Britain, 1689–1746* (London, 1980); B. Lenman, *The Jacobite Clans of the Great Glen, 1650–1784* (London, 1984).

3 Brewer, *Party Ideology and Popular Politics*; Rogers, *Whigs and the Cities*.

Ambivalences of English Identity in the Eighteenth Century

a popular chord. Out of the fracas over General Warrants would emerge the potent slogan 'Wilkes and Liberty'. The defence of the 'liberties of Englishmen' would be a central concern of radical politicians from the 1760s through to the 1832 Reform Act and beyond.[1]

The encapsulation of English liberties has a curious, complex and even contradictory history. It embraced: Anglo-Saxon myth — the witangemot as proto-democracy destroyed at Hastings by 'William the Bastard and his armed banditti';[2] Angevin misconstruction — King John's being forced to concede by Magna Carta at Runnymede liberties under the law extracted from him by a public-spirited baronage; different types of anti-Stuart romanticism — Leveller declarations in the 1640s about the political rights of the 'poorest he'[3] and the Glorious Revolution's final destruction of 'monarchical tyranny' in 1688;[4] Protestant triumphalism — the freedom of Englishmen guaranteed against the return of Catholic absolutism by North-German princes as unEnglish as they were unattractive; and, from the later eighteenth-century onwards, European enlightenment ideology anglicised and popularised by the likes of Tom Paine in *Rights of Man* (1791−2).[5]

From such a mosaic, varieties of Englishness may be tentatively reconstructed. The reconstructions do not always cohere, nor do they invariably distinguish (as Scots, Welsh and Irish assuredly would) between Englishness and Britishness. Nevertheless, national identity is powerful in eighteenth-century life if only as a weapon of propaganda, and it is important to ask

---

1 Rudé, *Wilkes and Liberty*; J. Brewer, 'The Wilkites and the Law, 1763−4', in *An Ungovernable People*, ed. J. Brewer and J. Styles, (revised edn, London, 1983); H.T. Dickinson, *Liberty and Property: Political Ideology in Eighteenth-Century Britain* (London, 1977), pp. 232−69; E.P. Thompson, *The Making of the English Working Class* (Harmondsworth, 1968); A. Goodwin, *The Friends of Liberty: The English Democratic Movement in the Age of the French Revolution* (London, 1979); J. Cannon, *Parliamentary Reform, 1640−1832* (2nd edn, Cambridge, 1980).
2 The phrase 'armed banditti' was coined by Tom Paine in *Common Sense*, published in 1776. See the discussion by C. Hill, 'The Norman Yoke', in *Democracy and the Labour Movement: Essays presented to Dona Torr*, ed. J. Saville (London, 1954).
3 A.S.P. Woodhouse, *Puritanism and Liberty* (2nd edn, London, 1974); *The Levellers in the English Revolution*, ed. G.E. Aylmer (London, 1975).
4 J. Miller, *Popery and Politics in England, 1660−88* (Cambridge, 1973); J. Miller, *The Glorious Revolution* (London, 1983).
5 The literature both by radicals in the era of the French Revolution and on artisan and rationalist radicalism in the 1790s is vast. In addition to Paine, James Mackintosh, *Vindiciae Gallicae: A Defence of the French Revolution and its English admirers* (London, 1792), Richard Price, *A Discourse on the Love of our Country* (4th edn, London, 1790), and William Godwin, *Enquiry Concerning Political Justice* (London, 1791), are central contributions to the debate. A good example of artisan-inspired literature is *Selections from the papers of the London Corresponding Society*, ed. M. Thale (Cambridge, 1983).

what conditions favoured both its formulation and its promotion.

*

The first, it may be thought, stresses Britain rather than England. War, from the last years of the seventeenth century onwards, brought England much nearer to the heart of international affairs than at any time since the reign of Elizabeth I, and more powerfully so than ever before. First England, then Britain, was involved in unprecedentedly costly wars against France both under William III at the turn of the eighteenth century and against Revolutionary/Napoleonic France at the turn of the nineteenth. Britain was also at war from 1739 to 1748, from 1756 to 1763 and, with less success, from 1775 to 1783. All these wars, with the partial exception of the last which secured the independence of the north American colonies, ended in treaties which recognised Britain's growing influence. As John Brewer has noted, Britain by 1760 'had become one of the heaviest heavyweights in the balance of power in Europe. She had also acquired an empire of ample proportions and prodigious wealth.'[1] It has even been argued that even the American War helped to foster distinctive national identity. The enemy then was not 'Catholicism' (though, of course, both Catholic France and Spain intervened on the colonial side in 1778), but 'the unloyal' in the shape of English and Scottish colonial emigrants, the great majority of whom were of dissenting stock.[2]

War on the scale frequently seen in the eighteenth century required the resources of the state to be mobilised. New taxes were raised and the demands of military and naval recruitment frequently involved closer liaison between central government and local authorities.[3] The relative decline of the power of 'localism' — an immensely strong force in seventeenth-century England — is one of the most significant features of the eighteenth century. New taxes and the raising of troops were controversial measures and helped to nurture in many English towns a vigorous 'oppositional' culture which will be considered later. However, success in war and the expansion of overseas empire seem to have produced pride in achievement and a greater

---

1 J. Brewer, *The Sinews of Power: War, Money and the English State, 1688–1783* (London, 1989), p. xiii.
2 L. Colley, 'Whose Nation ? Class and National Consciousness in Britain, 1750–1870', *Past and Present*, 113 (1986), pp. 100–1.
3 Brewer, *Sinews of Power*; W. Kennedy, *English Taxation, 1640–1799* (London, 1913); P.K. O'Brien, 'The Political Economy of English Taxation, 1660–1815', *Economic History Review*, 2nd series, xli (1988); P.K. O'Brien, *Power with Profit: The State and the Economy, 1688–1815* (London University Inaugural Lecture, 1991); J.V. Beckett and M. Turner, 'Taxation and Economic Growth in eighteenth-century England', *Econ. Hist. Rev.*, 2nd series, xliii (1990).

Ambivalences of English Identity in the Eighteenth Century

sense of identity with the nation.

As Linda Colley has suggested, however, this nation was Britain (or perhaps England-as-Britain). Growing English interest, and even sympathy, was beginning to be evinced by the end of the century in the Welsh and Scottish dimensions. Collections of Celtic ballads were published and, among the middle and upper classes, tourist visits to countries previously considered remote, barbarous and inhospitable were beginning to be made. Such visits were also made to the English Lake District, about which more or less identical reservations had been held. It is worth asking to what extent the greater knowledge about Britain as an entity, fostered by 1800 in the production of better maps, new topographical guides and accounts and (crucially) improved road communications, was a process of discovery about the northern and western Highland regions by English folk usually resident in the Lowlands.[1]

Romantic concerns about the literature and customs of the Celtic nations did not, however, extend to the nurturing of their separate languages. Indeed, as foreign observers noted, linguistic uniformity was an important element in their perception of the overall coherence of Britain. Use of a single language which could be understood by roughly five million people at the beginning of the eighteenth century and double that number by the end was a major exception to the European pattern. Even in a large and established nation like France, for example, well into the second half of the nineteenth century, French was a second language for about half of the population if accessible at all. The English, and increasingly the Scots and Welsh, spoke in different dialects and with different accents but they were comprehensible to one another. The use of language was often a social weapon; it was rarely a barrier to communication.[2]

Furthermore, the pressure for Scots and Welsh — particularly those with careers to make and English contacts to develop — to conform became intense. The Anglo-Welsh Acts of Union of 1536 and 1543 had proscribed Welsh as an official medium of communication and the middle and upper classes increasingly abandoned it. The process seems to have quickened during the eighteenth century and, by the early nineteenth century, although perhaps 60 per cent of ordinary folk still spoke Welsh (far more in North Wales), more than half of these were bilingual.

There was considerable debate among visitors to Lowland Scotland about

---

1 Colley, 'Class and National Consciousness in Britain', pp. 104, 110−12. This theme of national identity enhanced during war is further developed in L. Colley, *Britons: Forging the Nation, 1707−1837* (New Haven and London, 1992), especially pp. 101−45, and 283−375.
2 Robbins, *Nineteenth-Century Britain*, pp. 31−45.

whether their differences of usage suggested that 'Scots' should be considered a dialect or a separate language. Better educated Scots were encouraged to conform to anglicised usage; as Lord Cockburn put it early in the nineteenth century, 'Our mere speech was doomed to recede ... before the foreign wave and it was natural for a young man to anticipate what was coming.'[1] By contrast, and despite (or perhaps because of) English attacks on the Highlands after Culloden, Gaelic remained tenacious among the lower classes there until the middle of the nineteenth century. It was not, however, a language much used by those of political or social substance.

Among several European influences on this heightened national awareness, the Romantic movement at the end of the century was encouraging exploration of nature in its wilder — and purer — manifestations. Lower down the social scale, long-distance movement in search of jobs and new opportunities accelerated the process of knowledge about the nation as a whole, although, of course, migration to London had been a feature of mobility for far longer.[2]

The growing importance of the press also heightened a sense of national awareness. Local newspapers began to grow in numbers early in the eighteenth century. In 1723 twenty-four provincial newspapers were being published.[3] This had risen to forty-one by 1745 and even more rapid expansion followed in the second half of the century. The frequent wars of the century undoubtedly increased sales and, thus, titles. Readers were eager to learn about alliances, strategy and, especially, deeds of heroism. By 1800, few towns of any size were without their own newspaper and several had more than one. Eighteenth-century local newspapers were filled to a much greater degree than are their twentieth-century counterparts with news and comment about war, government and national politics. The increase in knowledge about Britain through newspapers is of prime importance to a growing sense of identity.

It may, of course, be asked to what proportion of the population such

---

1 *Ibid.*, pp. 38–9.
2 P.J. Corfield, *The Impact of English Towns, 1700–1800* (Oxford, 1982), pp. 68–70; M.J. Daunton, 'Towns and Economic Growth in Eighteenth-Century England', in *Towns in Societies*, ed. P. Abrams and E.A. Wrigley (Cambridge, 1978); C.W. Chalklin and M.A. Havinden, *Rural Change and Urban Growth, 1500–1800: Essays in English Regional History* (London, 1974); *Migration and Society in Early-Modern England*, ed. P. Clark and D. Souden (London, 1987); I.D. Whyte, 'Migration in Early Modern Scotland and England', in *Migrants, Emigrants and Immigrants*, ed. C.G. Pooley and I.D. Whyte (London, 1991).
3 G.A. Cranfield, *The Development of the Provincial Newspaper, 1700–60* (Oxford, 1962); G.A. Cranfield, 'The London Evening Post, 1727–44: A Study in the Development of the Political Press', *Historical Journal*, vi (1963).

literate communication was accessible. The question is unanswerable with precision, but knowledge of national events was certainly widely available, and not just among the upper and middle ranks of society. Coffee-houses, as is well known, were an increasingly fashionable means of discussing events, and London coffee-house society was rapidly emulated in the provinces, particularly in the administrative and legal centres and in spa towns such as Bath and Buxton.[1]

What coffee-houses did for the well-off, public houses increasingly did for the craftsmen, small master manufacturers, skilled workers and even apprentices. Extensive politicisation of urban Britain, once considered to have happened outside London only at the very end of the century under the impact of the French Revolution, is now known to have occurred in the provinces from the 1730s and to have embraced a wider proportion of the total population. Public houses were valuable meeting places for political discussion. Newspaper articles castigating Walpole in the 1730s over his excise scheme, the Pelhams' ineffective war strategy in 1756, Bute's leadership in the early 1760s, or Grenville's American policy could be read out loud for the benefit of those with insufficient literacy and to form the basis of discussion.[2]

During the 1790s, of course, the authorities kept a careful watch on pubs where radical 'Jacobins and atheists' consorted to celebrate the Rights of Man and to argue for increased political representation. In Britain by the end of the eighteenth century, political awareness was widespread and well established. It would be quite wrong to suggest that the national consciousness which was part of this burgeoning political culture was restricted even to that diverse and extended elite which was yet another distinguishing feature of eighteenth-century British society.[3]

*

The evidence above seems clearly to support Dr Sharpe's contention that 'By 1760, despite the persistence of localism, a shift had occurred towards a sense of national consciousness.'[4] By the middle of the eighteenth century,

---

1   Corfield, *Impact of English Towns*; P. Borsay, 'The English Urban Renaissance: The Development of Provincial Urban Culture, c.1680−c.1760', *Social History*, v (1977); P. Borsay, *The English Urban Renaissance: Culture and Society in the Provincial Town, 1660−1760* (Oxford, 1989); P. Borsay, *The Eighteenth-Century Town: A Reader in English Urban History, 1688−1820* (London, 1990).
2   Rogers, *Whigs and the Cities*, especially pp. 347−89.
3   C. Emsley, *British Society and the French Wars, 1793−1815* (London, 1979); J. Stevenson, 'Popular Radicalism and Popular Protest', in *Britain and the French Revolution, 1789−1815*, ed. H.T. Dickinson (London, 1989).
4   J. Sharpe, *Early Modern England: A Social History* (London, 1987), p. 120.

if not earlier, the nation was certainly richer and probably more self-confident and self-aware than any other in Europe. It was also linguistically and culturally more unified and, further down the social scale, more knowledgeable about itself and its political processes than any other in Europe.

One crucial caveat must be entered, however, and one question remains. The caveat concerns politics. National awareness in no way implied consensus. Bitter political and ideological battles raged throughout the century. The old orthodoxies about eighteenth-century political history now seem little more than travesties. Broadly speaking, the traditional view was as follows. The feuding between Whig and Tory political elites which characterised the reign of Queen Anne (1702–14) was followed by a long period of 'oligarchy' in which corrupt, and increasingly complacent, Whig politicians ruled England much as they wished, enmeshing Tory opponents and ignorant Hanoverian monarchs alike in intricate exclusivist intrigues. This oligarchy broke up in the reign of George III (1760–1820). However, although issues such as the American colonies, religious toleration and, especially, the French Revolution, were divisive they were so substantially among the great landowners, rather than across social divisions. Landowners continued to exercise control, if no longer by the 1790s effortlessly then certainly successfully, at least until the passage of the Great Reform Act in 1832.[1] Meanwhile the independent powers of the monarchy, formally reduced by the Revolution Settlement of 1689 and practically much more so by the Whigs after 1714, continued to decline.

The ways in which this picture needs to be modified in the light of recent scholarship tells us much about the nature of national identity. At its simplest, political awareness was by no means so socially exclusive as the oligarchical model implies. Dr Rogers's work has indicated the extent to which the growing political sophistication of the urban commercial classes, especially in London, developed as a political factor with which the governing elite had to deal. The City of London became, in Rogers's words, 'the critical source and springboard for nation-wide campaigns' against what was seen as the increasingly extensive powers being taken by the Whig landowners and, interestingly, their leading commercial allies. Thus the role taken by the City from the 1730s was increasingly that of the spokesman for 'English liberties' against excessive taxation and monopolising tendencies in

---

[1] J.V. Beckett, *The Aristocracy in England, 1660–1914* (Oxford, 1986), pp. 436–56. See also J.C.D. Clark, *English Society, 1688–1832* (Cambridge, 1985); and, for the exercise of political influence by the landowners, J.A. Phillips, *Electoral Behavior in Unreformed England* (Princeton, 1982), and F. O'Gorman, *Voters, Patrons and Parties: The Unreformed Electorate of Hanoverian England, 1734–1832* (Oxford, 1989).

commerce.[1]

The City, therefore, spoke for the 'middling' sort and increasingly adopted attitudes which might be seen as a natural extension of the concerns of Tories in the reign of Queen Anne. Hanoverian politics brought a different focus of attention, of course, but the City increasingly adopted the role of spokesman for independence from oppressive government and guardian of the liberties of Englishmen.

In this, they were following and developing the ideas of Henry St John, Viscount Bolingbroke, who tried to fashion an effective principled opposition to Walpole in the 1720s and 1730s on the basis of eliding the old distinctions between Whig and Tory and asserting that the government of England had fallen into the hands of a corrupt faction.[2] This line of argument appealed to a large number of non-Jacobite Tories since it could deflect direct criticism from the crown, for them the unquestioned symbol of all temporal authority. On this construction, the first Hanoverian monarchs, George I and George II, had been duped by Walpole and his gang into conceding rights which were now used to destroy the liberties of the people. In Bolingbroke's words, these 'mercenary and abandoned wretches ... have dared to lead for a dependence of the parliament on the crown; not for the dependence of the several parts of the government on one another'. 'The greatest good of a people is their liberty.'[3]

On Bolingbroke's analysis, this liberty derived from the Glorious Revolution which had defined, albeit negatively, the powers of the crown in relationship to parliament. From 1689, for example, the monarch could not constitutionally govern without parliament, war could not be levied, or a standing army maintained, 'without consent of parliament'. Bolingbroke took the logic of this position an important step further. The monarch could no longer *ipso facto* symbolise the nation and it became possible to argue that Englishmen could owe a higher allegiance to their country than to an individual monarch. Thus, in contradistinction to the absolutist monarchy as nation ('L'Etat, c'est moi', as Louis XIV famously had it), Bolingbroke urged that 'the limitations on a crown ought to be carried as far as it is necessary to secure the liberties of a people'.[4]

Opposition politics asserted the constitutional propriety of their desperate struggles on behalf of those liberties of Englishmen which were endangered

---

1 Rogers, *Whigs and the Cities*, p. 6.
2 H.T. Dickinson, *Bolingbroke* (London, 1970); Dickinson, *Liberty and Property*, pp. 163–92.
3 *Ibid.*, p. 175.
4 Viscount Bolingbroke, *The Idea of a Patriot King*, quoted in J.H. Shennan, 'The Rise of Patriotism in 18th-century Europe', *History of European Ideas*, xiii (1991), p. 693.

not by an illegitimate monarch but by a corrupt Court. Government actions were scrutinised by libertarian yardsticks, many of which were derived from those historical, or mythical, precedents referred to above. Thus, the Salt Tax of 1732 and the excise proposals which gave Walpole so much anxiety in 1733−4, and from which arguably his position never entirely recovered, were 'portrayed as a massive assault upon English liberties as much as impositions upon the productive classes that brought dubious benefits to landed proprietors'. When the excise was withdrawn, there were massed celebrations in at least twenty towns. In Newcastle upon Tyne, the merchants of the city gathered to light candles in celebration of the 'WORTHY PATRIOTS who for the LIBERTY of their COUNTRY and the GOOD of TRADE, made so glorious a STAND against the Increase of Excise Laws'.[1]

Again and again government taxation was presented as ruinous to the interests of ordinary Englishmen. This theme produced variations to be embroidered upon for upwards of a century.[2] As late as the middle of the nineteenth century, as Dr Taylor's work has shown, John Bull iconography was much more prominently displayed in representations against the burdens of taxation than on any other cause. The freeborn Englishman, it almost seemed, should always resist paying taxes since these were invariably used to line the pockets of the governors and to shore up corrupt government.[3]

Simplified populist rhetoric of this sort provided a link between 'country Tories' of the City of London in the 1730s and 1740s and democratic radicals in the late eighteenth and early nineteenth centuries. For William Cobbett in the 1820s, as for Viscount Bolingbroke in the 1730s or the spokesman of the City of London, William Beckford, in the 1750s, the cause of the people's miseries was misgovernment, and this misgovernment was only perpetuated by corruption.[4] It was patriotic to alert the people to the threat from government; thus the language of patriotism was as easily appropriated by the left of the political spectrum (in conventional twentieth-century terms) as by the right.

1   Rogers, *Whigs and the Cities*, p. 373.
2   The low-taxation, liberty and patriotism theme has served the British Conservative Party well throughout the 20th century. The Conservatives find it profitable to castigate their opponents as parties of 'high taxation': high taxes impose heavy burdens on the people, thus sapping their energies and capacity for individual initiative. This strategy was potently deployed as recently as March-April 1992, during the general election campaign; for a particularly crude, and vigorous, example of its deployment, see the strongly pro-Conservative *Daily Mail*, 7 April 1992, p. 1.
3   Taylor, 'John Bull and the Iconography of Public Opinion'.
4   M. Peters, *Pitt and Popularity: The Patriot Minister and London Opinion during the Seven Years War* (Oxford, 1980); D. Green, *Great Cobbett: Noblest Agitator* (Oxford, 1985).

Ambivalences of English Identity in the Eighteenth Century

English patriotism appealed to a sense of right: to forms, beliefs and attitudes assumed to lie in the ancient past and from which all liberties and right order derived. In the eighteenth century, of course, as Bolingbroke saw, a more immediate, and precise, focus presented itself in the Glorious Revolution of 1688−9. Not surprisingly, much political debate turned on which groups were the more valid interpreters of the constitution which was supposed to guarantee the liberties of Englishmen.

Patriotic argument and rhetoric was not exclusively concerned with liberty, with maintaining the purity of the constitution and with distrust of the executive. The patriots of the mid-eighteenth century were also concerned with the proper role of England abroad, and with the supremacy of the Anglican Church. London merchants trading with the Americas were to the fore in criticising Walpole in the 1730s for not adopting a more aggressive foreign policy and for neglecting the interests of the empire. Anti-French attitudes neatly linked old anti-Catholic prejudices and newer commercial concerns.

The other patriotic stick with which to beat an allegedly corrupt government was found in its devotion to the interests of Hanover over those of England. William Pitt the Elder came to prominence as an ally of the London opposition in his attacks on 'Hanoverianism'.[1] The government was taxing the nation in order to pay subsidies to continental allies and for expensive and fruitless campaigning. Patriots embraced a 'blue water' policy which, once again, linked the prospects of commercial advantage with the historic strength of England as a maritime nation, and recalled its famous heroes such as Frobisher and Drake.

The supremacy of the Church of England was an issue for which the seventeenth-century royalists had fought hard. Catholicism was the issue which had brought about the downfall of James II. Tories in the reign of Queen Anne furiously upheld the interests of the Church against the threat from dissent, and made much political capital from the increasingly important links between Whiggery and nonconformity.[2] Mid-eighteenth-century patriots argued that in the strength of the Church of England lay the security of the nation. This was a less sensitive, and contentious, issue after a couple of generations of Whig control of ecclesiastical patronage, which saw the appointment of a number of low-church bishops and the increasing

---

1 Rogers, *Whigs and the Cities*; P.D. Brown, *William Pitt, Earl of Chatham* (London, 1978).
2 G. Holmes, *British Politics in the Age of Anne* (2nd edn, London, 1987), especially pp. xix−xii, 51−115; G. Holmes, *The Trial of Dr. Sacheverell* (London, 1973); *The Divided Society: Party Conflict in England, 1694−1716*, ed. G. Holmes and W.A. Speck (London, 1967).

influence of erastianism.[1] Nevertheless, attacks on church supremacy still roused 'country' interests and could cause embarrassment for the Whig establishment. Walpole ran into severe difficulties over proposed relief for Quakers for vexatious prosecution for non-payment of tithes due to the Church in 1736. The Jewish Naturalisation Bill of 1753 ran into heavy criticism orchestrated from London and had to be withdrawn by a Whig government fearful of heavy reprisals in the forthcoming election of 1754.[2] The London opposition, as so often, combined 'English' sentiment with commercial interest. The target, of course, was the increasing Jewish influence in high finance and the links between finance and the Whig government of Henry Pelham, but seeing Jewish naturalisation as an oblique attack on the integrity of Christianity was an acceptable way to deflect charges of bigotry. The ability of opposition politicians to rouse popular hostility to any measures which might seem to weaken the Church goes a long way towards explaining why measures to remove political disabilities from Dissenters had to wait until the end of the third decade of the nineteenth century.

The political figure most readily associated with 'patriotic' values was the Elder Pitt, whose victories in the Seven Years War were an important staging post in the identification of national pride and status. Significantly, the early Hanoverian monarchs were not accorded much popular respect, still less veneration. Nor was George III early in his reign. The Bute episode and the series of blunders over the American colonies alike served to render him a figure of popular suspicion, if not downright hostility. In the second half of George III's reign, however, and especially after his famous victory over the 'infamous' Fox-North Coalition at the end of 1783 which led to the Younger Pitt's becoming prime minister, the king began to emerge as a national symbol to be venerated and celebrated.

This process has been charted by Linda Colley, who sees in what she calls 'the apotheosis of George III' a new dimension to Englishness.[3] Increased wealth and the need for an appropriate outlet to demonstrate civic, as well as national, pride were one element in this. Growing expertise at channelling in 'patriotic' directions major events which threatened to career riotously out of control is another. However, the outbreak of war against

1 N. Sykes, *Church and State in England in the Eighteenth Century* (Cambridge, 1934); N. Sykes, *From Sheldon to Secker: Aspects of English Church History, 1660–1768* (Cambridge, 1959), chapter 6; G.F.A. Best, *Temporal Pillars: The Queen Anne's Bounty, the Ecclesiastical Commissioners and the Church of England* (Cambridge, 1964).
2 Rogers, *Whigs and the Cities*, pp. 89–93, G. A. Cranfield, 'The London Evening Post and the Jew Bill of 1753', *Historical Journal*, viii (1965).
3 L. Colley, 'The Apotheosis of George III: Loyalty, Royalty and the British Nation, 1760–1820', *Past and Present*, 102 (1984).

Ambivalences of English Identity in the Eighteenth Century

Revolutionary France in 1793 appears to have been decisive. By that time, George had been on the throne for thirty-three years, considerably outliving all of his earlier ministers. He was therefore an appropriate symbol. France was also the national enemy. After 1793, however, George could stand as a symbolic defender of the old order and civilised values against the dangerous, and unchristian, ethic of the French Revolution.[1] George III was a Christian king but, for nationalist propaganda purposes, he was a constitutional monarch. Thus a dynasty, which for many 'patriots' during the course of the eighteenth century represented unwise European entanglements, undue Court influence and a repression of the people's liberties, came in the person of the ageing, and by 1809 mentally unstable, person of George III to symbolise the nation.

It was a curious, if not entirely irrational, rite of passage. Opposition to the values of the French Revolution, and to the threat from radicals within Britain, was the prime unifying force among propertied Englishmen by the end of the eighteenth century. Englishmen may not have known what they were for, but they were well aware of what they were against.

Finally, there is the question of 'identity'. The reader will be well aware that, although national identity has been the central feature of these speculations, it has not always been clear whether this identity properly relates to England or to Britain. The ambivalence is intentional since it reflected contemporary uncertainty. The national pride stimulated by economic growth and increasingly impressive achievements on the world stage was, for the most part, British, although the extent to which Scots and Welsh would have welcomed the often unconscious incorporation is unclear. The imperial glosses of the last years of the eighteenth century emphasised Britain, but to a surprising degree did so within a southern-English frame of reference. Expressions of national identity which depended upon historical reconstruction and older cultural reference are much more likely to be specifically 'English'.

Patriotism, although it was effectively used as a buttress to national resistance against the French at the end of the century, was not a government preserve; nor did it invariably have anti-representational ideological overtones.[2] Though national identity was making increasingly substantial

---

1 *Ibid.*, pp. 108–10; R.R. Dozier, *For King, Constitution and Country: The English Loyalists and the French Revolution* (Lexington, 1983); A. Booth, 'Popular Loyalism and Public Violence in the North-West of England, 1790–1800', *Social History*, viii (1983); W. Stafford, 'Religion and the Doctrine of Nationalism in England at the time of the French Revolution and the Napoleonic Wars', in *Religion and National Identity*, ed. S. Mews (Oxford, 1982).
2 Taylor, 'John Bull and the Iconography of Public Opinion'; H. Cunningham, 'The Language of Patriotism, 1750–1914', *History Workshop Journal*, xii (1981).

inroads into 'localism' with its emphasis on social leadership by gentry and by the Anglican clergyman, local interests remained important. For many MPs, at least until 1832, 'independence' remained the paramount virtue. They appeared at Westminster specifically to represent local interests rather than to support party causes.[1]

That Britain was a nation with a sense of identity by the end of the eighteenth century is certain. That identity was focused on a successful commercial nation, loyalty to which was channelled through a 'constitutional' monarchy. Whether a separate sense of 'English' national identity existed, as opposed to a series of local perspectives and cultural concerns, is much less clear. A bold attempt to encapsulate England as an *Ancien Régime* 'Confessional' state, with the Church of England at its core, has recently been made, but has not found widespread acceptance.[2] It is difficult to suggest any alternative, and distinctive, national identifier. It is not tidy or heroic, but it may not be entirely inappropriate to suggest that 'Englishness' looks backward while dominant 'Britishness' (albeit with a strong English cultural dominance) anticipates the Victorian age of industry, empire and profit.

---

1 The role of 'independency' in parliament is discussed in most of the political histories of the period. See, particularly, J.B. Owen, *The Eighteenth Century* (London, 1974), pp. 94–122, 277–94; W.A. Speck, *Stability and Strife, 1714–60* (London, 1977); I.R. Christie, *Wars and Revolutions, 1760–1815* (London, 1982); P. Langford, *A Polite and Commercial People, 1727–83* (Oxford, 1989); B. W. Hill, *British Parliamentary Parties, 1742–1832* (London, 1985); N. Gash, 'The English Constitution in the Age of the American Revolution', in N. Gash, *Pillars of Government* (London, 1986). For an interpretation which places particular stress on the stability and conservatism of politics and society in the 18th century, see Clark, *English Society 1688–1832*.

2 J.C.D. Clark, 'England's *Ancien Régime* as a Confessional State', *Albion*, xxi (1989), is a development, with particular reference to the position of the Church of England, of his thesis in *English Society 1688–1832*. For Clark's many critics, it is perhaps most useful to refer to J. Innes, 'Jonathan Clark, Social History and England's *Ancien Régime*', *Past and Present*, 115 (1987), not least for its extensive bibliography of the controversy.

Patriotic Perceptions: Denmark and Sweden, 1450–1850

Jens Rahbek Rasmussen

In 1671, eleven years after absolutism had been introduced in Denmark-Norway, the first anointing of a Danish king took place at Frederiksborg Castle — a ritual repeated at every accession to the throne until 1840. It was an opportunity not to be missed by Danish poets, most of them clergymen hoping for promotion to more lucrative posts should the king approve of their poetic efforts. With the exception of *Hosiannah* by Thomas Kingo, the greatest poet of the baroque age (and, incidentally, of Scottish descent), most of these servile outpourings are by now deservedly forgotten; but one contribution, that by Henrik Gerner, will repay consideration in the present context, though less for its literary merits than because it throws an interesting light on our subject of Danish-Swedish relations.[1]

After a Latin introduction, Gerner has the various lands which belonged, or had belonged, to the Danish king step forward to pay homage. So Denmark, Norway, and Iceland, all indisputably parts of the Danish realm when Gerner wrote, are followed by two more surprising contributors: Sweden, independent since 1523, and England, which had briefly been part of King Canute's North Sea empire in the eleventh century. From a formal point of view, the latter is of considerable interest, as the Oxford-educated Gerner showed off by writing it in English.[2] Sweden is less exotic in that

---

1 Both Kingo's and Gerner's poems can be found in the excellent anthology *Dansk Barokdigtning*, ed. E. Sønderholm (Copenhagen, 1969–70), i, pp. 281–6; ii, pp. 156–71.
2 Whereas every single professor at the University of Copenhagen in the 16th and 17th centuries is known to have written Latin poetry (see H.P. Schepelern's contribution to *Latinen i Norden, 1500–1700* [Copenhagen, 1977], p. 16), English verse was a rarity indeed. This may perhaps justify a quote, though Dr Johnson's remark about women preachers may come to mind.

What could yet *Denmarck* better chuse?	That she shall never headlesse stand,
How could she make a better use?	Nor want a King within her land,
of which She last has heir'd?	Nor without Ruler be.
She gave her to your *Father* selfe	*Her Kings* are crowned all one day,
For lesser years agoe then twelve	Anoynted onely is the way,
& what himselfe desir'd;	that makes them ever free
But she got Satisfaction	From profane hands & Tyrants mindes
In gaining Kings extraction,	That makes them Stand for Stormy windes
For *Soueraignitie*.	With god et men agree.

she, like Norway and Iceland, speaks Danish (though contemporaries would have appreciated that the metre was taken from a well-known Swedish song). The message however is interesting. Addressing the Danish king as a neighbour and a brother, she expresses her hope that in future the two countries may live in peaceful co-existence; if only they cooperate in mutual trust, no enemy can possibly harm or defeat them:

> Ret Aldrig skal nogen os skade
> Hvormeget de monne os hade;
> Naar vi vende Rygge
> Med trygge
> Til hin anden fast
> Uden Svig og Last
> Baade Skib oc Mast
> Staar med anden brast
> Ingen skal os tvinge
> Beringe
> Fiende hver for Borde skal springe.[1]

Given the historical situation in general and Gerner's personal experience in particular, this is truly extraordinary. For in 1671 Denmark and Sweden had been bitter enemies for generations, and the latest clash between the two rivals had very nearly cost Denmark its political existence, and Gerner his life.[2] But it does reveal the curious ambivalence in the relations between Denmark and Sweden for almost four hundred years: the two nations were *arvefjender*, hereditary enemies, but also *broderfolk*, sister nations. This can be seen, and most often is, as a chronological sequence in which political

---

1   This defies translation, but English readers may be interested to know that it is remarkably similar, in tone and expression, to Daniel Defoe's praise of the Union of 1707; see *The Faber Book of English History in Verse*, ed. K. Baker (2nd edn, London, 1989), p. 235.

2   In 1657 Sweden, in response to a Danish declaration of war, launched a surprise invasion of Denmark across the frozen Belts. In the Peace of Roskilde (1658) Denmark ceded Skåne (Scania), Halland and Blekinge (in what is now southern Sweden), the island of Bornholm, and parts of Norway. In a new war, Sweden's attack on Copenhagen in February 1659 was repelled, and great power interests ensured the *status quo*, more or less, in the Peace of Copenhagen (1660). But the Scanian provinces remained Swedish, and attempts to regain them (in the 1670s and the 1710s — see the following note) failed. In 1659 a resistance movement operating in North Zealand hit upon the daring idea of trying to take Kronborg, then in Swedish hands. The plan involved a Colonel Hutchinson, and Gerner came in handy as an interpreter. But the plan was betrayed, and the participants were caught and tortured; one was executed. Gerner was sentenced to death, but was reprieved and exchanged for a Swedish officer in Danish captivity.

Denmark and Sweden, 1450–1850

conflict gave way to peaceful cooperation; but I shall try to show that the two attitudes also co-existed in the centuries dominated by fratricidal wars. In 1523 Sweden broke away from the Union of Kalmar, which since 1397 had united, under Danish monarchs, the kingdoms of Denmark, Norway, and Sweden (with Finland). On four earlier occasions the Union had been patched together again, but this time the breach proved final; the enormity of the Bloodbath of Stockholm in 1520, in which the Danish King Christian II had some eighty Swedish bishops and nobles executed, precluded reconciliation. Sweden emerged as an independent monarchy under Gustav Vasa, and three centuries of rivalry began between Sweden and Denmark-Norway involving no fewer than eleven separate wars.[1]

It is a moot point whether the armed conflicts before 1523 should be seen as precursors of the later national wars, though neither early modern propaganda nor later nationalist historiography had any doubt that they should. In almost all cases 'Swedish' nobles and yeomen could be found on the 'Danish', that is the pro-Union, side, and parts of the aristocracy clearly adopted a Scandinavian rather than a national perspective. But in looking at the creation, persistence and eventual decline of Danophobia (and Swedophobia), the medieval conflicts are indeed relevant. For it was precisely during these wars that the anti-Union forces in Sweden succeeded in whipping up national prejudice against the Danes, thus creating an image which was to stay in the Swedish mind for centuries. Denmark followed suit, but there is no doubt as to where the initiative lay.

One of the chapters in Vilhelm Moberg's *A History of the Swedish People* is aptly called 'How the Swedes learned to hate Danes' ('Hur danskarhadet uppstod i Sverige').[2] Drawing on extensive research by Swedish scholars, Moberg shows that the loathing and hatred felt by many, if not all, Swedes toward the Danes was anything but spontaneous. Once established, it may have been kept alive by the horrible experience of the recurrent wars; but that is not how it began. The origins lay in a deliberate

1 These were: the Scandinavian Seven Years War (1563–70), the War of Kalmar (1611–13), the Torstensson War (1643–5), the First and Second Carl Gustav Wars (1657–60), the Scanian War (1675–9), the Great Northern War (1700, 1709–20), and three minor conflicts in 1788, 1808–9, and 1813. (Several of the wars have different names in Sweden and Norway.) A popular survey of the Danish-Swedish conflicts, L. Lindeberg, *Arvefjenden* (Copenhagen, 1985), is superficial but comprehensive, often entertaining and worth consulting for the lavish illustrations.
2 V. Moberg, *A History of the Swedish People*, translated by P.B. Austin (London, 1973). A prolific writer, Moberg is perhaps best known for *Utvandrarne* (*The Emigrants*), a saga about a Swedish family emigrating to America in the 1860s, later made into both a movie and a TV series directed by Jan Troell and starring Max von Sydow and Liv Ullman. The two volumes giving his radical-populist version of his country's history up to the mid-16th century sold more than 300,000 copies in Sweden.

and systematic effort by the various political leaders to inculcate hatred of the Danes into the Swedish people. Songs, ballads and chronicles written in simple, powerful rhymes were mass-produced in the chancery of the Swedish regents (*riksföreståndare*) and kings, and spread by itinerant singers to towns and villages. Like the verse, the message conveyed was unsubtle but effective: the Danes (usually called *jutar*, that is, Jutlanders) were portrayed as cruel, greedy, untrustworthy cowards with a ridiculous language and strange eating habits. Unfortunately they were also smooth-tongued and cunning, and made up for their obvious deficiencies in courage and warfare by being sly negotiators. This image was first established around 1450 by, for example, *Gotlandsvisan*, which compared the Danes to scorpions:

> The scorpion useth to play
> embraceth with his mouth alway;
> with his tail stingeth;
> so do the Danes
> when they parley.[1]

From then on the same image is taken up again and again, and new negative features are added; thus, *Karlskrönikan* accuses the Danes of habitually and indiscriminately killing women, children and invalids. Sweden's last Catholic archbishop, Johannes Magnus, wrote a history of Sweden in Latin which spread this 'black legend' to the whole of Europe, not least through a powerful speech attributed to a former archbishop, Hemming Gad. After a fairly complete inventory of Danish faults, shortcomings and character blemishes, Gad concludes: 'With few exceptions all the Danes and their kings have been such cruel tyrants and bloodthirsty persecutors of all pious folk and good people that two drops of milk cannot be more like to each other than they are like Caligula, Nero, Heliogabalus, Pharaoh and other tyrants who in human form have exercised bestial cruelties.'[2]

It is interesting to note that Magnus's work (published posthumously in 1554 by his brother Olaus) was written in Rome, where the author had found exile after the reformation in Sweden. National interest transcended religious differences, and as an ideology of integration Danophobia was clearly useful to the new Swedish monarchy. Indeed, Gustav Vasa's chancery continued the production of anti-Danish ballads. One of them,

---

1 Moberg, *History of the Swedish People*, ii, p. 65. For the use of *jutar*, see N. Ahnlund, *Svenskt och nordiskt från skilda tider* (Stockholm, 1943), pp. 209–11.
2 The quote is from *Denmark: Praise & Protest*, ed. A.M. Williams (Copenhagen, 1969), p. 8; see now K. Johannesson, *The Renaissance of the Goths in Sixteenth-Century Sweden: Johannes and Olaus Magnus as Politicians and Historians* (Berkeley, 1991).

Dalavisan, celebrated the prowess and courage of the *Dalecarlians* (that is, the men from the province of Dalarna where Gustav's national revolt began). It was, however, written around 1530, at a time when, regrettably, they were demonstrating these admirable qualities not in fighting the Danes, but in protest against the centralising monarchy and its Church. Obviously the ballad was meant to flatter them and remind them of their role in getting rid of the Danish oppressors. It did not work. The rebellion spread from Dalarna to other provinces, and in 1542−3 the so-called Dacke Revolt swept Sweden. Reflecting social as well as religious discontent, it was brutally put down by Gustav Vasa — with help from the Danish king, Christian III. The two kings were united in their desire for political stability and in their fear of the former king of Denmark and Sweden, Christian II. In their lifetime this superseded national enmity and their mutual suspicion.[1]

But in 1563 the first major war broke out, followed by several others until 1720. Why these wars were fought need not detain us here. Suffice it to say that both countries tended to use as justification their fear of being encircled or 'strangled' by the other. Sweden feared that Denmark and Russia would prevent them from getting out of the Baltic; Denmark that alliances between Sweden and the house of Gottorp (for centuries in partial control of Holstein) would expose them to a two-pronged attack. But by 1720 it was clear that the great powers would not allow the Scandinavian *status quo* to be challenged by either country (three later minor confrontations were due to Denmark and Sweden backing opposing European alliances).[2]

Of course the Danes engaged in propaganda as well, and their stereotype of the neighbour and enemy will be strangely familiar: the Swede could not be trusted, habitually broke pledges, attacked without warning, committed all kinds of war crimes, and so forth, whereas the Dane was noble, upright and modest, fighting only according to the rules and for good patriotic reasons. The methods were also largely the same. Pamphlets and other writings made as well as refuted accusations, often in painstaking and slightly ridiculous detail; thus in 1497 King Hans obtained a sworn statement from the *landsting* of Funen, denying a Swedish claim that the impoverished Danish peasants had to let women pull the plough for lack of oxen and

---

[1] See Moberg, *History of the Swedish People*, ii, pp. 174 ff., 219 ff., and M. Roberts, *The Early Vasas* (Cambridge, 1968), index under 'Dacke' and 'Dalarna'.

[2] A useful survey of Scandinavian history can be found in *Encyclopaedia Britannica*, 15th edn, s.v. 'Scandinavia, History of'. (Later editions have separate entries for the individual countries.) Chapters 1 and 14 in H.A. Barton's excellent *Scandinavia in the Revolutionary Era, 1760−1815* (Minneapolis, 1986) may also be helpful. M. Roberts, *The Swedish Imperial Experience, 1560−1718* (Cambridge, 1979), evaluates various interpretations of Swedish expansion and the struggle for *dominium maris Baltici*.

horses. And, as in Sweden, popular ballads were seen as a useful weapon: in his 1520 campaign, Christian II brought with him 'official' poets who used written accounts of the campaign as a basis for versified propaganda. During the Seven Years War 'all kinds of ballads were written and published, as usually happens', according to Anders Sørensen Vedel's introduction to his ballad collection, *Hundredvisebogen* (1591); and later wars were no exception. How many of these ballads were actually commissioned we do not know, but not all of them were as spontaneous as the reader or listener was led to believe. 'A soldier's ballad of Kalmar' (1612), for example, was hardly that, given that its motto 'He writes best of war who participates' comes from the Greek historian Polybius, not a likely favourite among professional soldiers.[1]

But, arguably, the Danish effort pales in comparison with the Swedish. Admittedly the subject has been more or less ignored by Danish historians, but this in itself needs explanation. It would seem that the Swedish propaganda was actually shriller, and that there was much more of it; Denmark never quite matched the enemy stereotypes in *Karlskrönikan*, nor for that matter the massive self-glorification of Olof Rudbeck's *Atlantica*.[2] Sweden seems to have suffered from an inferiority complex which the rise to great power status did little to lessen: it was all very well to create a glorious Gothic past stretching back to the sons of Noah, but filled with rude and uncouth warriors as it was, it became something of a liability in a Europe of increasingly refined civilisation.[3]

Be that as it may, we need to ask how far this propaganda influenced popular perceptions. Broadly speaking it may be said to have targeted three groups: the home front, the population in the provinces fought for (and in), and the international community. Leaving aside reactions abroad, the effect in the provinces of Småland and Skåne, where most of the fighting took place, is likely to have been modest. The local population tried to lie low and to defend their family and property as best they could. They were in a no-win situation where one day they would be forced to give food and money to one army, only to be charged with treason when the other army

---

[1] See K.-I. Hildeman, *Politiska visor från Sveriges senmedeltid* (Stockholm, 1950); J.H. Koudal, 'Klassekamp på vers: Politisk visesang omkring feudalismens krise i Danmark i første halvdel af 1500-tallet', *Modspil*, 3 (1978), and P. Brask in *Dansk Litteraturhistorie*, ii (1984), pp. 450–1.

[2] At least not in Danish. The until recently largely neglected corpus of neo-Latin literature includes several anti-Swedish epics; see K. Skovgaard-Petersen, 'Danish Neo-Latin Epic as Anti-Swedish Propaganda', *Proceedings of the Seventh International Congress of Neo-Latin Studies, Toronto ... 1988* (Binghamton, NY, 1991).

[3] See D. Kirby, 'Imperial Sweden: Image and Self-Image', *History Today*, November 1990, and Roberts, *Swedish Imperial Experience*, pp. 70–5. I hasten to add that nor was Denmark seen as fully civilised by outside observers.

Denmark and Sweden, 1450–1850

moved in the next. We have a moving description of this experience in Sthen Jacobsen's chronicle of the Scanian war — the author himself was caught in the middle, tried to remain neutral in spite of Danish sympathies, and was horrified by the atrocities of war.[1]

On the home front, we have seen how the rebellious Dalecarlians ignored the propaganda in the 1530s, as they were to do again in 1743 (see below). A Danish ballad, 'O Danmark din synd begræd' ('O Denmark, lament thy sin'), from 1645 bewails the Swedish occupation of Jutland, but blames it on human sinfulness in general and on the cowardice of the Danish nobility in particular.[2] These reactions may not have been typical of popular response to the official propaganda effort — no doubt many Swedes actually 'learned to hate Danes', and vice versa — but they do show that it was not necessarily accepted by everyone.

Incidentally, the propaganda which was so massively produced during the actual conflict could become a problem in peacetime. An attack upon a country's honour almost equalled an attack on its frontiers, and could be part of a *casus belli*. Several peace treaties contained clauses banning all sorts of scurrilous writings, or demanding that offending visual presentations of historical scenes be destroyed. A Danish vicar, Jon Jensen Kolding, was taken to court in 1595 when his Latin history of Denmark came to the attention of the Swedes. Among the alleged violations of the 1570 Peace of Stettin were a hostile portrait of Erik XIV, the use of various pasquils, and possibly the fact that Kolding enumerated no fewer than twenty-nine Danish kings to whom the Swedes had had to swear allegiance. The government complied with the request for trial, and Kolding was sentenced to one year's suspension, though he was in fact reinstated after six months. If this was less than draconian — technically he could have been sentenced to death — it still shows that the government felt it had to act on such complaints, at least in certain situations.[3] In 1766, when in a diplomatic move Christian VII's sister married the later Gustav III of Sweden, the Danish government, in an attempt at appeasement, decided to abolish the 'Day of Thanksgiving', February 11th, celebrating the capital's miraculous deliverance from the

---

1 The chronicle was only published much later: Sthen Jacobsen, *Den Nordiske Kriigs Krønicke*, ed. M. Weibull (Copenhagen and Lund, 1897; reprinted 1972).
2 'En vise fra Svenskekrigen 1643–45. Meddelt af Karl Fredstrup', *Danske Magazin*, 5th series, ii (1891).
3 Jon Jensen Kolding, *Daniæ descriptio nova* (Frankfurt-am-Main, 1594); and see the postscript in the new Danish translation by A.A. Lund, *En ny Danmarksbeskrivelse 1594* (Aarhus, 1980). On other occasions it was more lenient. The Peace of Roskilde in 1658 stipulated that Karel von Mander's tapestries at Frederiksborg Castle, depicting the War of Kalmar and the coronation of Christian IV, should be taken down, but in spite of several Swedish representations, they were not.

Swedes in 1659. This was much regretted by Danish patriots who saw it as a useful national holiday, and in fact it remained popular.[1]

But of course the governments could not monitor all expressions of enmity and hostility, even had they wanted to; and visitors abroad often came across examples of blatant defamation. The Swedish theologian Sven Bredberg visited Copenhagen in 1708 and had a friendly enough reception, but in the University Library he happened to see a pictorial description of various Danish-Swedish battles where 'the Swedish actions were mightily belittled' ('the swänska handlingar mächta woro förringade'); and in Stockholm, Mathias Paulsen in 1699 was shown what was effectively a public museum to the Stockholm Bloodbath:

> One can scarcely describe the hatred of the Danes which the Swedes inculcate into their children. They still conserve the room and the window at Stortorget from where King Christian watched so many innocent people and children being killed. In the same room is found his portrait and below that an account of his cruel tyranny, and on holy days, if the weather is agreeable, the common people take their children there, and explain to them in detail what happened then. And the story is then continued in their almanacs that it may always be fresh in their memory, and the common people by such impression may come to hate all the more.[2]

But in spite of these persistent efforts, the feeling of belonging to the same Scandinavian nation surfaced again and again. We shall now take a look at this proto-Scandinavism.

Already around 1540, the Swedish reformer Olaus Petri regretted in his *Swedish Chronicle* the enmity between the two nations. In his view, neither people could claim to be on the side of truth and justice, and neither stood to gain from future conflicts; therefore one ought not to believe the national propaganda emanating from both sides. 'Wherefore little doth it behove the Swedes to laud themselves for all they have won in Denmark, no more behoveth it the Danes to boast of what they have gained in Sweden: great damage and ruin hath befallen both parties.'[3] His wise words did not see print until 1818, though his chronicle is known to have circulated in

---

1 *Dansk Identitetshistorie*, ed. O. Feldbæk (Copenhagen, 1991−2), i, pp. 56, 138.
2 Bredberg, quoted in H. Ilsøe, 'Lærde forbindelser mellem Danmark og Sverige ca. 1660−1720', in *Bøger, biblioteker, mennesker: Et nordisk festskrift tilegnet Torben Nielsen* (Copenhagen, 1988), p. 564; for Paulsen, see Georg Christensen's edition in *Karolinska Förbundets Årsbok* (1923), pp. 215−33, and his article 'Danskes rejser i Sverige', *Samlaren: tidskrift för svensk litteraturhistorisk forskning*, new series, iii (1922).
3 Moberg, *History of the Swedish People*, ii, p. 71.

Denmark and Sweden, 1450—1850

manuscript; but others expressed similar sentiments. In 1688 the Swede Johan Hadorph wrote to his Danish fellow-scholar, Thomas Bartholin, that 'we are one people using the same language, though ruled by different kings';[1] again, this was a private communication, but it is curiously reminiscent of something which Gerner said publicly in 1681 in his versified chronicle of the Scanian war. Here he concluded his description of the battle of Lund (with some 7,000 Danish and 3,000 Swedish casualties) with an 'epitaph' which began:

> Her ligger kecke Mend, hvis' Been oc Blod er blandet
> Iblandt hinanden saa, at ingen siger andet
> End de er aff een Slect de var oc aff een Troe
> Dog kunde de med Fred ey hos hinanden boe.[2]

Contacts during or even immediately after a war, which might be construed as fraternising with the enemy, were carefully avoided.[3] But otherwise communication resumed remarkably quickly, as if nothing had happened. Jacob Bircherod, who was a member of the Danish negotiation team in Stockholm in 1720, wrote a light-hearted account in which he confirmed that both nations regarded the other as utterly false (if children fell through the ice, the Swedes would say that 'the ice is Danish'), but that for his part he had yet to encounter a dishonest Swede. Anders Spole, a professor of astronomy, fought for Sweden in the Scanian war, and his house and observatory were burnt down during the battle of Lund, yet a few years later he was involved in a friendly correspondence with Danish scholars.[4]

Thus from the late seventeenth century, we can observe a kind of literary and cultural Scandinavism coming into existence. But, politically, there was still a long way to go. In 1743, that constitutional curiosity, the Peasants'

---

1 Ilsøe, 'Lærde forbindelser mellem Danmark og Sverige', p. 554; and H. Ilsøe, 'Danskerne og deres fædreland: Holdninger og aspekter ca. 1550—1700', in *Dansk Identitetshistorie*, i.
2 *Dansk Barokdigtning*, ed. Sønderholm, i, p. 205. It translates roughly as:
   Brave men are here interred, their corpses intertwined,
   Their blood and bones so mixed that everyone shall find:
   They were of common stock, to the same God they prayed,
   Yet failed to live in peace. Here are their bodies laid.
3 Ilsøe, 'Danmark og Sverige', p. 562.
4 *Jacob Bircherods Rejse til Stockholm 1720*, ed. G. Christensen (Copenhagen, 1924), pp. 59, 93; Ilsøe, 'Danmark og Sverige', p. 558. In some cases people were almost too quickly off the mark: when the scholar-librarian Rasmus Nyerup in 1810 crossed from Elsinore to Helsingborg, rumours of a border closure left him 'anxiously speculating what might now once again be afoot between the two countries so soon after peace has been concluded'. See *Rasmus Nyerups Rejser til Stockholm i Aarene 1810 og 1812* (Copenhagen, 1816), pp. 3—4.

Estate in the Swedish Diet, supported the candidature of the Danish King Christian VI as heir to the Swedish throne, arguing that he 'was the one most closely related to us Swedes, be it through the purity of religion, the accordance of the laws, the similarity of manners, or the very unity of language'. But they failed to carry the day; and the election of Adolf Frederik of the house of Gottorp, Denmark's perennial enemy to the south, ensured heightened political tension for decades until the problem found its diplomatic solution in 1773.[1]

During the reign of the unstable and megalomaniac Gustav III (1772 – 92), the atmosphere can best be described as one of cold war. Gustav repeatedly tried to engineer attacks on Denmark and Norway, though only when Denmark in 1788 reluctantly honoured its alliance with Russia and declared war on Sweden did it actually come to a (minor) battle. The mood of the time may be gauged from two events on the cultural front. The first opera in Swedish, the super-nationalistic 'Gustav Wasa' with a libretto written jointly by Johan Henrik Kellgren and the king himself ('Flee, foes! Revenge and death / follow brave Svea's path'), was performed to an enthusiastic audience in 1786. The king's sister-in-law noted in her diary that 'the battles in it, where the Swedes defeat the Danes, were applauded with special vigour, a consequence of the always vivid hatred between the two nations; I have never witnessed such noisy behaviour in the pit'.[2] The Danish contribution was less spectacular though more durable: Johannes Ewald included in his play 'Fiskerne' the later royal anthem, 'Kong Christian stod ved højen mast' (or, in Longfellow's version, 'King Christian stood by the lofty mast'). Celebrating three Danish naval heroes, whose fame of course stemmed from battles with the Swedes, the anthem tells us of King Christian IV that 'His sword was hammering so fast / Through Gothic helm and brain it passed'; of Niels Juel that he 'smote upon the foe full sore'; and of the Norwegian-born Peder Wessel Tordenskjold that 'Terror and Death glared where he went'.[3]

In 1794, when the two countries were briefly united in a defensive alliance, a more conciliatory note was struck. The clergyman Andreas Wöldike in a sermon called Sweden 'the very honourable sister country

---

[1] Quoted in Lindeberg, *Arvefjenden*, p. 256. Similar plans for uniting the two crowns, in 1810 and 1850 respectively, also failed.
[2] *Ibid.*, pp. 262 – 3. A recent production in Stockholm, with Nicolai Gedda as the villain Christian II, was a complete failure with not just the pit but almost everyone booing the performance (*Politiken*, 6.10.1991).
[3] See H.W. Longfellow, *The Poetical Works* (London, 1908), pp. 40 – 1. The anthem is still sung enthusiastically, e.g. at gala performances at the Royal Theatre in Copenhagen, though probably few in the audience realise that 'the Goths' and 'the foe' refer to the Swedes.

Denmark and Sweden, 1450—1850

(*broderland*)', and he criticised the 'stupid national animosity' that had led to so many wars. Denmark, Norway and Sweden were in his view *trillingeriger*,[1] and he piously hoped that they would always remain united and 'from now on love each other for ever and ever'.[2] This was the kind of sentiment which carried over into the Scandinavism of the nineteenth century, of which more below; only the wars were not yet over.

In the Napoleonic wars, Denmark and Sweden ended up on opposing sides. Denmark tried to stay neutral as it had done so profitably for most of the century. But in two pre-emptive strikes, in 1801 and 1807, Britain defeated the Danes and took their navy lest it fall into French hands (adding for good measure a terror bombardment of the civilian population of Copenhagen). Denmark responded by entering into an alliance with Napoleon. Sweden, on the other hand, opposed France, and during the Franco-Russian rapprochement it supported a Russian attack on and conquest of Finland (1808—9). This, of course, created diplomatic problems when Sweden and Russia eventually both came out on the winning side, and the solution was to have momentous consequences for Scandinavia: Russia was allowed to keep Finland, while Sweden in 1814 got Norway by way of compensation. Denmark was thereby reduced from a not unimportant second-rank power to a definitely minor European state.[3]

Not surprisingly, this gave rise to a new round of mutual insults and incriminations. N. F. S. Grundtvig — later to become famous as a prolific hymn-writer and creator of the *folkehøjskole* movement — attacked Sweden bitterly for its treachery, and adduced a number of historical examples to buttress his point. 'Far be it for me in any way to inflate or sanction the disastrous hatred that for centuries, perhaps for millennia, was passed on to the Scandinavian peoples (*Nordens folkefærd*)', he wrote, but in this case the spirit ruling Sweden must be condemned: 'My country is in this the servant of God and Truth, whereas Sweden is the servant of Falsehood and Evil.' The verbal battle was joined by the (rightly forgotten) Swedish writer Lorenzo Hammarskjöld who under the punning classical motto *Timeo Danaos et dona ferentes* offered his version of the Scandinavian wars through

---

1 Literally 'triplet realms', a pun on the word *tvillingerige* ('twin realm') used to describe the dual monarchy of Denmark and Norway. The neologism never caught on, partly because the alliance soon broke down, partly because it was already being used for the *helstat*, i.e. the monarchy which consisted of Denmark, Norway and Holstein.
2 Quoted in M. Bregnsbo, 'Præsterne og de fremmede', *Siden Saxo*, vii:4 (1990), p. 46. Another clergyman said much the same thing in 1810. Mr Bregnsbo, whose book *Gejstlighedens syn på samfund og øvrighed 1775—1800* appeared in 1992, kindly let me have access to his unpublished data. See also his article 'Clerical Attitudes towards Society in the Age of Revolution', *Scandinavian Journal of History*, xvi (1991).
3 For the (rather complicated) history of these years, see Barton, *Scandinavia in the Revolutionary Era*.

the centuries. Of course he saw Denmark as untrustworthy and Sweden as brave and magnanimous; and anyway Denmark ought to dissolve itself and take advantage of the beneficial rule which Sweden had always bestowed on its conquered provinces.[1]

Similarly, there is a good deal of evidence that the mutual hatred and prejudice survived, especially if not exclusively among the less educated. The common people in the Swedish province of Småland, which had had more than its fair share of war, believed around 1800 that the Danes were really a kind of werewolves![2] And as late as 1911 — it emerged in a heated debate on national character in the Danish periodical *Tilskueren* — it was proverbial in Sweden that 'if you do business with a Dane, you will be deceived every time'. The Swedes had for centuries looked upon the Danes 'with some of that envy and resentment which the uneducated feel towards their betters', and even now the typical Swede viewed the Dane 'as an officer views a cunning trader'.[3] In Denmark, where the verb *at svenske* at least in 1830 meant to cheat or to steal, there was a similar undercurrent, and Scandinavism was seen by many as an intellectual craze confined to the capital and unlikely to catch on in the provinces. One of the Danish leaders in the nationally contested duchy of Schleswig, Laurids Skau, indirectly confirmed this when he claimed, in 1845, that 'the Scandinavian sympathies are much stronger among the peasants here in Schleswig than they are in the same class in the kingdom [i.e. Denmark proper]; there you can still find national enmity towards the Swedes, which is unknown here'.[4]

In spite of such residual resentment, however, Danish-Swedish relations rapidly improved. Cultural contacts intensified, and many intellectuals and writers became 'Scandinavised' — in some cases very quickly. Grundtvig

---

[1] Lindeberg, *Arvefjenden*, p. 283; Å. Holmberg, 'On the Practicability of Scandinavianism: Mid-nineteenth-century Debate and Aspirations', *Scandinavian Journal of History*, ix (1984), p. 178.

[2] See Roberts, *Swedish Imperial Experience*, p. 68.

[3] *Tilskueren*, 1911:ii, pp. 361-8, 433-7. Note that here for once the usual symmetry of perception (Danes/Swedes are cruel and false, Swedes/Danes are noble and trustworthy) gives way to the idea of an empirical difference, i.e. Sweden as a military versus Denmark as a commercial nation.

[4] H. Becker-Christensen, *Skandinaviske drømme og politiske realiteter: Den politiske skandinavisme i Danmark 1830–1850* (Aarhus, 1981), pp. 34–5; Skau to Carl Ploug, 3.1.1845, in *Brevveksling med politiske venner i København*, ed. H.V. Gregersen (Copenhagen, 1966), pp. 552–3. Similarly, in 1838 Chr. Flor maintained that 'the Scandinavian awakening will come sooner among the people of Sønderjylland than among the so-called real Danes'. But both Skau and Flor were hoping to get Sweden-Norway involved in the Danish struggle against the Germans, and may well have been indulging in wishful thinking. 'Scandinavism never really caught on among the farmers in Slesvig', is the verdict of L. Rerup in *Dansk Identitetshistorie*, ii, p. 384 (Flor is quoted at p. 366).

Denmark and Sweden, 1450–1850

forgot his anger and in 1838 suggested that a Scandinavian *folkehøjskole* be established in Gothenburg. Another interesting example of the change in attitude is offered by Hans Christian Andersen. In 1830 he wrote a solemn poem about 'The Danes and their King', praising God for the nation's narrow escape from Swedish conquest in 1659. Three years later, however, he wrote home from Rome about the planned Christmas celebrations 'where Swedes, Norwegians and Danes become one nation; Rome reunites the Scandinavian (*nordiske*) countries!' In 1839, he produced a sort of Scandinavian anthem ('Vi er et Folk, vi kaldes Skandinaver'); and in 1851, in his travel account *I Sverrig*, he admitted that both countries had behaved abominably over the centuries, and praised the new understanding between them.[1]

*

Are there are any historical lessons to be drawn from the Scandinavian experience, any recipes for peaceful solutions of ethnic conflicts? I am afraid not. Rather, two specific factors made it possible to transform the old *arvefjender* to *broderfolk*. First, there was no longer anything to fight for. Second, new enemies emerged to engage the attention of Sweden and Denmark: Russia and Germany.

Russia's designs on Finland were obvious from the early eighteenth century, and gradually Russia became Sweden's Enemy No. 1. As early as 1615 Muscovy was referred to as 'our old hereditary enemy, the Russian' (*vår gamble Arffiende Ryssen*), and the stereotype of the Muscovite, which survived well into our century, was of 'an insolent, treacherous barbarian, whose Christianity was at least doubtful, whose morals were deplorable, who was individually contemptible, but alarming by reason of his overwhelming numbers'.[2] The Danes also feared Russia, but the new hereditary enemy was Germany. Already in the late eighteenth century, a mixture of cultural xenophobia and early nationalism made the Germans and their language (then widely spoken in the Danish monarchy) very unpopular. When nationalism gathered momentum from the 1840s, the Danes and the (not yet united) Germans for decades fought over the duchies of Schleswig and Holstein, Prussian intervention eventually ensuring German victory. The

---

1 Becker-Christensen, *Skandinaviske drømme*, pp. 35–6; J.R. Rasmussen, 'Fra svenskekrige til fodbold: Danmark og Sverige som arvefjender', in *Fjendebilleder og fremmedhad*, ed. K.K. Kristiansen and J.R. Rasmussen (Copenhagen, 1988), pp. 150–1.
2 Roberts, *Swedish Imperial Experience*, p. 68. In a cartoon which at the time (*c.*1900) was very much a jest in earnest, Albert Engström has a grammar school inspector praise a teacher for his pupils' patriotism: 'Very commendable, Mr. Nilsson. Been giving them rousing speeches, have you?' 'No,' the teacher replies, 'but I have shown them the Russian alphabet.'

loss of Schleswig or Sønderjylland, including the Danish-speaking parts, in 1864 created a national trauma of a wholly different magnitude from the one in 1814.

Thus both Denmark and Sweden had good national motives for co-operation: a 'new Union of Kalmar', as it was often called, would improve their position *vis-à-vis* the great powers. Steen Steensen Blicher, a Danish poet and liberal (of sorts), put it concisely when he said that if a Scandinavian federal union (*Foederativstat*) was not created, Sweden would be swallowed by Russia, Denmark by Germany, and — an unusual but interesting suggestion — Norway by England.[1]

Because Scandinavism was a cultural as well as a political idea, it appealed to a broad political spectrum. The cultural cooperation built on the literary and scholarly contacts during the seventeenth and eighteenth centuries, and was readily accepted even by conservative intellectuals.[2] Even the two royal houses were reconciled once the two old kings involved in the events of 1810–14 had passed away: in 1846, Oscar I of Sweden visited his fellow monarch Christian VIII in Copenhagen, no doubt also in an attempt to pre-empt the Pan-Scandinavian movement.[3]

Liberals, on the other hand, saw the Pan-Scandinavian movement as eminently political. Even in the 1840s, both Sweden and Denmark were ruled in a fairly autocratic manner, and liberal politics were seen as subversive; furthermore, in Denmark a conservative establishment favouring the non-national *helstat* or confederation of Denmark, Schleswig and Holstein faced opposition from the national-liberals advocating a state which, at least in theory, was purely Danish. Scandinavism was thus very useful as a cover for liberal politics. Conversely, the establishment nervously assumed that Scandinavian topics invariably implied a liberal message, and even speakers on historical subjects were warned 'not to meddle in politics'.[4]

---

1 On Scandinavism in general, see Holmberg, 'On the Practicability of Scandinavianism', and H. Denman, 'Political and Cultural Scandinavism', *Scandinavica*, xiv (1975). On Blicher, see K. Sørensen, *St. St. Blicher* (Copenhagen, 1984), pp. 183–96.
2 See Denman, 'Political and Cultural Scandinavism'. Ironically, one of the leading conservative advocates of cultural Scandinavism, Chr. Molbech, actually first went to Sweden in 1810 as a Danish spy!
3 Becker–Christensen, *Skandinaviske drømme*, p. 177.
4 Thus C. Brix was warned in 1847 before giving a lecture on Scandinavia around 1750 (*ibid.*, p. 183). In 1842, *Videnskabernes Selskab* in Copenhagen suggested a prize essay on the Union of Kalmar, but this was turned down as too risky given 'the present chimaeric ideas of a Scandinavian union'. Instead, the society chose the presumably safer topic of Danish forests! See N. Clemmensen, 'En forening bliver til: Chr. Molbech og dannelsen af Den danske historiske forening', *Historisk Tidsskrift*, xc (1990), p. 19.

Denmark and Sweden, 1450–1850

It is interesting to observe that Norway (whose union with Sweden was a loose one virtually confined to a common king and foreign policy) stood somewhat aloof from the movement — possibly because Norway felt threatened neither by Russia nor by Germany, and had had a liberal constitution since 1814.[1] For practical purposes, pan-Scandinavism was therefore a question of Danish-Swedish relations.

It is true that many foreign observers viewed the possibility of a union with considerable scepticism — with the exception of some not entirely disinterested German nationalists.[2] The Russian ambassador, Nesselrode, regarded a Scandinavian union as politically impossible because the Swedes hated the Danes (this in 1844!) and felt superior to the Norwegians. The Scottish travel writer Samuel Laing in 1838 thought that the economic self-sufficiency of the three countries ruled out such a union (as opposed to the one between 'the three British nations'), and that anyway a population of five or six millions was too small to form a 'mass of power'.[3]

The obvious reply to that was, of course, that individually they were even less significant, and one important motive for Scandinavian cooperation was precisely to create an ethnic and linguistic unit which could survive. Theories of nationalism in the nineteenth century did not accept any miniscule ethnic community. The 'Europe of nations' foreseen by Mazzini in 1857 comprised only twelve such, most of them multi-national by our standards; and it was often argued that countries like Belgium (with 4.5 million inhabitants in 1850) were too small to constitute viable nations. The unification of Germany pointed in the same direction. All in all the idea of Scandinavian union was a practical proposal in tune with the time, not the

1 Becker–Christensen, *Skandinaviske drømme*, p. 168.
2 Well-known German nationalists pronouncing on Scandinavism included Ernst Moritz Arndt, F.L. ('Turnvater') Jahn, and Jacob Grimm. Jahn hoped that a united Scandinavia together with a united Germany would become a 'Manheim' whose calling it would be to carry world history forward and defend liberty against the Latin and the Slav peoples. Grimm predicted that Denmark would split, with Jutland becoming part of Germany, and the islands joining Sweden-Norway. See Holmberg, 'On the Practicability of Scandinavianism', pp. 178–9; *Dansk Identitetshistorie*, ii, p. 365; and I. Adriansen, *Fædrelandet, folkeminderne og modersmålet* (Sønderborg, 1990), p. 52.
3 Becker-Christensen, *Skandinaviske drømme*, pp. 135–6, 259. Laing's *A Tour in Sweden in 1838* is quoted by Holmberg, 'On the Practicability of Scandinavianism', pp. 171–2. But Scandinavism did have its moments abroad. In 1845, the national-liberal historian C.F. Allen wrote from London to Laurids Skau: 'Mind you, here in England the Scandinavist idea has already become reality. Nobody cares about the difference between Stockholm and Copenhagen, or between Christian VIII and King Oscar. In English discussions these kings often exchange thrones, and likewise the cities move from one country to another.' Letter of 3.8.1845, in *Danske politiske Breve fra 1830erne og 1840erne*, ed. P. Bagge and P. Engelstoft (Copenhagen, 1945–58), iii, p. 83.

idealistic pipe-dream it has often been described as.[1]

Vilhelm Moberg once wrote pessimistically that he had never heard of two neighbouring countries who had been hereditary friends (*arvevenner*): 'It seems as if only hostility between peoples is hereditary and abiding on this earth.'[2] But Scandinavian relations after 1814 seem to belie this: centuries of hatred and hostility were forgotten as close links were forged between the (eventually five) Scandinavian countries, and war between them became unthinkable. The real touchstone here was the so-called Union Crisis in 1905 when Norway seceded from the union with Sweden; in spite of considerable tension and a certain amount of sabre-rattling, this crisis was solved without recourse to war.

The more ambitious Scandinavian projects have, admittedly, failed (the abortive plans for a defensive union in 1948−9, a customs union in 1958−9, and an economic union in 1968−70 are three recent examples), but Nordic cooperation has in fact created a community which is in many respects closer than the European Community, even after the completion of the single market. The new Conservative prime minister in Sweden, Carl Bildt, when asked if he could mention just one case where his government did not face problems, quickly answered: 'Relations with Denmark.'[3] If not exactly a recipe for world peace, Scandinavian cooperation does at least show that mutual perceptions can change over time, and that it is not perhaps entirely impossible to imagine two neighbouring nations becoming hereditary friends.[4]

---

1   E.J. Hobsbawm, *Nations and nationalism since 1780* (Cambridge 1990), pp. 30−3. An interesting interpretation of the political failure of Scandinavism in the light of Stein Rokkan's theory of modernisation and state-building (which however seems to ignore Hobsbawm's point) can be found in K. Krüger, 'Der Skandinavismus im Lichte der Modernisierungstheorie', *Nordeuropa Studien*, xxvii (1990).
2   Moberg, *History of the Swedish People*, ii, p. 70.
3   Interviewed on the Swedish news programme 'TV−Aktuellt', 4.10.1991.
4   See the recent, very interesting anthology of articles dealing with Scandinavian identities: *Nationella identiteter i Norden — ett fullbordat projekt?*, ed. A. Linde-Laursen and J.O. Nilsson (Stockholm, 1991).

The Intensification of National Consciousness in Modern Europe

Ralph Gibson

This is really an essay on *popular* nationalism: about the way in which the great mass of the population in Western European countries came (or did not come) to identify with their country, especially in the course of the nineteenth century. The case studies are restricted to France, Germany and Italy; I much regret the absence of the Scandinavian countries, and above all of Russia (which would provide some fascinating contrasts). In each case, the mass of the population with which the essay is concerned was basically rural. Urban population did not outstrip rural population until 1891 in Germany and until 1931 (theoretically) in France. Italy, it is true, did have a surprisingly high rate of urbanisation (see appendix II), but much of that was due to the old localised heritage of the city-state and to the widespread existence in the south of 'agro-towns', most of whose inhabitants worked the land;[1] even after the Second World War, 44 per cent of the Italian labour force was still employed in agriculture.[2] We are dealing, therefore, with basically rural populations in all three countries. In the course of the nineteenth century — and essentially in the half century before the First World War — the rural populations of France and Germany came to think of themselves as French or German. Most of those who lived in the Italian peninsula did not; well after 1861 Italy remained, if no longer a mere geographical expression, still very far from being an emotional reference point for her inhabitants.

Modern French nationalism is often dated from the Revolution, or from certain aspects of Rousseau's ideas.[3] For the great mass of those who inhabited 'the hexagon' in the late eighteenth century, however, France was still a largely meaningless concept. For some areas this has long been abundantly clear. Thus in the west, the counter-Revolutionary war was at

---

1 See, *inter alia*, A. Blok, 'South Italian Agro-Towns', *Comparative Studies in Society and History*, xi (1969).
2 M. Clark, *Modern Italy, 1871–1982* (London and New York, 1984), p. 349.
3 See B. Jenkins, *Nationalism in France: Class and Nation since 1789* (London, 1990), chapter 2. This valuable book appeared after this paper was presented, and has not been integrated into it.

least precipitated by the levy of 300,000 men in 1793 to fight for France, in the face of which the young men did much the same as many young Frenchmen did after 1942 when called upon to serve a foreign power: they took to the *maquis*. But it was not only the inhabitants of the inland west who rejected the idea that they had anything to do with something called 'France'. Refusal to fight on behalf of that concept was extraordinarily widespread during the Revolutionary and Napoleonic Wars, as Alan Forrest's recent book has shown. When an amnesty was granted in 1803, for example, some 175,000 fugitives from conscription took advantage of it.[1] They had avoided the draft with as clear consciences as those young Americans who took the train to Canada in the 1970s. The future Saint John Vianney, the *curé d'Ars* (now officially the patron saint of parish priests the world over), deserted in 1809 and hid in the hills for eighteen months; despite his intense sense of personal sinfulness, he never repented of what he had done.[2] One might object that it was possible to identify with France without being willing to put one's life on the line. I am convinced, however, that the opposition to conscription under the Revolution and Empire was merely symptomatic of the fact that the vast majority of 'Frenchmen' did not consider themselves to be anything of the kind.

Matters would remain that way in France for a long time. Half a century before the First World War, there were still some striking examples of the durable localism of rural populations. Theodore Zeldin has made famous the story of the school inspector in the Lozère in 1864 who asked the children of a village school, 'In what country is the Lozère situated?', to which none knew the answer; or: 'Are you English or Russian?', which elicited no reply.[3] In the 1880s, a school inspector in the same area reported of its inhabitants that 'they often say they are in the Lozère, and when they cross the mountains they go *to* France'.[4] Now, this is merely anecdotal evidence: the school-children of 1864 probably simply thought to themselves, 'Who is this latest loony they've sent to us from the town?' The Lozère was, furthermore, a notoriously isolated and backward part of France. But Eugen Weber has demonstrated, to my mind convincingly, that the failure to identify with France was still widespread at the beginning of the Third Republic (in the 1870s); it was only in the course of the next half century that many peasants

1 A. Forrest, *Conscripts and Deserters: The Army and French Society during the Revolution and Empire* (Oxford, 1989), p. 70. The author is at pains to emphasise the dubiousness of all such statistics.
2 P. Boutry and M. Cinquin, *Deux pèlerinages au XIXe siècle, Ars et Paray-le-Monial* (Paris, 1980), p. 24.
3 T. Zeldin, *France, 1848–1945*, ii: *Intellect, Taste and Anxiety* (Oxford, 1977), p. 3
4 P.M. Jones, *Politics and Rural Society: The Southern Massif Central, c.1750–1880* (Cambridge, 1985), p. 272.

would become — or be made into — Frenchmen.[1]

One would expect that those who lived in the newly-established Germany in 1871 had similar difficulties in identifying with their new fatherland. The push for unification had clearly come from the professional and commercial bourgeoisie. Bismarck had taken up the nationalist cause (hitherto anathema to him) in order to seduce the middle-class liberals of Prussia who were attacking Hohenzollern absolutism in the 1860s; as Hans-Ulrich Wehler remarks, the wars of unification 'were used as a device to legitimise the prevailing political system against the striving for social and economic emancipation of the middle classes'.[2] The rest of the population were pretty much spectators in this elite power game. That is not terribly easy to demonstrate in a hard-and-fast way, but it is, for example, striking that in the Prussian elections of 1862 and 1863, when the unification issue loomed large, members of Class One of the three-class franchise (the richest 4.5 per cent of the electorate) were more than twice as likely to vote as were those of Class Three (the poorest 82.7 per cent).[3] And that was Prussia; in the states which the process rather inaccurately known as German unification brought under Prussian imperialism, the failure to identify with 'Germany' must have been much stronger. Many a school child must have felt what Julius Sturm had put into the mouth of one of their predecessors in 1850:

Die Länder kenn ich selber,
Nur Deutschland seh' ich nicht.[4]

The case of Italy scarcely needs dwelling on. Denis Mack Smith made it clear years ago that unified Italy contained scarcely any Italians. Certainly no more than 2.5 per cent of them were fluent in Italian — and the proportion outside Tuscany and Rome was very much lower.[5] Victor Emmanuel spoke for preference a Piedmontese dialect, and when Cavour declared 'Je suis Italien avant tout', he said it in French.[6] Mazzini and Garibaldi were really very peripheral figures. Sicilian and south Italian peasants had certainly no concept of being Italian (when Garibaldi told them about 'Italia', they thought he was talking about his mistress). When Italian

---

1 E. Weber, *Peasants into Frenchmen: The Modernization of Rural France, 1870–1914* (London, 1977).
2 H.-U. Wehler, *The German Empire, 1871–1918* (Leamington Spa, 1985), p. 26 (translation of *Das deutsche Kaiserreich, 1871–1918* [Göttingen, 1973]).
3 T.S. Hamerow, *The Social Foundations of German Unification, 1858–1871: Struggles and Accomplishments* (Princeton, 1972), p. 182.
4 'For my part, I know the states; only I don't see Germany at all.' See Appendix I, below.
5 T. de Mauro, *Storia linguistica dell'Italia unita* (2nd edn, Rome and Bari, 1979), i, p. 43.
6 R. Bosworth, *Italy and the Approach of the First World War* (London, 1983), p. 10.

unification turned out in practice to be merely the imposition on the south of the rather more efficient government of Piedmont, many southerners took to the hills in the endemic brigandage of the 1860s, which was put down with exemplary ferocity by Piedmontese troops with more loss of life than in all the wars of the *Risorgimento* put together.[1]

*

All this is fairly well-trodden territory. Identification with one's country, for the mass of the people, depended on a process of state-formation and modernisation which was not even begun in Italy in 1870, very partial in Germany, and still far from complete in France. One's sense of social identity remained for a very long time very largely local. This was, I think, basically the consequence of the kind of agriculture which had for centuries dominated in Europe. Eric Wolf has suggested that the three commonest 'ecotypes' in pre-industrial peasant society have been: (a) slash-and-burn farming; (b) hydraulic systems, dependent on large-scale irrigation (as in rice cultivation); and (c) Eurasian grain farming.[2] Slash-and-burn farming is clearly not of a sedentary nature; those who practice it regularly have to move on. Those who operate in hydraulic systems are tied to their irrigation works, but the complexity of those works is such that they tend to be organised by some kind of overarching state. Eurasian grain-farming, however, tends to encourage constant habitation of one spot, and does not require the regular presence of a wider authority. For a very long time, such had been — with exceptions — the chief characteristics of European agriculture. It encouraged sedentariness, and did not bring those that practised it into much contact with an overarching state.[3]

It should be added, perhaps, that not every historian agrees that, at least by the eighteenth century, European peasant farming had these characteristics. Jean-Pierre Poussou, for example, has concluded from his massive study of the South-West of France that 'the idea of parishes turned in on themselves, in terms of which historians have been too willing to describe French society of former times, needs to be seriously amended'.[4] He sees a very considerable amount of migratory movement (the only

1   The best short statement of 'Mack Smithery' is the first chapter in D. Mack Smith, *Victor Emmanuel, Cavour and the Risorgimento* (Oxford, 1971). See also his earlier chapter in the *New Cambridge Modern History*, x (Cambridge, 1960).
2   E. Wolf, *Peasants* (New Jersey, 1966), chapter 2.
3   A not dissimilar and very useful analysis of the impossibility of nationalism in agrarian society is to be found in E. Gellner, *Nations and Nationalism* (Oxford, 1983), chapter 2 (especially the diagram on p. 9).
4   J.-P. Poussou, 'L'immigration bordelaise, 1737–1791: Essai sur la mobilité géographique et l'attraction urbaine dans le Sud-Ouest de la France au XVIIIe siècle' (Thèse pour le Doctorat-ès-Lettres, University of Paris-Sorbonne, 1978), p. 552.

exceptions being the peasant proprietors who were indeed tied to a particular spot by ownership of the land in a system of Eurasian grain farming), and an active trade in diverse agricultural and proto-industrial products. Also, at a national level, Charles Tilly has argued that by the end of the eighteenth century the French countryside was heavily involved in production for the market, and that thus local solidarities were already very much weakened.[1] These are weighty authorities. I, however, would argue (with Peter Jones) that participation in market networks did not necessarily do much to widen local horizons;[2] sale and purchase were an essential part of most peasants' lives before the agricultural revolution, but it was a relatively small part, and was regarded as an unfortunate expedient to make economic and social autarky work. I think, too, that the mobility of peasant populations, at least in France, can easily be over-emphasised. Endogamy is a good indicator. In the three parishes of the Bas-Quercy studied by Jean-Claude Sangoï, in the second half of the eighteenth century over a third of marriages involved a man and wife from the same parish, and over 80 per cent of the partners who came from another parish did so from within a range of ten kilometres.[3] Many other village studies tell a similar story. In any case, a long personal acquaintance with the history of peasants of south-west France in the nineteenth century has convinced me that the great majority moved about very little, and that their mental horizons remained very largely local — at least until the second half of the century.[4]

It is generally accepted that by 1914 this situation had radically altered, at any rate in France and Germany. The young men who marched off to war may not have been 'tickled to death to go',[5] but their attitude was quite different from those who had been conscripted for Napoleon's wars. The French High Command had predicted a 13 per cent disobedience to call-up, but in the event it was only 1.5 per cent.[6] Even in the Lozère, where half a

1 C. Tilly, 'Did the cake of custom break?', in *Consciousness and Class Experience in Nineteenth-Century Europe* (New York, 1980).
2 Jones, *Politics and Rural Society*, pp. 56–9.
3 J.-C. Sangoï, 'Histoire démographique de trois communes rurales du Bas-Quercy de 1751 à 1872: Démographie et groupes sociaux dans la paysannerie' (Thèse de 3e cycle, University of Toulouse-Le Mirail, 1982), pp. 161–2.
4 Abel Châtelain estimates that in the early 19th century, out of a population of 29 million, about 200,000 were affected by temporary migration; by 1850, the number was about 500,000 — and over 800,000 at harvest time (A. Châtelain, *Les migrants temporaires en France (1800–1914)* [Lille, 1977], i, pp. 42–3). These are considerable figures, but they concern only a peripheral element of French rural society, which was fundamentally peasant-based and sedentary.
5 'Tickled to death to go' comes from the First World War popular song *Good-by-ee*, now immortalised in *Oh! What a Lovely War*.
6 R. Girardet, *La société militaire dans la France contemporaine, 1815–1939* (Paris, 1953), p. 246.

century earlier the school-children had perhaps not known whether they were English or Russian, it was only 2.7 per cent.[1] Those who did disobey were marginal figures, such as a small peasant who had not even heard that the war was on; or the tiny handful of conscious anti-war protesters of anarcho-syndicalist conviction, like the stonemason who declared that he didn't want to get his head bashed in for the rich, that he didn't give a sod if he was French or Prussian, that he had no capital to defend, that the capitalists and the priests were responsible for the war, and that he'd rather emigrate than fight.[2] (He got a six-month suspended sentence from a court martial, and no doubt suffered soon thereafter the fate of Uriah the Hittite. This nameless protester may be recommended to our prayers.) He was, however, one of only a tiny minority. Popular mentalities seem to have been almost identical in Germany — which was the excuse given by the SPD leaders for failing to take any action against mobilisation.[3] On both sides of the Rhine, the population at large identified with their country, and accepted the requirement to defend it by arms.

It is true that the traditional picture of wild patriotic enthusiasm in 1914 does need to be modified. British people are particularly likely to be led into error here, having been brought up on old photos of the rush to enlist — photos evoked by Philip Larkin:

> The crowds of hats, the sun
> On moustached archaic faces
> Grinning as if it were all
> An August Bank Holiday lark.

But the high profile of those who rushed to enlist can easily make us forget the much greater number of those who did not. There seems to have been no systematic investigation of this possibility with respect to Britain.[4] But whatever the case, the situation on the Continent was very different, inasmuch as the mass armies were armies of conscripts: men did not have any choice. Official and newspaper reports, of course, presented these conscripts as being eager to defend their *patrie*. Records of public opinion kept by schoolteachers at the outbreak of the war, however, tell a rather different story. Jean-Jacques Becker's analysis of these reports suggests that

1 J. Maurin, *Armée—Guerre—Société: soldats languedociens (1889–1919)* (Paris, 1982), p. 379.
2 J.-J. Becker, *1914: Comment les Français sont entrés dans la guerre* (Paris, 1977), pp. 354–5.
3 J. Joll, *The Second International, 1889–1914* (2nd edn, London, 1975), p. 179.
4 There is some useful material in P. Simkins, *Kitchener's Army: the raising of the New Armies, 1914–16* (Manchester, 1988), chapter 2, but it does not really tackle this problem. The picture which seems to have inspired Larkin is reproduced on pp. 50–1.

the mass response to mobilisation was 'reserved' — though enthusiasm did build up as the patriotic fanfare got under way. People did perhaps accept the need to defend their country — but less with enthusiasm than *la mort dans l'âme*.[1]

Nevertheless, the transformation of popular mentalities in France and Germany over the preceding century had been immense. In Italy, such a transformation had hardly taken place at all: if Italy had been made in 1861, it would take much longer than half a century to make Italians. Popular response to the outbreak of war in 1915 may, of course, have been complicated by the fact that Italy had switched sides, which did tend to make it rather unclear what one was supposed to be fighting for. There is, at any rate, ample evidence that the war was not popular with most of those who had to fight it. Prefectoral reports commissioned in April 1915 made it clear that the agrarian masses felt no enthusiasm for the war.[2] In the villages of Sicily, according to Filippo Sabetti, there was 'an almost plebiscitary rejection of the war as a useless slaughter'; by 1917, there were more than 20,000 Sicilian draft-dodgers and deserters roaming the countryside.[3] Soldiers from southern Italy had to be driven into battle by a mixture of alcohol and military policemen with machine guns behind the line.[4] Even northern peasants experienced the war as 'a form of obscure punishment'[5]; Piedmontese peasant wives were happy to welcome the large number of deserters who hid out in local farms — happier in fact than they would be to welcome the partisans of 1943−5.[6] It is no wonder that Italy's military effort collapsed after two years. John Gooch has explained Italian military performance in the First World War in terms of the unpreparedness of the military. No doubt this was a major reason, but I remain convinced that the fundamental reason for the failure of Italian mass armies was that they had no concept of what they were supposed to be defending.[7]

*

1   Becker, *Comment les Français sont entrés dans la guerre*, especially pp. 284−302.
2   Bosworth, *Italy and the Approach of the First World War*, p. 93.
3   F. Sabetti, *Political Authority in a Sicilian Village* (Rutgers, 1984), pp. 120−1.
4   F.M. Snowden, *Violence and the Great Estates in the South of Italy: Apulia, 1900−1922* (Cambridge, 1986), pp. 150−1.
5   A.J. Cardoza, *Agrarian Elites and Italian Fascism: The Province of Bologna, 1901−1926* (Princeton, 1982), p. 246.
6   A. Bravo, 'Italian Peasant Women and the First World War', in *War, Peace and Social Change in Twentieth−Century Europe*, ed. C. Emsley, A. Marwick and W. Simpson (Milton Keynes, 1989), especially pp. 111−12. The article is republished from *Our Common History: The Transformation of Europe*, ed. P. Thompson and N. Burcharat (London, 1982).
7   J. Gooch, 'Italian Military Competence', *Journal of Strategic Studies*, v (1982). Professor Gooch's contribution to the present volume (below) emphasises more strongly the factors under discussion here.

Why, in the fifty or hundred years before 1914, did people living in France or Germany come to think of themselves as French or German, while those living in Italy developed little sense of being Italian? It will be suggested here that it was the consequence of two parallel processes (at least one of which was rather weak in Italy): a rapid increase in the geographic range of social interaction, and the conscious indoctrination of nationalist fervour by states whose range of action was also rapidly increasing.

It scarcely needs demonstrating that it was in the second half of the nineteenth century, in France and Germany, that the range of social interaction began dramatically to escalate, in all kinds of ways.[1] Appendix II documents some of them: urbanisation and migration; literacy, newspaper reading, and the universalisation of a national language; participation in the political process through the ballot-box: the list could be extended indefinitely. Here attention is merely drawn to one item that is often forgotten: the escalation of postal traffic. Particularly spectacular was the development of the postcard as a means of rapid communication. In the years before the First World War, the postcard came to serve many of the functions of a telephone call today. Postcards of that time are now collectors' items, and their imagery has been studied. What has not been studied — so far as I know — is the messages that they transmitted.[2] Postcards are just one, under-documented, example of a revolution in the scale of human interaction in the half-century before the war. Postal traffic is also a good example of how far Italy lagged behind in this revolution: in 1913, Italians sent fifteen letters or cards per head, French people forty-eight, and Germans eighty. Is it any wonder that the French and Germans had a stronger sense of belonging to a national community?

A revolution in the scale of human interaction would not, however, *by itself* lead to a more intense national consciousness. It seems to me that in order to identify with a country, people needed to be *told* that it was there that they belonged. This task was largely carried out by the representatives of the French and German states — and of the Italian state, but with much less success, since the social infrastructure was not there. It must be remembered that this was a period, especially in France, of rapidly expanding state activity. This is not desperately easy to demonstrate in a precise manner. There are some figures in Appendix II, which — although I

---

1   The thesis that nationalism has been fundamentally a consequence of escalating human interaction is examined by K.W. Deutsch, *Nationalism and Social Communication: An Inquiry into the Foundations of Nationality* (2nd edn, Cambridge, Mass., 1962).
2   The messages on postcards would, I imagine, be an excellent Ph.D. subject. A limited but useful starting point is A. Ripert and C. Frère, *La carte postale: Son histoire, sa fonction sociale* (Lyon and Paris, 1983).

am rather dubious about them — suggest a certain increase in the activity of the state. Furthermore, the *nature* of that activity was changing. When Karl Marx talked, in 1875, of the withering away of the state, he was thinking of its repressive functions, which to men of his generation practically constituted its *raison d'être*. But the late nineteenth-century state, in France and Germany at least, began to offer people certain things that they positively wanted. Education is the most obvious example: state expenditure on education in France increased from less than 50 million francs a year in the late 1870s to 300 million by the eve of the First World War. Perhaps even more importantly, however, the expansion of state activity gave people jobs, even in the most isolated areas. In the Lozère again, in the small upland *bourg* of Pont-de-Montvert, by 1890 the public purse was paying not only the *curé* and the *pasteur* (as it had done since 1801), but also four male and three female schoolteachers, three road-menders, two tax-collectors, one forest guard, three policemen and two postmen; in all likelihood, more money was coming into Pont-de-Montvert in their wage packets than was going out in taxes from the whole population.[1] National government was thus no longer a distant force which taxed you, conscripted you and put you in jail: it wore a human face. Ordinary people were thus much more disposed to listen favourably to its spokesmen when those spokesmen transmitted the ideology of the state: nationalism.

And transmit it they did, especially in the rapidly expanding school system, and most notoriously in the teaching of history. This phenomenon has been much studied, so I shall limit myself to one little-known example, taken from a Bavarian teachers' manual at the turn of the century, where a sample lesson was given of how to teach the poem 'The Triumph of Vionville', concerning a costly Prussian (*sic*) victory in the war of 1870–1:

> If during the treatment of such a piece the eyes of our boys do not flash, the cheeks do not glow, the heart does not pound, if the fist is not clenched with the thought: If only I could have ridden there! — then either the discussion or the delivery lacked the proper inspiring fire, or the boy is no good.[2]

The teaching of French history tended to be less militaristic, but its function was much the same. Italian teachers did try, too: pupils wrote essays on 'Why do you love Italy?', and were fed a diet of stories of heroic deeds on the battlefields of the *Risorgimento*.[3] But the impact was not the same: the

---

1 P. L.-R. Higonnet, *Pont-de-Montvert: Social Structure and Politics in a French Village, 1700–1914* (Harvard, 1971), p. 105.
2 K.D. Kennedy, 'Lessons and Learners: Elementary Education in Southern Germany, 1871–1914' (Stanford University Ph.D. Thesis, 1982), p. 262.
3 Clark, *Modern Italy*, p. 38.

necessary revolution in the scale of human interaction was as yet too incomplete, and in any case too many of Italy's children did not go to school.

It seems to me that nationalism is the natural ideology of a powerful state apparatus, and that it is therefore scarcely surprising that the personnel of that apparatus purveyed it.[1] Clearly, however, they also had another — and perfectly overt — purpose: social control. It is now rather unfashionable to say this (at least in the German case), so let me dwell on it for a moment. In the first place, identification with one's country had certain logical implications of a conservative nature, particularly where obedience to its laws was concerned. This is made clear by a wall poster of 1892 used in the primary schools of the French Third Republic (replacing the religious exhortations of a previous generation).[2] It listed, among other duties, 'duties towards your country'; they included:

> Love of one's country
> Obedience to its laws
> Compulsory education
> Military service
> Paying one's taxes
> Exercising the right to vote.

The primary schoolteachers who used this kind of document may not have been consciously using nationalism for purposes of social control, but when they talked about obeying laws and paying taxes that is clearly what they were doing. In Germany, at least according to Hans-Ulrich Wehler, it was done very deliberately. The Prussian educational regulations of 1854, for example, prescribed reinforcement of patriotic feeling and loyalty to the monarchy as primary teaching objectives. 'In this way (Wehler remarks) the teaching of history was used as an anti-revolutionary mind-drug for the inculcation of a patriotic mentality.'[3]

Wehler is, in fact, the high priest of this 'manipulation model' of German history under the *Kaiserreich*. He argues (though he was certainly not the first to do so) that the pre-industrial elites of Germany, notably the Junkers, deliberately used the appeal of *völkisch* nationalism (and anti-

---

[1] I am looking here at the purely indoctrinatory aspects of mass state-run education. Ernest Gellner develops a much more subtle thesis about the inevitability of such education in industrial society, about its culturally homogenising effect, and how this means that nation and culture become for the first time synonymous, making nationalism almost inevitable. See his *Nations and Nationalism*.
[2] Reproduced in M. Ozouf, *L'Ecole, l'Eglise et la République, 1871–1914* (Paris, 1963), p. 112.
[3] Wehler, *The German Empire*, p. 121.

semitism) to rally mass support against the forces of industrial modernity that were pushing in a democratic direction. This was most evident in the *Nationalvereine*, the nationalist organisations of the late nineteenth and the early twentieth centuries, such as the *Bund der Landwirte*, the *Flottenverein*, the *Alldeutscher Verband*, and so on. Such is Wehler's 'manipulation model', whereby elites blind the masses to their true interests by mobilising them under the banners of anti-modernism, anti-semitism and nationalism.

It is vehemently contested by a group of anglophone historians led by Geoff Eley and David Blackbourn. Their counter-interpretation has almost managed to establish itself, in this country at least, as neo-orthodoxy. What they argue is that organisations like the *Nationalvereine* were not so much elite initiatives to rally the masses behind interests that were not their own, as elite concessions to popular mobilisations of a spontaneous kind. At the very least, they were the product of *interaction* between elite action and that of the mass of the membership. Thus, according to Eley, 'To capture the real changes at work in German society ... the notion of mass politics has to imply not only manipulation from above, but also militant pressure from below.'[1] Blackbourn (a little more cautiously) claims that one is looking at 'the interaction between, on the one hand, aggrieved and demanding rural populations and, on the other, social and political elites of different political colours who saw themselves required to head off and somehow absorb these pressures'.[2] They are arguing, in effect, that the masses cannot simply be manipulated by feeding them the pap of nationalist or anti-semitic rhetoric; concessions to their own interests have to be made as well. Hegemony, states Eley (claiming to draw on Gramsci) must be *negotiated*; it is not simply the result of the triumph of the ideology of the ruling class, but of a process of *interaction*.[3]

Well, I remain unconvinced. It may be true that anti-semitism was a spontaneous demand of elements of German rural society: southern peasants, for example, had direct experience of Jewish cattle-dealers who were noticeably 'other', and who were probably as crooked as anybody else. I find it difficult to imagine, however, that the concept of one's nation can arise spontaneously out of personal experience. In nineteenth-century rural Europe, at least, people had to be *told* what nation they belonged to. Those

---

1 G. Eley, 'The Wilhelmine Right: How it changed', in *Society and Politics in Wilhelmine Germany*, ed. R.J. Evans (London, 1978), p. 125.
2 D. Blackbourn, 'Peasants and Politics in Germany, 1871–1914', *European History Quarterly*, xiv (1984), p. 50.
3 Eley, 'Wilhelmine Right', p. 125. The passage by Gramsci usually referred to is in *Selections from the Prison Notebooks of Antonio Gramsci*, ed. and translated by Q. Hoare and G. Nowell Smith (London, 1971), p. 161. But a careful reading of this text suggests that it will not carry all the weight of interpretation that is put upon it.

Ralph Gibson

who controlled the education system were acutely aware of this, which is why the rapidly expanding state systems of the late nineteenth century made national identity the keystone of their curricula. Of course, such indoctrination would only work under certain conditions: I have pointed in particular to a revolution in the geographic extent of social interaction and to the development of a state with a human face.[1] In Italy, these conditions were often absent — with the result that no amount of indoctrination would work (see John Gooch's contribution to this volume). But where such conditions were both present — as they certainly were in France, and in Germany so far as rural society was concerned — the process of indoctrination was spectacularly effective. Without it, I doubt whether the kind of war the First World War turned out to be could have been fought.

---

1 One should also emphasise that simple indoctrination, unaccompanied by any tangible rewards, will probably not work. In this connection the Eley/Blackbourn analysis, emphasising the interactive nature of the negotiation of hegemony, is very relevant. The point that for indoctrination through education to work it has to offer some concrete advantages to the indoctrinated is well made by Weber, *Peasants into Frenchmen*, pp. 325–9.

Appendix I

Aus der Schulstube

Ich weisz noch, wie mich's narrte,
Das ich mein Vaterland
Nicht auf der Länderkarte
In unsrer Schule fand.

'Ei, seht den dummen Hansen!
Beim Himmel, das ist arg!'
Es rief es und liesz tanzen
Den Stock der Schulmonarch.

Dann muszte mich ein Knabe
Belehren, wo es sei;
Der zeigte mit dem Stabe
Der Länder mancherlei.

'Die Länder kenn ich selber,
Nur Deutschland seh' ich nicht.'
Da ward vor Zorn noch gelber
Des Alten Angesicht.

Den Bakel wieder liesz er
Nun tanzen fürchterlich,
Dann mit der Nase stiesz er
Auf seine Karte mich.

'Hier Österreich, hier Preuszen,
Hannover, Baierland,
Und wie die andern heiszen:
Das ist das deutsche Land.

Nun weiszt du, wo's gelegen?'
Und ob ich's gleich nicht sah,
Mir graute vor den Schlagen,
Und heulend rief ich ja.

(Julius Sturm, 1850)

My father showed me this poem long ago, and I have lost the reference. It is a piece of perfect doggerel, but it illustrates quite nicely the difficulty children might have had in putting any meaning into the concept 'Germany'.

Appendix II. The Increasing Range of Social Interactions

Table 1. Railways

	Kilometres of track (millions)			Passenger-kilometres		
	France	Germany	Italy	France	Germany	Italy
1853:	3954	7147	808	1375	1050	—
1873:	18139	23890	7223	4347	5700	—
1893:	35350	44340	15004	10010	12700	2184
1913:	40770	63378	18873	19300	41400	5000

SOURCE. B.R. Mitchell, *European Historical Statistics, 1750–1970* (London, 1975), pp. 581–3, 601–5.

Table 2. Urbanisation

(A)

	% of pop. in towns >5,000			% of pop. in towns >100,000		
	France	Germany	Italy	France	Germany	Italy
1861:	23.3	—	26.8(?)	7.7	—	5.4
1881:	—	28.7	55.3	10.5	7.2	8.0
1901:	35.9	42.3	59.3	14.0	16.2	9.3
1911:	38.9	48.8	62.3	14.8	21.3	10.9

(B) Number of towns with more than 10,000 inhabitants

	France	Germany	Italy
1500:	32	23	44
1600:	43	30	59
1700:	55	30	51
1800:	78	53	75

SOURCES. P. Flora, *State, Economy and Society in Western Europe, 1815–1975* (Frankfurt, London and Chicago, 1983–7), ii, pp. 259, 262, 267; J. de Vries, *European Urbanization, 1500–1800* (London, 1984), appendix III.

Table 3. Internal Migration

(A) France (2 departments): % change

	Seine	Lozère
1836–51:	+23.8%	−6.8%
1851–66:	+43.3%	−12.3%
1872–91:	+36.2%	−15.6%
1891–1911:	+29.7%	−20.0%

(B) Germany: % of population born in a different region

	All Germany	Brandenburg & Berlin
1880:	4.3%	18.7%
1890:	6.2%	24.4%
1900:	7.9%	27.5%
1907:	8.7%	29.5%

This analysis divides Germany into six large regions, of which Berlin and Brandenburg is one. Smaller units of analysis would give much higher figures for geographic mobility.

SOURCES. J. Pitié, *Exode rural et migrations intérieures en France: l'exemple de la Vienne et du Poitou-Charentes* (Poitiers, 1971), pp. 106−9, 120−3, 140−3, 156−9; W.G. Hoffmann, *Das Wachstum der deutschen Wirtschaft seit der Mitte des 19. Jahrhunderts* (Berlin, 1965), pp. 178−80.

Table 4. Emigration

Known emigrants per 100,000 inhabitants

	France	Beyond Europe Germany	Italy	Italian emigration within and beyond Europe
1871:	20	185	65	158
1881:	12	486	145	479
1891:	16	241	616	964
1901:	12	39	859	1638
1911:	13	35	749	1521

SOURCE. *Annuaire Statistique, 34 (1914−15)* (Paris, 1917), p. 165* (partie rétrospective).

Table 5. Literacy

(A) % of military recruits able to read

	France	Germany	Italy
1875:	82%	98%	48%
1885:	86%	99%	54%
1895:	93%	—	62%
1914:	96%	—	67%

(B) Signing of the marriage register

	% grooms able to sign			% brides able to sign		
	France	Prussia	Italy	France	Prussia	Italy
1875:	80%	—	46%	69%	—	25%
1885:	87%	97%	56%	80%	95%	34%
1895:	94%	99%	62%	90%	98%	46%
1914:	98%	—	78%	97%	—	67%

(C) % of Italian population aged over five able to read

	North	Centre	South	Sicily	All Italy
1871:	45.8%	28.2%	16.6%	14.8%	31.3%
1911:	81.0%	59.7%	41.1%	42.0%	62.4%

SOURCE. Flora, *State, Economy and Society in Western Europe*, i, pp. 80–2.

Table 6. Newspapers

(A) France

1861:	Circulation of national newspapers (political):	236,510
1880:	Circulation of Parisian dailies:	1,984,521
1912:	Circulation of Parisian dailies (not sporting or financial):	5,270,000

(B) Germany

	Titles	% Dailies	Avge. distr.	Total copies
1866:	1525	20%	—	—
1900:	3500	—	5000	c.17,500,000
1913:	4200	45%	6000	c.25,200,000

(N.B. in 1913 the S.P.D. had 90 papers, total circulation c.1,465,000.)

(C) Italy

Easily the largest in 1871 was *Il Secolo* (Milan): circulation, c.30,000

SOURCES. C. Bellanger et al., *Histoire générale de la presse française*, ii (Paris, 1969), pp. 258–60, and iii (Paris, 1972), pp. 234, 296; K. Koszyk, *Deutsche Presse im 19. Jahrhundert* (Berlin, 1966), pp. 307–8; Clark, *Modern Italy*, p. 40.

Table 7. Postal Traffic

Millions of items

	France Letters	Cards	Germany All post	Letters/Cards per head France	Germany	Italy
1873:	341	16	563	—	—	—
1883:	620	35	1042	17	19	7
1893:	791	50	1917	—	29	7
1903:	1062	196	4019	25	53	9
1913:	1752	401	7024	48	80	15

SOURCES. *Annuaire Statistique, 1914–15*, pp. 63*, 205*; Hoffmann, *Wachstum der deutschen Wirtschaft*, pp. 420–1.

Table 8. Language

(A) France
In 1789, 50% did not speak French at all, and only 12−13% spoke it 'correctly'.
Survey of patois-speaking, 1863: *Lozère*: 26% of 7−13 year-old schoolchildren 'do not speak French'; 49% could speak it but could not write it. (Presumably the vast majority of those who did not go to school spoke no French.) *France*: in 18 out of 89 departments, more than 25% of schoolchildren (aged 7−13) 'do not speak French'.
(The 1863 survey was the last one.)

(B) Germany
There were an estimated 3−500,000 readers of German in the age of Goethe and Schiller, but many fewer who actually spoke the *Hochsprache* for everyday purposes.

(C) Italy
At the time of unification, about 400,000 Tuscans, 70,000 Romans, and 160,000 others were 'fluent in Italian'. That accounted for around 2.5% of the total population. Of the non-Roman and non-Tuscan population, only about 0.8% spoke Italian fluently.
SOURCES. E.J. Hobsbawm, *Nations and nationalism since 1780: Programme, myth, reality* (2nd edn, Cambridge, 1992), pp. 60−1; Weber, *Peasants into Frenchmen*, pp. 498−501; De Mauro, *Storia linguistica dell'Italia unita*, i, p. 43

Table 9. The Franchise

(A) The system

	France 1871	Germany 1866	Italy 1861
Suffrage:	universal manhood	universal manhood	very limited*
Government:	responsible	non-responsible†	'responsible'

* Italian Franchise: 1861−80: 3−4%; 1882−1909: 25−35%; after 1909: 'universal' (c.90%).
† German *Reichstag* had very limited powers.

(B) Participation rates: (i) Prussia, 1862−3 (unification issue important)

	% of electorate (October 1863)	% of each class voting April 1862	October 1863
Class I:	4.5%	61.0%	57.0%
Class II:	12.8%	48.0%	44.0%
Class III:	82.7%	30.5%	27.3%
Total:	100%	34.3%	30.9%

(C) Participation rates: (ii) national elections

	France	Germany	Italy
1876/77:	73.9%	60.6%	59.2%
1912/13/14:	74.6%	84.9%	60.4%

SOURCES. Flora, *State, Economy and Society in Western Europe*, i, pp. 113−14, 117−18, 127−8; Hamerow, *Social Foundations of German Unification*, p. 182.

Table 10. Government Expenditure

(A) General and central expenditure (in millions of francs/marks/lire)

	France General	France Central	Germany General	Germany Central	Italy Central
1872:	3348	2817	—	1380	1224
1880–1:	4180	3566	1827	536	1329
1890–1:	4289	3580	3072	1043	1775
1900–1:	4932	3557	4852	1671	1711
1906–7:	5111	3538	7130	2487	2086
1912–13:	6091	4264	9685	3418	3100

As % of National Domestic Product:

	France	France	Germany	Germany	Italy
1871:	11.6%	9.7%	—	10.8%	12.8%
1880–1:	15.4%	13.1%	12.5%	3.7%	13.1%
1890–1:	15.0%	12.5%	15.2%	5.2%	17.3%
1900–1:	15.2%	11.0%	17.4%	6.0%	15.2%
1906–7:	14.6%	10.1%	18.7%	6.5%	16.2%
1912–13:	12.0%	8.4%	20.4%	7.1%	16.9%

(B) General government personnel

France	Germany	Italy
1866: 374,000	1871: 204,000	1871: 282,233
1906: 562,200	1913: 460,000	1911: 444,884

(C) State expenditure on education in France (millions of francs p.a.)

1875–79:	45.6	1900–04:	219.8
1880–84:	102.6	1910–14:	300.0
1890–94:	178.2		

SOURCES. Flora, *State, Economy and Society in Western Europe*, i, chapter 4, and pp. 209, 214–15, 219; L. Fontvielle, *Evolution et croissance de l'Etat Français, 1815–1969* (Cahiers de l'Institut de Sciences Mathématiques et Economiques Appliquées, série AF, no. 13, 1976), annexe II.

Table 11. Consequences?

(A) French response to outbreak of war, seen by primary teachers

| | Mobilisation | | Departure | |
	Gen. pop.	Workers	Gen. pop.	Workers
Reserved:	61%	78%	20%	38%
Calm:	23%	14%	30%	28%
Enthusiastic:	16%	8%	50%	34%

The 'general population' figures represent only six departments, those for 'workers' only the department of the Gard.

(B) Military casualties, 1914–1918

	Total deaths	% of males aged 15–49
France:	1,327,000	13.3%
Germany:	2,037,000	12.5%
Italy:	578,000	7.5%
Allied total:	5,421,000	2.7%
Cental Powers total:	4,029,000	11.5%

SOURCES. Becker, *Comment les Français sont entrés dans la guerre*, pp. 319, 341; J.M. Winter, *The Great War and the British People* (London, 1985), p. 75.

Nationalism and the Italian Army, 1850−1914

John Gooch

Between 1848 and 1870 the army first of Piedmont and then of Italy fought five campaigns and united Italy. Although its feats of arms were frequently inglorious, they were not unsuccessful. They were scarcely over before a glorious past became a political necessity, not least because Italians saw their own unification being compared with that of Germany and did not wish to admit that their military virtues were not equal to those of Prussia. Thus the army, which had a practical importance in the years up to 1870, also came to have a high symbolic importance after that time. Its role in the formation of national identity changed, however, with the fall of Rome on 20 September 1870. Great deeds — or, at least, deeds which had greatness thrust upon them — gave way to more humdrum occupations. 'The age of poetry is over,' King Victor Emmanuel II remarked gloomily, 'the age of prose has begun.'[1]

The Italian army was to bear a heavy burden in the years to come, one which went well beyond the task of national defence. Although nominally united, Italians possessed no shared culture and no common system of ideas, worked through no universal means of communication and recognised no obligations owed to the new state by all its members. Political unity had been imposed upon almost a dozen states, and upon many more regions and localities of varying degrees of isolation. Although the beginnings of industrialisation were apparent in the north, particularly in the cities of Turin and Milan, the Italian population was predominantly rural and peasant, its mental world shaped by the closed relationship between local culture and local *patois*. Far from feeling any strong sense of nationalism, most members of the new state defined their loyalties in terms of the family and of *campanilismo*. Italy had been made but it remained, as Massimo d'Azeglio remarked, to make Italians. That task fell primarily to the army.

In mid-nineteenth century Europe regional isolation was being broken down partly through the spread of the railway. Italy's economic and industrial backwardness meant that she lagged far behind other European powers in this regard. Tennyson's 'ringing grooves of change' were in short supply in the new state, and were to remain so: in 1861 Italy possessed only

---

1 B. Croce, *Storia d'Italia dal 1871 al 1915* (Bari, 1953), p. 2.

2,100 kilometres of track and in 1888 the figure had risen to a mere 11,800 kilometres (none of it double-tracked). Austria had twice that amount, France three times as much and Germany could almost quadruple it.[1] Statistics of every kind — length of track, numbers of locomotives, numbers of passenger and goods waggons — both before and after 1900 all went to demonstrate the same thing: that the means for Italians to move around their country were and remained limited.

If transport could break down the physical barriers which stood in the way of nationalism, education was the most effective means to overcome the mental barriers to unity. Schools were one of the most important means the state could employ for the purposes of national propaganda, and they were used to notable effect by Jules Ferry in France in the 1880s. Here Italy was perhaps even more backward than in the matter of railways. In 1863, when the population numbered some twenty-five millions, only 27,000 Italians over the age of eleven attended school. Primary education was not made obligatory until 1877, and then only for children between the ages of six and nine. That remained the extent of the state's obligations in this field until the First World War. A secondary education was and remained the privilege of the wealthy: in 1901 only 4.6 children in 1,000 received it.[2] In these circumstances illiteracy rates were naturally high: according to the 1861 census, 78 per cent of the population was illiterate, and by 1901 the proportion was still 56.3 per cent. The army had thus to become the school of the nation in more senses than one.

One final impediment to the generation of nationalism among Italians ought to be mentioned, and that is the absence of a state-recognised Church. Religion is not always merely an arm in the arsenal of the state, and Catholicism could divide as much as it could unite. Nonetheless, the dispossession of the Papacy in 1870 and the withdrawal of Catholicism from national politics after 1872 generated tensions and divisions in a society which was already marked by the number and depth of the shatter-lines that ran through it. The hostility between Church and state in the years up to 1914 meant that nationalism and religious belief were competitors and not partners.

The manner in which Italy was unified determined the army's main task in forging nationalism among Italians. The 'Piedmontisation' of Italy involved exporting Sardinian political and legal institutions to the rest of the

---

1 J. Gooch, 'Italy before 1915: The Quandary of the Vulnerable', in *Knowing One's Enemies: Intelligence Assessment before the Two World Wars*, ed. E.R. May (Princeton, 1984), p. 219.
2 G. Candeloro, *Storia dell'Italia moderna*, vi: *Lo sviluppo del capitalismo e del movimento operaio* (Milan, 1970), pp. 256–68.

country and imposing upon it the Savoyard monarchy in the person of Victor Emmanuel II. Only a minority of Italians had fought under the nationalist banner during the wars of the *Risorgimento*, and the remainder had to be taught patriotism. Two sorts of national feeling had to be developed: loyalty to the monarchy and ready acceptance of the obligations and exactions imposed by the state. Since the latter included such unwelcome and unpleasant novelties as the general imposition of military conscription after 1860 and the *macinato*, an extremely unpopular tax on the milling of grain which provoked extensive rioting when it was introduced in 1869 and great relief when it was abandoned in 1884, the task of drumming up enthusiasm for the new state was far from easy.

The importance of the military element in Italian nationalism is readily apparent in the picture of the crown which was conveyed to the populace. The house of Savoy created the image of a military monarchy of the most active kind — though as the crown passed from hand to hand its military enthusiasms became less practical and more academic. Victor Emmanuel II, promoted with the dizzying rapidity experienced only by royalty and by Napoleonic marshals, was a lieutenant at eleven and a general at twenty-six. In the wars of 1859 and 1866 he took command in the field despite the pleading of his more level-headed advisers. Disguising the extent of his military incompetence became one of the major occupations of Italian historians during the years that followed.[1]

His son, Umberto I, who succeeded to the throne in 1878, rarely appeared out of uniform and, although he never commanded in the field, took great delight as colonel-in-chief of a German hussar regiment in personally leading his troops over the assault course during annual manoeuvres in Frankfurt. Victor Emmanuel III also underwent the customary military education, but being of a more reflective cast of mind than either of his predecessors he preferred military history to active soldiering.[2] Like his father and grandfather, he manipulated military symbology in order to maintain the close association between nationalism and the crown; unlike them he was an unenthusiastic soldier who could not be bothered to see his army off to the Libyan war in 1911.

Important though it was as a symbol, the army was of far greater practical importance in the genesis of Italian nationalism. It was the only national institution which directly touched the lives of more than a fraction of the population. Its activities could therefore exert a vital influence on the

---

1 P. Del Negro, 'Villafranca: La leggenda di un re "nazionale"', in P. Del Negro, *Esercito, stato, società* (Bologna, 1979); D. Mack Smith, *Victor Emmanuel, Cavour and the Risorgimento* (Oxford, 1971).
2 D. Mack Smith, *Italy and its Monarchy* (Yale, 1989).

people, either directly or indirectly. Accordingly issues such as the length of military service and the proportion of each annual class actually called to the colours directly influenced the spread of civic consciousness among the population. The decisions which were taken about these matters were coloured by the acknowledged need to foster *Italianità*. Indeed, no other army in Europe devoted more consideration to the problems of educating soldiers — in the broadest sense of the word.

War had forged the Italian state, and throughout the years between the capture of Rome in 1870 and the outbreak of the First World War some nationalist politicians from both left and right were inclined to argue that another war was exactly what was needed to unify the nation. They were always in a minority, and there was never a moment when Italy came anywhere near fighting a war in Europe — although in 1888 Crispi did try to start one.[1] She did, however, undertake colonial wars first in Ethiopia (1885–1896) and then in Libya (1911–12). Although the circumstances of these wars were different, and although there is still dispute among historians about their causes, both episodes had broad features in common. They were opportunistic essays in great power policy overseas, undertaken primarily as a result of political calculation, partially clothed with the garb of commercial gain (which proved entirely illusory in both cases) and justified by reference to a 'civilising mission' which was belied by the behaviour of Italian troops overseas. The army was by no means unanimous in its enthusiasm for either venture, but took little or no part in the decisions to undertake them: it was always a functional elite held at arm's length by Italian politicians.

Since those politicians by and large doubted the army's capabilities they were not much inclined to gamble on it to win nationalist support. In 1896 Crispi did try to overcome his domestic difficulties by urging his field commander in Eritrea to win a glorious victory, but the outcome was the battle of Adua — the most decisive defeat suffered by any white nation during all the colonial wars of the nineteenth century. Considerable nationalist enthusiasm greeted the outbreak of the Libyan war in September 1911, but it soon began to fizzle out as it became apparent that the war was going to be a difficult one to win. While military activity overseas was sporadic and often disappointing, the domestic use of the army in the cause of nationalism was both continuous and calculated.

Like almost all other European armies, the Piedmontese army of the 1850s was a 'barrack army', designed to provide a small, professional, well-trained standing force but lacking reserves. Of an annual class of 50,000

---

1   R. Mori, *La politica estera di Francesco Crispi (1887–1891)* (Rome, 1973), pp. 117–20.

young men, only a quarter were required to do any military service at all, the remainder being sent home after qualifying for social exemptions or failing on health grounds.[1] Only a portion of the unlucky group was called on to serve with the colours; and whilst legally bound for eight years, most of them were released after five.[2] In order to make fuller use of the army as an instrument for national education, it was necessary to shorten the period of service and to put larger numbers of young men through the regular army; however financial and other considerations dictated that the term of service remained legally fixed at eight years until 1871, when it was lowered to four. In 1875 the term was again lowered to three years, and in 1910 to two. At the same time attempts were made to increase the size of the army and therefore extend its influence. For most of the period, then, the vehicle for the indoctrination of the Italian people was a short-service army.

As the *Risorgimento* gathered pace after 1859 Piedmont began to extend her sway, adding first Lombardy, then the central duchies and finally the kingdom of Naples to her domains in the course of little more than a year. In March 1860, in the middle of this process of expansion — which was a difficult one for the military — a decision was taken which determined the shape of the Italian army until the First World War. Doubtful of the loyalties of the newly-acquired states, and particularly of their armies, the minister of war, Manfredo Fanti, ordered that in future all regiments should be composed of recruits from at least two different parts of Italy and that they should always be stationed in regions other than those from which they drew their members.[3]

In turning their backs on territorial recruiting, the generals were making a conscious effort to foster Italian nationalism. The official justifications for this system, which were frequently repeated during the years up to 1900, rested upon both positive and negative assumptions. On the positive side it was believed that by mixing recruits together in this way, soldiers would hear and come to understand different dialects, and would gain a better appreciation of Italians who came from other parts of the country than their own. Being stationed away from home was also held to be an advantage since it would mean that recruits would come to know other parts of the country at first hand. On the negative side lay deep-seated fears of regional separatism and an awareness of the danger of re-creating provincial armies

---

1 B. Farolfi, 'Dall'antropometria militare alla storia del corpo', *Quaderni storici*, xlii (1979).
2 V. Ilari, *Storia del servizio militare in Italia* (Rome, 1989), i, pp. 317–76; G. Rochat and G. Massobrio, *Breve storia dell'esercito italiano dal 1861 al 1943* (Turin, 1978), pp. 18–20.
3 F. Bogliari and C. Traversi, *Manfredo Fanti* (Rome, 1980), p. 39; J. Whittam, *The Politics of the Italian Army* (London, 1977), p. 60.

which was inherent in any system of regional recruiting, a fear which greatly exercised President Thiers in France in the early 1870s.[1] There was also a feeling — which was not often voiced openly but which was deeply felt — that whilst the inhabitants of northern Italy were inherently reliable, those from central Italy and particularly from the south were not. *Romagnoli* and Sicilians needed, as one commentator put it, to be scattered through the army like pinches of spice.[2]

By the 1870s, national recruitment was firmly established and Italian regiments were drawing their manpower from five or six different districts, and sometimes from as many as ten. At the same time regiments were rotated around Italy. In the 1870s the average regiment moved three times every decade, but by the early years of the twentieth century this rate had slowed down to two moves every ten years. A variety of reasons were used to justify this policy, of which the fostering of nationalism was one; others included the fact that certain parts of Italy were too pestilential for any unit to be based there for more than a fairly short period, and the argument that the army would be a less secure instrument of civil power if units were allowed to stay very long in the same place, when they would be likely to form links of all sorts with the local populace.[3]

Whether Italian nationalism was significantly enhanced as a result of the policy of national recruitment is difficult to say, but the evidence available suggests that it was not. Contemporary memoirs speak of the disdain of northerners for the south which they saw as backward and corrupt, a perception which first-hand acquaintance served only to strengthen. That the system could have effects which were exactly the opposite of those intended was shown all too clearly at Pizzofalcone in 1884. There, in a barracks near Naples, a gang of northerners surrounded two Calabrians and taunted them about their southern origins. One of the two, a non-commissioned officer named Misdea, went to his dormitory, returned with his rifle and fired over fifty shots, killing seven soldiers and wounding six more. After a trial at which some of the members of the tribunal could not understand what he was saying because of the thickness of his Calabrian accent, Misdea was found guilty of murder and shot. While the trial was taking place a *carabiniere* was killed under similar circumstances, also at Pizzofalcone. The response of the War Ministry was to order that soldiers no longer be allowed

---

1 A. Mitchell, 'Thiers, MacMahon, and the Conseil Supérieur de la Guerre', *French Historical Studies*, vi (1969), p. 238.
2 'L'altra campana', *L'Italia militare e marina*, 31 October/1 November 1895.
3 P. Bertinaria, 'Lo stanziamento dell'esercito italiano in età liberale, 1869–1910', in *Esercito e città dall'unità agli anni trenta: Convegno nazionale di studio* (Perugia, 1989), p. 18; G. Rochat, 'Strutture dell'esercito dell'Italia liberale: I reggimenti di fanteria e bersaglieri', in *ibid.*, pp. 33–4, 48–9.

to keep live rounds in barracks.[1]

Such was the strength of feeling about the dangers of regionalism that only one exception was made to the general system of national recruitment. The need to be able to react quickly to an attack by France and to bar the Alpine passes dictated a locally recruited military force; otherwise troops could not hope to be on the spot quickly enough. Accordingly in 1872 special regional mountain units — the *Alpini* — were created. The old guard of the Piedmontese army inveighed against this move, warning that troops recruited in this way would lack discipline and would amount to no more than companies of smugglers; but the *Alpini* seem to have served efficiently and effectively. However when reservists were recalled in order to suppress the riots in Milan in 1898, the highest number of absentees was recorded in an *Alpini* regiment.[2]

Whatever its putative social advantages, national recruitment was militarily extremely disadvantageous: the process of mobilising the army for war was severely slowed down as a consequence of the requirement that reservists travel to their regimental depots in other parts of the country, a problem which had been all too clearly demonstrated in the French army at the start of the war of 1870. By the 1890s, fortified by the opinion of outside observers such as Archduke Albrecht of Austria-Hungary, the army was in a mood to abolish Fanti's system and replace it with territorial recruitment.[3] But the politicians were not, and when proposals were put to parliament in 1895 — against a background of agrarian rioting in Sicily and growing socialist agitation in northern Italy — they were peremptorily rejected by liberals and conservatives alike on the grounds that regional recruitment would mean renouncing 'the most potent means of Italianisation'.[4] Against this argument military logic alone could make no progress and subsequent attempts to alter the system all failed, despite strong backing from the Italian general staff.

The third factor affecting the army's capacity to influence civilians directly through military service, alongside the term of service and national recruitment, was the size of the annual contingent which was incorporated for service with the colours. Here economics played a central role, for Italy was simply too poor to be able to afford to take into the army every young

---

1 J. Gooch, *Army, State and Society in Italy 1870–1915* (London, 1989), p. 63.
2 Ilari, *Storia del servizio militare*, ii, p. 234.
3 Rome, Ufficio Storico dello Stato Maggiore dell'Esercito, MS. Adetti Militari: Vienna busta 7: Brusati despatch, 2 April 1891, no. 43.
4 L. Pelloux, *Quelques souvenirs de ma vie*, ed. G. Manacorda (Rome, 1967), p. xliv; Del Negro, *Esercito, stato, società*, p. 217; 'Il sistema territoriale', *L'Italia militare e marina*, 8/9 October 1895.

Nationalism and the Italian Army, 1850–1914

man who was physically capable of service.[1] Other considerations also played a part in the process of calculating the military arithmetic, including the desire to provide means by which the sons of the bourgeoisie could evade some or all of their military obligations; the result was a lengthy list of the grounds on which exemption from military service could be granted. Nevertheless, the outcome was that until the eve of the First World War, when the system was tightened up and the list of exemptions drastically pruned, on average no more than a quarter and sometimes only a fifth of the annual class ever donned a uniform and saw the inside of a barracks for more than a few days each year. In numerical terms this amounted to an annual intake ranging between 60,000 and 90,000 men.

Of all features of the Italian military system during the years following reunification, this last is perhaps the most important. What it meant was that, appearances to the contrary, there was less of a difference than might be supposed between the long-service, professional Piedmontese 'barrack army' of the 1850s and the short-service Italian conscript army of the 1880s and 1890s as far as direct military influence on the population went. Limitations on the size of the annual contingent meant limitations on the degree of nationalist influence the army could hope to exercise, even at its most effective. As military commentators pointed out with growing frequency after 1900, when the pressures on the army to do more in the way of educating the nation and do it better increased, most of the nation was out of its reach.[2]

The Piedmontese army of the 1850s, and the Italian army which succeeded it in 1861, was in no sense a genuine citizen army: it was relatively small, isolated from society and composed of people most of whom, for one reason or another, were unable to avoid military service. It was also largely illiterate. These circumstances shaped the concepts of the social function of the army which prevailed from 1850 to 1870: that it should teach its members to read and write and instill in them a respect for authority. The means adopted were accordingly a combination of education and military discipline. Regimental schools were created in the aftermath of the war of 1848–9 and they remained an important part of military life until 1892, when they were abolished. Time was set aside each week for instruction and the authorities provided reading primers which used simple moralistic stories as their vehicle to literacy.

After taking into account the tendency of officialdom to inflate any figures in its own favour, the army's literacy campaign seems to have been something of a success up to 1892. It was aided by the fact that incoming

1 L. De Rosa, 'Incidenza delle spese militari sullo sviluppo economico italiano', *Atti del primo Convegno Nazionale di Storia militare* (Rome, 1969).
2 'Per le armi della Patria', *L'Italia militare e marina*, 9/10 December 1902.

205

recruits appear to have been of a higher educational standard than the population at large: from the 1870s to the early 1890s about 50 per cent of the annual intake were illiterate, while the national figure never fell below 67 per cent. Its success probably had much to do with the provision that those who passed an approved literacy test could be released from military service early. The army's claims of literacy rates of over 90 per cent on discharge need to be viewed with a degree of caution, but even left-wing Italian historians accept that the system of regimental schooling played a significant part in diminishing the national levels of illiteracy during these years. After the regimental schools were abolished, rates of illiteracy on exit jumped sharply from under 10 per cent to 25 per cent.[1]

An army which discharged only some 40,000 time-expired soldiers into society each year could not hope to exercise much in the way of direct influence on a population of over thirty millions. Rather, its alumni were expected to provide an example which it was hoped others would follow. Imbued with simple *Risorgimento* myths and accustomed through the ready acceptance of military discipline to obey superiors, they would be ejected into society imbued with patriotism, love of work, a sense of national dignity and the *spirito militare*. Conservative politicians, however, were sufficiently distrustful of their population not to want to introduce a shorter term of military service and thereby spread these qualities more widely through society.

Literacy was an important instrument in the development of Italian nationalism, particularly when allied to military themes, and the last years of the 'age of poetry' witnessed a spate of books which were designed to develop just this form of patriotism. The best known was undoubtedly Edmondo de Amicis's *La vita militare*, published in 1868 as a counter-blast to an anti-militarist novel which had appeared the previous year. Adopting a new literary approach to military life, De Amicis avoided both the traditional glorification of the army and the dry style of specialised military journals, and instead sought to present the army as simply a part of the natural world. De Amicis's example spawned a great many imitators and a whole genre of military romances began to appear thereafter. Their interest lies not so much in the fact that a large number of them were written by soldier-authors as in that many of them were aimed at soldiers as well as civilians. Intended to be educative as well as entertaining, they stressed the themes of military pride, loyalty and adherence to authority.[2]

1 Ilari, *Storia del servizio militare*, ii, pp. 399–400.
2 D. Maldini Chiarito, 'Alcune osservazioni a proposito della vita militare nella narrativa e nella memorialistica dell'ottocento', in *Esercito e città dall'unità agli anni trenta*, pp. 19–26; P. Del Negro, 'De Amicis versus Tarchetti: letteratura e militari al tramonto del Risorgimento', in Del Negro, *Esercito, stato, società*.

While the army was still fighting for Italian independence its role as educator of society was necessarily somewhat circumscribed, but by the late 1860s, when only Rome remained to be won, it was clear that Italy was on the point of entering a new age in which the role of institutions such as the army would have to change substantially. The beginnings of a new strain of thinking were apparent when, in 1868, the Pedagogical Society of Milan held a conference entitled 'The Italian army in peacetime in relation to the education of the masses and national unification.' This produced the blueprint for a conservative nation-in-arms, identifying two paramount roles for a peace-time army: civic education and the development of feelings of national identity.

The intellectual impetus behind the Milan congress came from the impact which positivist ideas of social psychology were beginning to make both on civilians and on military thinkers. Herbert Spencer's views on the need for a new kind of education to meet new needs, in contrast to the inaptness of ideas based upon military discipline, struck a chord in a society which was keen to substitute the lay educator for the priest. On their own, such ideas would probably have made only slow progress in affecting the army; but they received a powerful external stimulus in 1870−1 when first the Franco-Prussian War and then the Paris Commune led military authorities to accept — sometimes reluctantly — that the old-style Piedmontese army no longer fitted either the military or the social needs of the new Italy.

The success of the Prussian short-service conscript armies in the war against France demonstrated quite unequivocally that the mass army of citizen-soldiers had arrived, and within a few years the German model was being copied by countries as far distant as Russia and Japan. In Italy there was much debate about the reasons for Prussia-Germany's success. Soldiers pointed to the crucial role played by the general staff; conservatives laid great stress on the principle of obedience which was characteristic of the semi-feudal Prussian state; and liberal reformists and the Left pointed to the military value of popular energy, properly harnessed.[1] Finally, the popularisation of Clausewitz's ideas about the importance of moral will in battle which was one of the consequences of Prussian success in 1870 alerted the military to the need to deal with soldiers as individuals and no longer to treat them as automatons.

The role of the army as educator of the nation took on a new importance as the needs of the politicians and the requirements of the soldiers came to coincide. The military saw battlefield success as the consequence of internal and not external factors acting upon citizen-soldiers: only a high level of

---

[1] F. Minniti, 'Esercito e politica da Porta Pia alla Triplice Alleanza (I)', *Storia contemporanea*, iii (1972).

national culture could provide the necessary psychological impulse to bring victory. Strong individual motivation was of even greater importance on the modern battlefield, where the volume of fire a defence could lay down dictated that troops could no longer fight in close order but had to be spread widely and operate in small groups. This necessitated fostering a greater degree of independence without losing the collective cohesion necessary to launch successful attacks. Therefore the officers wanted better-educated soldiers who were imbued with patriotism. For their part, the politicians wanted more patriotic citizens and were prepared to see the army undertake an educative function that the state could not — or would not — afford. Moltke's oft-quoted remark that Prussia's armies owed their success to the Prussian schoolmaster found a ready audience in Italy where educational ideas were beginning to move in a similar direction.

After 1870, the idea that the army should be the educator of the nation was the central theme of a stream of books and articles which flowed from the pen of Italy's leading military authority, Nicola Marselli.[1] Marselli was much influenced by Herbert Spencer's ideas and in 1871 he applied them to an analysis of the social questions underlying the Paris Commune. His conclusion was that, if political upheaval were to be avoided, a modern society needed a system of moral education to spread concepts of patriotism, nationalism and loyalty to institutions. Education was to be the integrator, and it was the army's role to provide it. For Italy the army was — in Marselli's much-quoted words — 'the crucible of the nation'.[2]

The military reforms of the 1870s, which reduced the term of service first to four years and then to three, created a degree of nervousness in the official mind about how to inculcate subordination into troops in what seemed to traditionally-minded officers to be an indecently short period under arms, and throughout the 1880s a school of thought existed which pressed the virtues of old-style discipline. However, the bulk of the officer-corps and the high command accepted the importance of their new role as educator of the nation, and indeed a new branch of learning came into existence to develop that role: it was christened *pedagogia militare*, and Marselli was its leading light.

A variety of means were adopted to transmit moral training to the troops. They included regimental schools and conferences, books and newspapers. Regimental schooling does not seem to have got much beyond imparting the simple rudiments of national feeling, emphasising the cult of the flag and

---

1 A. Visintin, 'Esercito e società nella pubblistica militare dell'ultimo ottocento', *Rivista di storia contemporanea*, xvi (1987), pp. 38–41. The best summary of Marselli's works is P. Pieri, *Guerra e politica negli scrittori italiani* (Milan and Naples, 1955), pp. 275–97.
2 N. Marselli, *Gli avvenimenti del 1870–1* (Turin, 1873), i, p. 142.

encouraging recruits to learn the names of members of the royal family.[1] The newspapers offered slightly more sophisticated fare. The most important of them, and the first one to be aimed specifically at conscripts as an organ of moral education, was *La caserma* ('The Barracks'). Founded in 1886, and praised by Marselli, it contained a judicious mixture of glorious episodes from the military history of various armies and comments on every-day affairs. Whilst there was a strong element of '*Risorgimento* nostalgia' about it, it did not shrink from discussing what were euphemistically labelled the 'difficult' episodes of the struggle for independence such as the naval defeat at Lissa in 1866, the civil uprising in Palermo in the same year, and the attack on Garibaldi at Aspromonte in 1867.

An 'idealist' view of the army prevailed during the 1870s and 1880s which correlated the moral education of the individual soldier with the effective functioning of the army and which held that the army had to take on the role of other, less efficient civil institutions. It came under attack from two directions. On the one hand it was argued that the nation's schools should serve the army and not the other way round, and that it was not the army's business to educate people, but simply to give them military training; while on the other, some acute observers pointed out that the nature of the raw material on which the army had to work was changing in important ways which made it necessary to revise both the content and the methods of military education. By the 1880s generations of recruits were coming into the army who had never known a divided Italy. They had had a more secular education than their predecessors; they were more individualistic; and they were more knowledgeable about citizens' rights. To instill nationalism into these young men was a task of a rather different order than it had been twenty or thirty years earlier.

The events of the 1890s, which more than bore out the gloomiest predictions of the most hardened conservatives, completely changed the army's role in society. Organised socialism made its appearance in northern Italy and its proponents began to attack the army as an instrument of reaction and social oppression. Agrarian disturbances in the south gathered pace and ferocity. Anarchists — all too commonly Italian — assassinated the president of France, the shah of Persia, the empress of Austria and finally, in 1900, King Umberto of Italy. The Catholics re-entered national politics on a platform of social reform, and even the French seemed to be making threatening noises. The court and the conservative political circles

---

1 N. Labanca, 'I programmi dell'educazione morale del soldato. Per un studio sulla pedagogia militare nell'Italia liberale', in *Esercito e città dall'unità agli anni trenta*, pp. 521–7; N. Labanca, 'Una pedagogia militare per l'Italia liberale: I primi giornali per il soldato', *Rivista di storia contemporanea*, xvii (1988), pp. 554–7.

surrounding it genuinely feared that Italy was on the point of dissolving little more than two decades after it had been unified, and in 1897 a few worried conservatives said that the dynasty and the monarchy needed a war to overcome the mounting internal divisions.[1] In these circumstances the army's role as the main prop of Italian nationalism underwent a radical change. Instead of being the nation's schoolmaster it became the nation's policeman.

From the middle of the 1890s up to 1914, the army found itself fighting a defensive action on behalf of Italian nationalism and the *Risorgimento* settlement against the social and political forces unleashed as a consequence of the spread of urbanisation and industrialisation, of workers' movements and of socialism. It was now required to fight a defensive action both inside and outside the barracks to try to neutralise the waves coming from society at large which threatened to smash the established fabric of the nation into atoms. In these circumstances the notion of 'military propaganda' took on an entirely new meaning. In the eyes of the military, the moral preparation of the country and of the army were being hindered by subversive theories and by utilitarianism, which were suffocating patriotism and military sentiment and which had to be fought with maximum energy.[2] The problem was that many of the officer-corps, particularly at the junior level, were ill-equipped for the task. Like their French and German counterparts, Italian officers found during these years that they needed a much higher level of education if they were to match their men in the arts of the dialectic and win them back to patriotic nationalism. They also suffered from a comparatively low level of professional competence and of general culture which made it hard for them to win the respect of their men on an individual basis. A promising reformist movement launched by junior officers during these years which aimed to change the whole basis of military discipline from a system based on punishment to one based on mutual respect was stifled by the higher reaches of authority.[3]

The army sought to combat the anti-patriotic attitudes of its recruits in two ways. A propaganda campaign was launched in the columns of a new military newspaper, the *Giornale del soldato* ('Soldier's Journal'), which was founded in 1899. It resorted to a crude form of guilt by association, labelling anti-militarists as 'anarchists, assassins and cowards', and charging them with being obstacles to the industrial and commercial development of Italy, of which the army and navy were an integral part. And it adopted a crude and narrow educational philosophy based on the proposition that what was needed to instill patriotism into the hearts of the nation was 'the history

1 D. Farini, *Diario di fine secolo*, ed. E. Morelli (Rome, 1962), ii, p. 1151.
2 Labanca, 'I programmi dell'educazione morale del soldato', pp. 532−4.
3 Ilari, *Storia del servizio militare*, ii, pp. 166−7.

of wars, of great deeds, of great men, of great things.' Its effect seems to have been small, not least because probably not much more than half the army could read.[1]

The second string to the military bow was the attempt to diffuse 'agrarian culture' throughout the army. This was done by means of lectures, practical exercises and lessons in agricultural techniques.[2] Since only 43 per cent of the annual intake were agricultural workers, this scheme was clearly designed, in part at least, to woo the intransigent proletariat to the supposedly conservative values of the peasant. It was a programme in which Victor Emmanuel III took a personal interest. The German army took much the same approach to the problem of reviving patriotism in its recruits; neither it nor its Italian *confrère* seems to have had very much success.

Little practical help was to be gained from the circulars sent around by the war ministry to the regimental officers who were struggling with a task which most recognised was beyond them. They were advised to talk to their men about civil rights and obligations; to make them understand the necessity of the laws which governed civil life; and to make them realise that liberty came from the scrupulous observance of these laws.[3] On the eve of the First World War they were keenly aware of the weakness of Italian patriotism and of the dangers this posed for the army, and looked with some envy at the Japanese — a light-hearted people who enjoyed life but who, as the Russo-Japanese War had revealed, were ready to sacrifice themselves in the cause of national honour.[4]

*

Fostering nationalism was always regarded as one of the primary tasks of the Italian army. It is much easier to chart the ways in which it sought to do this, and to identify the stages through which it passed between 1850 and 1914, than to gauge its success. On the other hand, a system of conscription does provide the historian with a plethora of statistics from which some tentative conclusions may be drawn.

Figures of the numbers of potential conscripts who failed to present themselves at the annual tribunals make it possible to construct a rather rough-and-ready map of Italian military patriotism. After a brief upheaval in the early 1860s, when Umbria and the Marches headed the lists for absenteeism, the national picture settled down and remained more or less

---

1 Labanca, 'Una pedagogia militare per l'Italia liberale', pp. 567–9, 577. For a contrary view, see Ilari, *Storia del servizio militare*, ii, pp. 391–2.
2 Visintin, 'Esercito e società nella pubblistica militare', p. 53.
3 'Le science social nell'Esercito', *L'Italia militare e marina*, 4/5 February 1902; 'Propaganda contro propaganda', *L'Esercito italiano*, 16 October 1904.
4 'Preparazione militare e virtù di popolo', *L'Esercito italiano*, 6 February 1910.

unchanged until 1914. The most patriotic regions were Sardinia, Piedmont, Tuscany, Lombardy, Umbria and Emilia Romagna, while the least patriotic were Sicily, Calabria and Basilicata, together with the city of Genoa. Used chronologically rather than geographically, the same statistics show a sharp fall in absenteeism after 1863, when the national figure was approximately 20 per cent, to rates of between 3 and 5 per cent during the 1870s and 1880s. Thereafter, perhaps in reaction to the unpopularity of the repressive actions of the state, the figure began to climb again: by 1898 it had mounted to over 7 per cent and in 1914 it reached 10.46 per cent.[1]

Statistics of the proportion of potential soldiers who failed to appear for military service are of course of somewhat limited use in assessing the effectiveness of the army's programmes for raising national consciousness. Slightly better guides are to be found in the rates of re-appearance after active service either for further training or when recalled for public order duties. Here the figures suggest varying degrees of failure rather than varying degrees of success. During the 1880s and early 1890s approximately 25 per cent of those recalled for obligatory training failed to show up, and by 1912 that figure had risen to almost 58 per cent. When summoned to suppress public disturbances, civilian soldiers showed somewhat more enthusiasm, though still being far from whole-hearted about the business. In 1898, a year of national rioting on an unparalleled scale, 14 per cent of conscripts failed to respond to recall orders. By 1912 that figure had risen to almost 30 per cent.[2]

The statistics suggest that the army was failing to meet the demand placed upon it to win the hearts and minds of generations of Italians who were coming under the influence of socialism and materialism. All the other available evidence points to the same conclusion. As late as 1907, Victor Emmanuel III told the British military attaché that his people still had 'to be educated, to be taught habits of discipline, obedience and orderliness', and that they had yet to learn what 'patriotism, in the broad national sense, means'.[3] On the eve of the First World War, the Italian officer-corps was deeply embittered by the failure of the civilian politicians to hold the nation together and by the weight of responsibility they were being asked to carry in attempting to bridge the chasms in Italian society. It was for this reason, among others, that the army was prepared to give qualified support to Fascism in Italy after 1922.

1 Ilari, *Storia del servizio militare*, ii, pp. 358–60; Del Negro, *Esercito, stato, società*, pp. 169–216.
2 Ilari, *Storia del servizio militare*, ii, pp. 175, 360.
3 London, Public Record Office, MS. Foreign Office Papers, F.O. 371/469/979: Delmé Radcliffe to Egerton, 14 December 1907.

Euskadi: Basque Nationalism in the Twentieth Century

Martin Blinkhorn

The experience of the Basques provides proof that a people does not necessarily equal a nation, nor does a nation have to form the basis of a state. This essay examines the emergence of a Basque national consciousness and nationalist movement during the course of the twentieth century. In doing so it touches upon the role of history as both reality and myth, upon the relationship between regionalism and nationalism, upon different conceptions of nationality — historical, territorial, linguistic, and so on — and upon a number of other questions which, despite the distance separating the Basque country from the North and Baltic Seas, ought to have some bearing on the wider matters discussed in this volume.

The modern Basque region is normally considered to comprise four Spanish provinces, Vizcaya, Guipúzcoa, Alava and Navarra, and three French districts within the department of Basses-Pyrénées, Benaparroa (Basse Navarre), Zuberoa (Soule) and Laburdi (Labourd). This region embraces all those who speak Euskera, the Basque language, today, together with many who do not. It includes the south of Navarre, where Euskera has not been spoken for at least 200 years, but excludes parts of Gascony which were certainly Euskera-speaking once upon a time. Of the 2.1 million inhabitants of Spain's Basque-Navarrese region, perhaps 600,000 actually speak Euskera, though many more would consider themselves ethnically Basque.

Nobody is certain where the Basques came from, how long they have been where they are now, or who they really are. There would seem to be three main possibilities as to their origins. The first is that they are the survivors of peoples who once inhabited a much greater area, perhaps even the whole of the Iberian peninsula. Although appealing to *Spanish* nationalists anxious to link the Basques' identity with that of Spain as a whole, and thereby diminish their exclusive link with 'the Basque country' as we now understand the term, this seems unlikely. The other two possibilities both link the Basques with roughly the area they now occupy, one being that they are, so to speak, the 'original' inhabitants of the western Pyrenean region and perhaps of a somewhat more extensive area radiating outwards from it, the second that they represent a 'freak', non-Indo-European element swept westwards during the Indo-European population movements of the Bronze Age.[1]

What *is* beyond dispute is the uniqueness of the Basques' ethno-linguistic character. Their language, Euskera, is a non-Indo-European, agglutinative tongue with no proven relationship with any other surviving language. Perhaps, as some early nineteenth-century Basque priests argued, Euskera was verily the language of the Creator, of Adam and Eve, and of the entire pre-Babel world. Perhaps it is true (though given the chronology of the Creation, this seems inconsistent with the previous theory) that the Devil himself tried and failed to learn the language, leaving the Basques uniquely untemptable and virtuous. More scientifically, attempts have been made since early in the nineteenth century to link Euskera with the languages of ancient Egypt, the Hittites or the Phoenicians; with those of northern or southern Amerindians; with Berber or ancient Ligurian; with Finnish or Magyar; with Georgian and other Caucasian languages; and with pre-Celtic Irish or — of course — Pictish. All have proved (to say the least) inconclusive.[2]

Language therefore tells us little that is certain about the Basques' origins, save that they are different from those of every other surviving European — and probably non-European — people. Nor does archaeological evidence tell us as much as we would like, though we may safely accept a continuous 'Basque' presence in mountainous districts of the western Pyrenees and eastern Cantabria from the Bronze Age. Only from the time of Christ is the Basques' presence in their present-day heartland clearly attested, by a succession of intrusive observers: Romans, Visigoths, Franks and Arabs — though no document in Basque exists from earlier than the mid-tenth century. The various Basque tribes appear to have co-existed harmoniously with the Romans, who (when not recruiting them for military service) mostly left them alone. Relations with the Visigoths were more disturbed; they gave the Basques their enduring reputation as warlike troublemakers. In the seventh century, a combination of population increase among the Basques and political instability among their neighbours enabled the Basques to spread northwards throughout much of what became Gascony, and perhaps southwards to reoccupy Alava, which they had at some earlier time vacated, and consolidate their presence in southern Navarre and present-day Rioja. This would appear to be the moment in historical time when the Basques occupied the greatest area of northern

---

1 R. Gallop, *The Book of the Basques* (London, 1930), pp. 1–22; R. Collins, *The Basques* (Oxford, 1986), pp. 1–8, 13–30.
2 *Ibid.*, pp. 8–12.

Spain and south-western France.[1]

With the emergence in the early ninth century of the independent principality of Pamplona we have what many Basque nationalists have regarded as the first Basque 'state', one which reached its apogee in the early eleventh century when, under Sancho el Mayor, what had now become the kingdom of Navarra encompassed all 'Spanish' Basque, and a substantial part of 'French' Basque, territory. With the subsequent division of the kingdom, Navarra herself embarked upon a historical course separate from that of the other three Spanish Basque provinces, Vizcaya, Guipúzcoa and Alava, whose fate became linked with that of what was to become the Castilian kingdom.[2]

It is important to stress that little or no *Basque* consciousness as such accompanied either the emergence of Navarra or the other provinces' relationship with Castile. Whether or not the concept of a 'Basque' Navarrese state has any validity, that of a medieval Basque *nation* certainly does not. Although it is likely (very little in this area is certain) that the ruling elites of the region continued to speak Basque well into the central Middle Ages, they, and much of the urban population of the region, also from an early date displayed signs of what might, in the broadest sense, be termed Latinisation, involving the embracing of a Latin 'high' and religious culture and, as it gradually emerged, the use of a 'Spanish' vernacular. Medieval Euskera produced no high culture analogous to that of Catalonia. Long before the union of the Spanish kingdoms in the late fifteenth and the early sixteenth centuries, Euskera had become the non-literary and seldom written language of the region's peasantry. During the early modern and modern periods, until its revival this century, spoken Euskera contracted not only sociologically but also geographically, retreating from the larger towns into the countryside, and in Alava and Navarra from south to north: a thorny problem for twentieth-century Basque nationalists eager to construct a 'greater' Euskadi whose borders would coincide with the limits of spoken Euskera in its heyday.[3]

With regard to the Basque-Navarrese region's historical relationship with Spain, two notable features require highlighting. The first is the constitutional relationship of Vizcaya, Guipúzcoa and Alava with the Castilian and later the Spanish monarchy, and that of Navarra with Spain following its incorporation in 1512. All were governed by a complex body of customary laws, the *fueros*, the overall effect of which was to allow both

---

1 *Ibid.*, pp. 100−1.
2 J. del Burgo, *Historia de Navarra: La lucha por la libertad* (Madrid, 1978), pp. 519 ff.; R. Bard, *Navarra: The Durable Kingdom* (Reno, Nevada, 1982), pp. 19−40.
3 M. Heiberg, *The Making of the Basque Nation* (Cambridge, 1989), pp. 46−8.

parts of the region a degree of administrative, economic and fiscal autonomy, and what later generations, at least, came to regard as internal democracy, which survived even after the *fueros* of other regions — Aragon, Catalonia and Valencia — had been destroyed by the Bourbons in the eighteenth century. Although the Basque-Navarrese *fueros* had nothing to do with 'Basqueness' in any ethnic or linguistic sense, their survival into the age of modern nationalism helped give the Basque provinces and Navarra a pronounced sense of their own identity and was to prove vital to Basque nationalist ideology. The knowledge that Navarra had once been a powerful, independent 'Basque' state, and the (disputed) conviction that the association of Vizcaya, Guipúzcoa and Alava with Castile, and thereafter with Spain, was a voluntary and dissoluble one, provided Basque nationalism with indispensable historical 'myths'.[1]

The second feature which needs to be stressed is the enduring, close integration of Basque and Navarrese elites into the public affairs of Spain: the court, the bureaucracy and the armed services. The disproportionate role played, for example, by Basque seafarers and Imperial officials in the opening up, settlement, administration and defence of the Spanish American empire was followed in later generations by the emergence of a financial and industrial elite whose affairs were utterly bound up with the interests of Spain. Although one might speak of these elites as possessing a very strong *regional* consciousness, linked with their autonomous institutions and casually labelled 'Basque', this had little to do with Basque culture, language or, therefore, nationality.[2]

*

The emergence of a self-conscious Basque nationalism from the late nineteenth century onwards can best be understood in terms of responses to two more or less parallel, even complementary, processes of transformation affecting the Basque-Navarrese region: first, the completion (however imperfect in detail) by the Spanish 'liberal' state of the centralising and rationalising process begun by the eighteenth-century Bourbons, a process from which the region had until the 1830s remained relatively immune; secondly, the economic, and with it the demographic and cultural,

---

1 S.G. Payne, *Basque Nationalism* (Reno, Nevada, 1975), pp. 14–15.
2 R. Barahona, 'Basque Regionalism and Centre-Periphery Relations, 1759–1833', *European Studies Review*, xiii (1983); Heiberg, *Making of the Basque Nation*, pp. 24–32. For detailed accounts of Basque economy and society, see especially E. Fernández de Pinedo, *Crecimiento económico y transformaciones sociales del País Vasco (1100–1850)* (Madrid, 1974), and P. Fernández Albadalejo, *La crisis del Antiguo Régimen en Guipúzcoa, 1766–1833: cambio económico e historia* (Madrid, 1975).

transformation of the coastal Basque provinces, Vizcaya and Guipúzcoa.

At the start of the nineteenth century, Basque consciousness, as distinct from the strong *regional* consciousness referred to above, remained low. Not only was Euskera spoken by a diminishing proportion of the region's population and within a contracting geographical area, but it was also largely confined to the more humble, least educated, least physically mobile members of the community. As a literary medium, or even a medium of written communication, Euskera barely existed, and unlike both Catalan and Galician it possessed no literary tradition capable of serving as the foundation of an imminent cultural renaissance. Although a handful of priests and lay intellectuals was beginning to study and codify Euskera, much as was happening with other 'suppressed' languages elsewhere in Europe, such activities were sluggish and took place in isolation from both the Euskera-speaking peasantry and the largely non-Euskera-speaking, hispanicised Basque elite. Whereas Catalan, and to a lesser extent Galician, enjoyed a cultural revival in the mid-nineteenth century, Euskera accordingly did not.

The nineteenth-century roots of Basque nationalism lie in protests against liberal centralisation and disentailment that were traditionalist and regionalist in character but lacked any appreciable stress upon nationality or ethnicity. The principal channel through which this sentiment flowed from the 1820s down to the 1870s was Carlism, a dissident monarchist cause which, behind a dynastic, ultra-clerical exterior, constituted an immensely complex, 'populist' vehicle for several strands of resistance to the changes associated with Spanish liberalism. In the Basque-Navarrese region, resistance to change took the distinctive form of defending the *fueros* against the centralising and secularising tendencies of both non-Basque and Basque liberals. During the First Carlist War (1833–40) Carlism's leaders, despite their essentially 'Spanish' horizons, calculatingly embraced the defence of the *fueros* in order to attract the support of a population restless at the encroachment of the Spanish state upon the four provinces' autonomous status, and at the threat to the economic benefits which that status was believed to guarantee them. Whether sincere or cynical, the tactic succeeded; thereafter the *fueros* became a Carlist principle and the Basque-Navarrese region a Carlist stronghold.[1]

Down to 1876 Carlism remained the customary form in which Basque-Navarrese regionalism expressed itself. But Carlism's repeated military

---

1 On the origins of Carlism and the First Carlist War in the Basque country, see R. Barahona, *Vizcaya on the Eve of Carlism, 1800–1833* (Reno, Nevada, 1989); J. Coverdale, *The Basque Phase of Spain's First Carlist War* (Princeton, 1984); and Payne, *Basque Nationalism*, pp. 33–60.

defeats — in 1839−40, in the late 1840s and finally in 1876 — brought about not the successful defence of the *fueros* but their steady erosion at the hands of a victorious liberal state. After 1876 Vizcaya, Guipúzcoa and Alava lost most of their former 'foral' rights; Navarra retained somewhat greater autonomy, which served to accentuate an already existing difference of outlook between the Navarrese and many of the inhabitants of the other three provinces. Throughout much of Navarra, Carlism was to retain its hold upon the mass of the rural population; in Guipúzcoa and Vizcaya especially, however, that hold now began to slacken. Having failed in practical terms to defend the region's interests, Carlism, in the eyes of many Basques, proceeded after 1876 to abandon a wholehearted commitment to the *fueros* in favour of an *españolista* (ultra-Spanish) strategy. One young Basque, Luis Arana y Goiri, spoke for many of his contemporaries when, early in the 1880s, he told his younger brother that Carlism had shown itself to be a 'false standard' as far as Basque freedoms were concerned. During the next decade the brother, Sabino Arana y Goiri, was to found modern Basque nationalism.[1]

By the 1890s two other developments were under way which contributed to the birth of a Basque nationalist movement. One was the appearance of a serious nationalist movement in Catalonia.[2] More by virtue of its mere existence than because of any specific characteristics which it exhibited, Catalanism served as an inspiration to the handful of Basque students and intellectuals who, during the 1890s, joined Sabino Arana in founding and running the clubs and periodicals out of which organised Basque nationalism emerged.

The second, more profound, development was the transformation of the coastal Basque provinces, Vizcaya especially, with the growth after 1876 of modern iron and steel, shipbuilding, armaments, paper and cement industries, together with the concentration there of the modern Spanish banking sector. Although Alava and Navarra remained predominantly rural and agricultural until well after the Spanish Civil War of 1936−9, large

---

1 On the links between Carlism and emergent Basque nationalism during this period, see V. Garmendia, 'Carlism and Basque Nationalism', in *Basque Politics: a Case Study in Ethnic Nationalism*, ed. W.A. Douglass (Reno, Nevada, 1985), and J. Real Cuesta, *El carlismo vasco, 1876−1900* (Madrid, 1985), especially pp. 225−7.
2 There is no satisfactory up-to-date study of Catalan nationalism in English, but see E. Allison Peers, *Catalonia Infelix* (reprint, New York, 1970); for a convenient account in Catalan, see J. Termes, 'De la revolució de setembre a la fin de la guerra civil, 1868−1939', *Història de Catalunya*, vi (Barcelona, 1987). S.G. Payne, 'Nationalism, Regionalism and Micronationalism in Spain', *Journal of Contemporary History*, xxvi (1991), offers a characteristically thoughtful and thought-provoking analysis of these phenomena.

areas of the coastal provinces became economically, socially and culturally 'modern' in the space of half a century. Here, industrialism, urbanism and modernity were swiftly superimposed upon a culture that, outside the Vizcayan metropolis of Bilbao, had hitherto been essentially conservative, introspective, devout, and culturally Basque if far from universally Euskera-speaking. In Bilbao, San Sebastián and other towns there formed a new version of those hispanicised elites that had for centuries been present in the Basque-Navarrese region, one which like its predecessors maintained close material and family ties with Madrid. From outside the Basque country, mainly from impoverished rural districts of Galicia, León and Old Castile, there flooded in immigrants, eager for work in the region's expanding industries. As regards the development of a sense of *national* identity among ethnic Basques, very many of whom had had little previous personal contact with any culture other than their own, this invasion of tens of thousands of non-Basques, bringing with it cultural conflicts and competition for jobs and resources, was enormously influential. There is, of course, a paradox here, and one with close parallels in very different European settings: that the ethno-national consciousness essential to the creation of a Basque nation came into being precisely when — and in part because — the Basque heartland of Vizcaya and Guipúzcoa was ceasing to be ethnically dominated by the Basque *people*.[1]

Politically speaking, the Basque oligarchy and its dependants came to constitute the local support, between 1876 and 1923, for 'Spanish' conservative and liberal parties. For their part immigrant labourers, plus a minority of genuinely Basque workers, provided the Spanish Socialist Party with one of its most important regional mass bases.[2] Between the Spanish oligarchic parties on the right and the centralist Spanish Socialist Party on the left, and between the socio-economic forces they represented, fell those layers of Basque society that were most traditionalist in outlook, most marginalised by and aggrieved at the economic and cultural convulsions affecting the region, and among which were to be found the highest proportions of Euskera-speakers: namely, the lower middle class of all but the larger towns, and the peasantry. It was among these sectors that Basque nationalism made its principal conquests during the first forty years of its existence.

*

The ideology and programme of Basque nationalism, as it evolved during the

---

1 Payne, *Basque Nationalism*, pp. 61–5.
2 J.P. Fusi, *Política obrera en el País Vasco (1880–1923)* (Madrid, 1975); J.M. Eguiguren, *El P.S.O.E. en el País Vasco (1886–1936)* (San Sebastián, 1984).

late 1890s and early 1900s, owed almost everything to the mind of its principal founder, Sabino Arana y Goiri. As the product of a devoutly Catholic, ultra-conservative, modestly bourgeois, Carlist background, yet politically shaped by a rapidly modernising urban environment, Arana was an archetypal example of the displaced petty-bourgeois intellectual. As such he epitomised a generation of young Basque Catholics, many of whom embraced his ideas and enlisted in the Basque cause. Arana's nationalist credo was very much of its time in its rhetorical aggressiveness, its stress upon racial purity and the moral superiority of the Basque community, its bitter hostility towards all things Spanish or deemed to be Spanish, and its assertive Catholicism. In the light of Basque nationalism's later development, however, it is important to record that Arana — who taught himself Euskera, imperfectly — laid relatively little stress upon either language or territory as means of defining nationhood, and that while unenthusiastic about the Spanish liberal system as a means of achieving either independence or autonomy for Euskadi — the Basque nation whose name he invented — he utterly rejected violence as a political tactic.[1]

Arana died in 1903 aged only thirty-eight, by which time his own ideological trajectory had begun to exemplify what were to prove two enduring tensions arising out of the Basque region's increasing social and ethnic complexity and the practical imperatives of everyday politics. The first was between an extreme, racially exclusive, ruralist traditionalism and a tendency to accept the urban society against which Basque nationalism embodied a revolt. From the earliest days Basque nationalism attracted a pragmatic, moderate element willing to accept the modern world whilst anxious to infuse it with 'healthy' rural and, of course, Basque values. By the time of his death, Arana himself was coming to accept the inevitability of industrialisation and accompanying socio-cultural change — to see industrialisation, indeed, as a Basque *achievement* which could, after all, be made compatible with the still desirable de-hispanicisation of Euskadi. The second, closely related, tension was between the desire for outright independence from Spain and acceptance of a more limited autonomy within Spain: autonomy which, unlike independence, might be acceptable to the large numbers of non-Basques resident within the region. Broadly speaking, 'urban', 'progressive' Basque nationalism tended to reject independence as impracticable (and perhaps economically damaging), and settle instead for autonomy; in this regard, too, Arana — to the distress of Basque

---

1 Arana's ideas are surveyed in Payne, *Basque Nationalism*, pp. 61–86, and Heiberg, *Making of the Basque Nation*, pp. 49–60. J.-C. Larronde, *El Nacionalismo Vasco: su orígen ysu ideología en la obra de Sabino Arana-Goiri* (San Sebastián, 1977), is the most serious scholarly study.

extremists — seems to have been moving quickly in a more moderate direction prior to his premature death.[1]

*

The actual growth of Basque nationalism up to 1923, when Spain's liberal parliamentary system, in a state of slowly advancing disintegration since her defeat by the United States in 1898, succumbed to the *coup d'état* of General Primo de Rivera, was slow and uneven, dependent upon the conjunction of activist proselytisation and grassroots nativism. Its core lay in the middle and lower reaches of the ethnically Basque middle class. After a very slow start, by the First World War the Basque Nationalist Party was also making inroads into the social layer from which it drew its mythic sustenance, namely the peasantry. Further advances were problematical. As an aggressively Basque cause hostile to Spanish immigration into the Basque country, self-evidently it held no attraction for an urban working class which was increasingly non-Basque and uninterested in all things Basque. Although, like other integral nationalist movements in early twentieth-century Europe, Basque nationalism zealously sought a working-class base, it achieved only modest success among a devout, ethnically Basque minority of urban workers. Despite a brief and opportunistic flirtation between Basque industrialists and nationalism during the years of the First World War, genuine converts were just as rare within the region's oligarchy.[2] When in September 1923 Primo de Rivera seized power in defence of public order and national, that is to say Spanish, unity, the Basque oligarchy, like that of Catalonia, unreservedly welcomed the *coup*.

The extent and limits of Basque nationalism's achievement before 1923 were demonstrated at the ballot box. Between the late 1890s and the end of the World War, large numbers of nationalists had been elected to local councils in Vizcaya and Guipúzcoa, and much smaller numbers in Alava and Navarra. In Vizcaya, particularly, a significant degree of parliamentary success was also achieved, reaching a peak in 1917, only to fall quickly back thereafter. By the early 1920s nationalism was still no more than a minority movement even in Vizcaya.[3]

To sum up, Basque nationalism between the 1890s and 1923 may be said to have assumed the role of a 'middle way' or 'third force' between the capitalist, Spanish-biased right and the Socialist, immigrant-based left, attracting lower-middle-class and later peasant support in districts directly or

---

1   Payne, *Basque Nationalism*, pp. 79–82.
2   J. Harrison, 'Big Business and the Rise of Basque Nationalism', *European Studies Review*, vii (1977).
3   Payne, *Basque Nationalism*, pp. 87–101.

indirectly affected by industrialisation and urbanisation, where social harmony was being fractured and where Basque nationalism, with its stress upon a new, racially-defined, basis of community, could appeal to those with no other political refuge. In most of Alava and Navarra, still largely untouched by industrialisation, a 'middle way' had little meaning; here, Carlism remained the dominant party of the political right and of rural and small-town Catholicism, and the nationalist cause languished.

The limitations of Basque nationalism's success were already, by the 1920s, revealing what were actually chronic problems. The appeal to 'middling people' who also happened to be, ethnically speaking, the most Basque layer of the population, was all very well, yet the identification of both left and right within the Basque heartland with Spain rather than with Euskadi meant that the chances of achieving independence were always meagre, and those of autonomy little better unless either right or left could be tempted or driven into tactically embracing the Basque cause. Since much of Basque nationalism's appeal to its loyalists lay in antagonism towards these 'anti-Basques' within their midst, this was to say the least a difficult dilemma, and one which was to surface in a number of guises during the decades to come.

A further, and potentially just as serious, problem was the continuing weakness of Basque nationalism among all social classes in Alava and Navarra, and indeed the absence in much of Navarra of any true Basque consciousness at all. Navarra's differentiation for the other three provinces lay, as it still lies, in her distinctive constitutional tradition; in her relative geographical detachment, with her southern half drawn economically and culturally southwards towards the Ebro valley, Aragon and Castile; and in the confinement of any sense of 'Basqueness' to her northern fringes. The result was *navarrismo*, a widely diffused *Navarrese* patriotism entirely compatible with loyalty to Spain. The problem of Navarra became all the more embarrassing as Arana's non-territorial conception of Euskadi, in which Basque nationhood, embracing all Basques from Vizcaya to Nevada, was more important than statehood, gave way to a more practical, territorially minded approach. To Basque patriots, Navarra, whose history after all did much to legitimate Basque nationalism's territorial aspirations, was (and is) an inseparable part of Euskadi; just as Ulster, to Irish patriots, was (and is) a part of Ireland. Thus, to continue the parallel (and Basque nationalists have always used the Irish case as an example), the presence in Navarra of what throughout the twentieth century has been a clear *españolista* majority created a problem as intractable as that created by a loyalist majority in Ulster. And indeed, whenever — in 1919, in the 1930s and after 1975 — the possibility of Basque autonomy has been seriously explored, the relationship of Navarra with the rest of the region has proved an insoluble conundrum.[1]

Despite this somewhat discouraging picture, the 1920s marked an important phase in the development of Basque nationalism. Twice in its history, Basque nationalism has undergone periods of political repression followed by unprecedented advance amid a newly liberal atmosphere. The period from 1923 to 1936 was the first of these. The Primo de Rivera dictatorship of 1923−30 suppressed Basque nationalism *politically* but tolerated non-political activity. Unwittingly Primo de Rivera thereby did the Basque nationalist cause a favour, for Basque nationalists channelled their energies into the fostering of Basque linguistic and cultural consciousness — with extraordinary success. The resulting explosion of interest in Basque culture embraced not only the region's intelligentsia and middle class but also the more numerous and symbolically more important peasantry. Most nineteenth- and twentieth-century European nationalist movements, among them Catalonia's, built political activity upon cultural foundations. Basque nationalism, in its early years, attempted to put the cart before the horse and create a political movement where such cultural foundations were very weak. During the 1920s the error, if such it can be considered, was substantially corrected, so that when Primo de Rivera fell in 1930 and more open politics returned, Basque nationalism at last stood poised for a breakthrough.

*

The breakthrough occurred during the Second Republic of 1931−6 when, with the collapse of the old party system of the monarchy and the emergence of genuinely popular and democratic politics, the Basque Nationalist Party (PNV) at last established itself as a major, though not a hegemonic, regional force. By 1933 it commanded 50 per cent of the vote (both male and female) in Vizcaya and Guipúzcoa and some 30 per cent in Alava, albeit only 10 per cent in Navarra.[2]

During this period the mainstream of the PNV abandoned the quasi-racist, integralist sentiments inherited from Arana in favour of a linguistic and cultural approach to nationalism and a generally Christian democratic stance towards everyday politics and social questions. It also effectively abandoned any serious idea of independence in favour of autonomy within a

---

1 S. Payne, 'Navarra and Basque Nationalism', in *Basque Politics: a Case Study in Ethnic Nationalism*, ed. Douglass, provides a valuable survey of this question. See also M. Blinkhorn, '"The Basque Ulster". Navarre and the Basque Autonomy Question under the Spanish Second Republic', *Historical Journal*, xvii (1974), and V.M. Arbeloa, *Navarra ante los Estatutos* (Pamplona, 1978).
2 M. Blinkhorn, *Carlism and Crisis in Spain, 1931−1939* (Cambridge, 1975), pp. 47−51, 60−4, 81−5; Blinkhorn, '"The Basque Ulster"'.

democratic Spain, as permitted by the Republican constitution of 1931. In pursuit of a statute of autonomy the PNV found itself dependent upon tactical alliances with 'Spanish' forces in an atmosphere of increasingly sharp left-right polarisation. Following a shortlived and unproductive alliance with the regime's extreme, essentially *españolista*, right, the PNV fumbled its way into accommodation with the parties of the moderate left. This is why, for all its Catholicism and general conservatism, the PNV found itself identified with the Republic in the civil war which began in July 1936.[1]

The combination of regional and national politics between 1931 and 1936 had the effect of reopening, or re-emphasising, the division between the two coastal provinces, Vizcaya and Guipúzcoa, where support for the PNV and the proposed autonomy statute was strong, and the inland provinces, Alava and Navarra, where the PNV was much weaker and support for autonomy insufficient to carry the issue in a referendum. When the Civil War broke out, Vizcaya and Guipúzcoa found themselves in the Republican zone (to be precise in *one* of the Republican zones), and in 1936−7 enjoyed an ephemeral and illusory existence as the Republic of Euskadi. Alava and Navarra, on the other hand, were revealed as strongholds not of Basque but of Spanish nationalism.[2]

*

Before commenting on the effects of the Franco regime upon Basque nationalism, it might be sensible to recapitulate some salient features of Basque nationalism as it developed between the 1890s and the end of the Spanish Civil War in 1939. In terms of recent attempts to classify types of minority nationalism, that of the Basques, before the Civil War, cannot be regarded as embodying a response to real *national* oppression, since Basque nationalism had not developed sufficiently for this to be an appropriate

---

1   On Basque Nationalism under the Second Republic, see J.P. Fusi, *El problema vasco en la II República* (Madrid, 1979); J.L. de la Granja, *Nacionalismo y II República en el País Vasco* (Madrid, 1986); J.L. de la Granja Sainz, *República y Guerra Civil en Euskadi* (Oñati, 1990); J.L. de la Granja, 'The Basque Nationalist Community during the Second Spanish Republic', in *Basque Politics: a Case Study in Ethnic Nationalism*, ed. Douglass; S. de Pablo, *Alava y la Autonomía Vasca durante la II República* (Vitoria, 1985); and, for a brief account, Payne, *Basque Nationalism*, pp. 117−56. Heiberg, *Making of the Basque Nation*, pp. 183−9, provides an interesting account of Basque local politics under the Republic. J.A. de Aguirre y Lekube, *Entre la Libertad y la Revolución, 1930−1935* (Bilbao, 1935), is the memoir of the leader of the Basque Nationalist Party during the Second Republic and the Civil War.
2   Granja, *República y Guerra Civil*, pp. 181−312; *La Guerra Civil en el País Vasco. 50 años después*, ed. C. Garaitaonaindia and J.L. de la Granja (Bilbao, 1987); Blinkhorn, *Carlism and Crisis*, pp. 250−70.

concept. Nor was it the expression of the political ambitions of an emergent bourgeoisie, inasmuch as the bourgeois elite of the Basque country was effectively hispanicised. Nor — though Arana argued otherwise — can the emergence of Basque nationalism be regarded as reflecting the discontent of a backward or exploited region, the victim of what nowadays is called 'internal colonialism'. Although this notion may be applicable to the *French* Basque region, neither the Spanish Basque region itself, nor (with some qualifications) its language, can be said to have been 'oppressed' by Spain or by Madrid; if Euskera was undervalued and regarded as an inferior means of communication, this was the doing as much of non-Euskera-speaking Basques as of 'Spaniards'. Far from being oppressed, either culturally or economically, the region was by Spanish standards developed, stable and prosperous; an importer of human resources not, as with Ireland, Brittany or Spanish Galicia, an exporter; not, again like Galicia, a 'forgotten' corner of Spain but one impossible to forget, if only because of the tentacular activities of Basque banks; not, like Catalonia, arguably overtaxed but fiscally privileged; not reaching upwards for parity of treatment so much as backwards after past or receding privileges.

Naturally, given the sheer uniqueness of Euskera, the distinctiveness of the region's constitutional traditions, and the continent-wide awakening of national consciousness in the nineteenth century, some sort of Basque nationalist movement was certain sooner or later to appear. Appearing as it did at the end of the century when *liberal* nationalism (characteristic, on the whole, of Catalonia) was everywhere yielding to a more aggressive, exclusivist, 'integral' nationalism, it is equally natural that Basque nationalism should have assumed the form that it initially did. Its early leaders and spokesmen were for the most part displaced, educated pettybourgeois, raised within an established political tradition — Carlism — yet feeling betrayed by it, tortured by the disintegration of an old socio-cultural order and desperate to find some means of recovering a sense of community. In many parts of Europe, where rapid change during the late nineteenth and early twentieth centuries disrupted deeply traditionalist cultures and societies, integral nationalism was the outcome. Basque nationalism falls within this category of nationalist movement. As for its support, this, as we have seen, likewise came mainly from the Basque equivalents of those social groups which in many parts of Europe responded to the impact of modernity by espousing one or other form of radical nationalism, some before the First World War and many more after. In this instance, the fact that in the Basque country both capital and urban labour were 'non-Basque', whilst it limited Basque nationalism's constituency, also allowed it a more 'independent' role than was often the case with radical nationalism elsewhere. And where many radical nationalist movements in the early twentieth century, even those

225

representing minorities, displayed a tendency to move increasingly rightwards, Basque nationalism was manoeuvred by the oscillations and peculiarities of the Spanish situation of the 1920s and 1930s into undertaking an 'opening to the left'.

*

It is this process, whereby, contrary to appearances and expectations in 1931, Basque nationalism came into confrontation with the Spanish right, that explains its anguish during the long years of Francoism and its subsequent radicalisation. The Basque nationalists' role in the Civil War thereafter doomed Vizcaya and Guipúzcoa, deemed to be 'guilty' provinces, to a degree of constitutional and political oppression never previously experienced, and Euskera to be subjected during the 1940s and 1950s to a policy of official discouragement never previously dreamed of by even the most fervent *españolista*. Navarra and Alava, on the other hand, were singled out for favoured treatment, as a reward for their enthusiastic commitment to the *Spanish* nationalist cause.

The effects of this clamp-down on a people whose national consciousness, that is its sense of itself *as* a people, had developed too rapidly during the 1920s and 1930s to be eradicated, can hardly be exaggerated. Down to the final years of the Franco regime, in no other region of Spain was opposition so widespread or intense. Given the history of the 1930s it is not surprising that in Vizcaya and Guipúzcoa hatred of the dictatorship, at least in the case of the region's urban and rural middle class, should express itself through nationalism. From the late 1950s onwards, nationalist sentiment of a sub-political kind was encouraged by the regime's gradual relaxation of restrictions upon Basque cultural, athletic and linguistic — though not political — activities.

The socio-economic climate of the Franco years also stimulated nationalist feeling in the Basque country. The revival of industrial activity in the region, accelerating sharply during the 1960s and now embracing Navarra and Alava for the first time, brought with it a 50 per cent increase in population between 1945 and 1973. Much of this was due to the arrival of new waves of immigrants from outside the Basque country. Like their early twentieth-century forebears during the first wave of mass immigration, many Basques saw their region's Basque character in danger of being 'swamped'; unlike their predecessors, however, the Basques of the 1960s and 1970s viewed this situation from an already nationalist standpoint.

During this time the Basque Nationalist Party succeeded in maintaining a reasonably active clandestine existence. Its ideological position, reflecting revulsion within the region against a rightist regime which crushed Basque and other democratic freedoms, was essentially that of Christian democracy;

any residual idea of independence from Spain, or of making common cause with French Basques, was abandoned in favour of autonomy within a future, democratic Spain; nationhood was therefore seen as separable from statehood, or at any rate as achievable via a state within a state.[1] Inevitably this moderation, and more particularly the PNV's tactical quietism *vis-à-vis* a regime that showed no signs of disappearing peacefully, incensed some, mainly youthful, radical nationalists. In 1959–60 these elements formed ETA (*Euskadi ta Askatasuna*); having broken away from the PNV, by the mid-1960s ETA had succumbed to the fashionable climate of the day by redefining its position in the language of Marxist-inspired national liberation movements.[2]

The emergence and development of ETA, in its bewildering variety of forms, demonstrate how the political climate of the dominant country influences 'subject' nationalism. While the early growth of Basque nationalism has to be seen in the context of a liberal Spain in crisis following the colonial 'Disaster' of 1898, and while Basque nationalism's surge and change of character during the 1930s can only be understood in terms of the complex politics of the Spanish Second Republic, the radical nationalism associated with ETA was unquestionably the by-product of Francoism and could not have emerged without it. Violence, seen by ETA in the 1960s as the only way of overthrowing the Franco regime and in the process giving birth to Euskadi, had after all played no previous part in either the theory or the practice of Basque nationalism. Rather than discussing ETA in detail, the rest of this essay will be limited to a number of salient issues with relevance to the wider themes explored in this volume.[3]

*

Like the original Basque nationalism of the 1890s, ETA was, and has remained, a movement of middle-class (chiefly male) youth, impatient with the lack of achievement of its elders (Carlists in the former case, the PNV in the latter). But, unlike the Arana generation, ETA has from the mid-1960s always contained a violent element. For all its extremism and the occasional

---

1 R.C. Clark, *The Basques: The Franco Years and Beyond* (Reno, Nevada, 1979), pp. 79–130; J. Sullivan, *ETA and Basque Nationalism: The Fight for Euskadi, 1890–1986* (London, 1988), pp. 1–26. See also S. Ben-Ami, 'Basque Nationalism between Archaism and Modernity', *Journal of Contemporary History*, xxvi (1991).
2 Sullivan, *ETA and Basque Nationalism*, pp. 27–60.
3 The Spanish-language bibliography on ETA is vast; the following are useful English-language studies: R.P. Clark, *The Basque Insurgents: ETA, 1952–1980* (Wisconsin, 1984); Sullivan, *ETA and Basque Nationalism*; and, for a fascinating social-anthropological approach, J. Zulaika, *Basque Violence: Metaphor and Sacrament* (Reno, Nevada, 1988).

accusations of critics, however, ETA has never embraced a biological or even strictly ethnic conception of Basque nationality. Where Arana's goals were moralistic and his notion of nationality vaguely racial, and where the PNV has gradually settled for a pragmatic, regionalist strategy according to which non-Basques can more or less comfortably embrace citizenship within an autonomous Euskadi, ETA's goals have been separatist, its vision of Euskadi explicitly territorial, and its notion of personal nationality primarily linguistic. ETA's vision has been one of an independent trans-Pyrenean Basque state comprising all four Spanish Basque provinces and the three Basque districts of France, with any inhabitant freely embracing 'Basqueness' via Euskera being acceptable as a Basque.

As with Basque nationalism throughout its history, and as with other modern nationalist movements, ETA has been torn by ideological dissension. This has to do less with actual conceptions of nationality, however, than with revolutionary strategy. Applying models drawn from China, Vietnam, Algeria and Cuba to the reality of the Basque country proved problematical, and the problem provoked a succession of schisms during the late 1960s, 1970s and 1980s. The schisms took two, sometimes overlapping, forms. The more easily graspable were those between devotees of violence and those who, frustrated or disgusted with violence, opted sooner or later for exclusively peaceful political action. More esoteric were differences consciously or unconsciously arising out of the distinctive sociological and ethnic composition of the Basque country: between those *etarras* keen to pursue the chimera of a cross-class 'national revolution', and those whose Marxism led them to stress the revolutionary role of the working class. The latter were repeatedly driven to seek alliances between a 'Basque' working class which mostly was *not* ethnically Basque and the workers of Spain as a whole, and successively drifted away from radical Basque politics in favour of other forms of revolutionary or extreme left-wing politics. Within the framework of radical nationalism, this tension may be regarded as a version of that conflict between out-and-out separatism and autonomy which has always been present within Basque nationalism as a whole.

Although both the numbers and the activities of ETA's men of violence have diminished considerably during the past few years — as Spain has become a democracy, as an autonomous region of Euskadi, comprising Vizcaya, Guipúzcoa and Alava, has come into being, and as the French authorities have become more amenable to anti-ETA co-operation with those of Spain — the movement has stubbornly refused to disappear altogether. This may prove nothing more than that, once a revolutionary, terroristic organisation exists and a related myth has grown up around it, a few hundred youthful zealots can at any time be attracted to it; and that such organisations are to say the least difficult to eradicate. More interesting, perhaps, is the persistence of substantial minority support within Euskadi, and even within Navarra, for the *Sinn Fein* of radical Basque nationalism, *Herri Batasuna* (Popular Unity). This is an issue which, requiring an essay of its own, cannot be pursued here. What it suggests is that over the course of the past century a Basque consciousness has come well and truly into being; that having once become a reality, the Basque 'nation' exhibits a chronic tension between (possibly symbiotic) pragmatists, content with nationhood within Spain, and eternally frustrated maximalists; that once ignited, national sentiment can always find fuel to keep it alight — in the case of present-day Euskadi, the decline of the region's traditional industries and irredentism towards Navarra. To put it in more generalised terms: national sentiment can be difficult to create, but once created it is even more difficult to control and downright impossible to destroy.